I0814880

The Hunting Falcon

The Hunting Falcon

The Story of WW1 German Ace Hans-Joachim Buddecke

Christopher A. Lawrence and
Jay Karamales

First published in Great Britain in 2024 by Air World,
an imprint of Pen & Sword Books Ltd, Yorkshire - Philadelphia

ISBN: 978-1-39908-501-4

A CIP catalogue record for this book is available from the British Library

Typeset in India by IMPEC eSolutions
Printed and bound in England by CPI

Pen & Sword Books Ltd incorporates the imprints of Pen & Sword
Archaeology, Air World Books, Atlas, Aviation, Battleground, Discovery,
Family History, History, Maritime, Military, Naval, Politics, Social History,
Transport, True Crime, Claymore Press, Frontline Books, Praetorian Press,
Seaforth Publishing and White Owl

For a complete list of Pen & Sword titles please contact:

PEN & SWORD BOOKS LTD
47 Church Street, Barnsley, South Yorkshire, S70 2AS, UK.
E-mail: enquiries@pen-and-sword.co.uk
Website: www.pen-and-sword.co.uk

or

PEN AND SWORD BOOKS,
1950 Lawrence Road, Havertown, PA 19083, USA
E-mail: Uspen-and-sword@casematepublishers.com
Website: www.penandswordbooks.com

From Jay Karamales

I dedicate this book to my grandfather, Thomas Angelo Karamales, who arrived in the United States in 1916 as an immigrant from Greece, and immediately enlisted in the U.S. Army as a translator to serve his adopted country. All of his sons followed his example, and served in the Army in World War II and Korea.

From Christopher A. Lawrence

This book is dedicated to my grandfather, William E. Catherall of Liverpool. In 1916 he lied about his age and went to sea at the age of 15. Served in the British merchant marine during the Great War.

Table of Contents

Illustrations and Maps

Acknowledgments

This book came about because of a side effort outside of our main areas of work at The Dupuy Institute. As such, there were really only two people primarily involved in this effort, Christopher A. Lawrence and Jay Karamales.

There are few others we would like to thank for their help and support: John Grehan, our editor at Pen & Sword, and an author in his own right. We received gracious support and assistance on this book from David S. Bremner of the UK (owner of Bristol Scout 1264), Paschalis Palavouzis of Greece, Bernard de Broglio of Australia, Dr Sterling Michael Pavelec of the Air Command and Staff College, Chris Whealy of the UK, Peter Kilduff of Connecticut, Tobias Weber of Germany, Dr Cigdem Oguz of University of Bologna, and Dr Lance J. Bronnenkant of New York. We would also like to thank the friends and associates who helped with Chris' various Great War air projects, including: Gillian Sells of the UK, E. Stiles Peabody of Virginia, Gary S. Schofield of New Zealand, Neal W. Bliven of Maryland, and Kevin Connor, the British film director.

Introduction

Sometimes I get tired of writing history. It is kind of a grind, especially if one is working on books on the Battle of Kursk larger than *War and Peace* (but without the peace). Therefore, as a side project I started looking into the history and stories of early Great War aces. One that caught my attention was Hans Buddecke because of his unusual journey. But there was no book on him in English. He was not a big name like German aces Immelmann, Boelcke, or Richthofen. I was able to find a book written in German by him and published in 1918.[1] As I was curious about his experiences in America, I sent it over to my friend and long-time colleague Jay Karamales to translate a few passages. Jay got interested in his account, and soon had translated the entire book. As I was reading through his rather unique account, I realized that this was a story worthy of publication and with a little support, would make for a unique and interesting book. So, this is what we have attempted to do here.

Our format is to let Hans Buddecke tell his story for two to four translated chapters, then we put in a chapter giving background and context to the events described. This is to round out the whole story. Then we continue with his narrative.

This allows him to tell his story and to place that story in context. As Buddecke's book was published in the spring of 1918, during the height of the Great War, there are names changed to protect his family and there are accounts of his time in America that we suspect were deliberately biased against Americans for wartime propaganda purposes. There is additional material on Buddecke that was published in the *Indianapolis Star*, as Buddecke's uncle was a major businessman in the Indianapolis area. This material was useful in that it provides both context and verification for the story he told. It was this research that led us down the path of writing a chapter for background and context after every two or four chapters of Buddecke's writing. We feel this is better than just translating and publishing his account without further comment, even though our background chapters are often larger than his chapters.

If one wants to read just Buddecke's account and bypass all our verbiage, just skip the prologue and Chapters 5, 9, 13, 16, 19, 20, and 22.

For Buddecke's narrative, we kept the arrangement of each paragraph as it was in his original book. He sometimes had a single sentence as a separate paragraph. We maintained this format.

— Christopher A. Lawrence

Prologue: The Start of the Great War

On 28 June 1914 in Sarajevo, the Austro-Hungarian Archduke Franz Ferdinand and his wife Sophie were assassinated by the Bosnian Serb anarchist Gavrilo Princip. This sparked a series of events that would lead to Austria-Hungary declaring war on Serbia a month later. On 30 July Russia ordered general mobilization in support of its Slavic client, and on 1 August 1914 Germany declared war on Russia in response. The war moved to Western Europe with Germany occupying Luxembourg on 2 August and declaring war on France on the afternoon of 3 August. Later that day, France reciprocated.

On the Western Front, the first skirmish of the war started on the morning of 2 August, at Joncherey, France, where an errant German cavalry patrol skirmished with a French garrison resulting in one dead on each side. On 4 August, Germany declared war on, and invaded, neutral Belgium. The United Kingdom issued an ultimatum to Germany to withdraw from Belgium, and when they did not, as of 11:00 p.m. that day, the United Kingdom considered itself at war with Germany. At this point, all the major powers in Europe were at war except for Italy and the Ottoman Empire (Turkey). The United States declared that it was neutral.

The German advance drove through Belgium, delayed at Lille by the hard-fighting Belgian Army, then rolled into France to the north and east of Paris. They continued pushing forward until 5 September, when they were nearly at the Marne River to the east of Paris. The Allies then initiated a massive multi-army counterattack against the over-extended Germans and rolled them back to the Aisne River near the Belgian border. The lines stagnated at that point, while the Germans and the Allies raced to the coast of the English Channel in attempts to outflank one another. The war settled into a stalemate over the winter until spring of 1915.

Hans Buddecke was a young German man of 23 living in America when the war started in Europe. He had been born in Berlin on 22 August 1890, in what was the Kingdom of Prussia in the German Empire. His father was in the German Imperial Army and Hans naturally followed his father's career. In the spring of 1904, he started his training as a cadet and in the spring of 1910 was commissioned as a lieutenant in the 115th Life Guards Infantry Regiment. It was the same unit his father had served in and was garrisoned in Darmstadt. The German Imperial Army had, before mobilization, 217 infantry regiments. There were eleven guard infantry regiments in the Imperial Army and the 115th was one of only two 'Life Guard' regiments.[2] It was an honor to earn such a posting, though Buddecke's may have been obtained with the help of his father. In the spring of 1913, he left the army and decided to travel to America. Buddecke had an uncle on his mother's side who was a very successful businessman in Indianapolis. During a visit to Germany by this American uncle and his daughter, Hans' cousin, they convinced him that his future should be in the United States, so he decided to emigrate there and his story picks up from that moment.

Chapter 1

Foreword

From the original memoir of Hans Buddecke[3]

As an expensive legacy of my beloved son, who sacrificed his life on the altar of the Fatherland on 10 March 1918, in an aerial battle on the Western Front, I present to the public his war memoirs. He wrote them down during his stay in Smyrna and completed them on his last home leave in his parents' home. Death has taken the weapon and the pen out of his hand, and just as his burning desire to witness the German final victory remained unfulfilled,[4] so he will no longer be able to enjoy the fruit of his spiritual work. But he has thus built a monument to himself that reveals the unique character of his humanity [or manhood] and love of aviation; leaves a gift to the Fatherland as thanks for the rich honors he enjoyed during his lifetime; and erected a landmark for German youth as an incentive to emulate his heroism.

Berlin, Spring 1918.

Albert Buddecke,
Lieutenant-Colonel and Deputy Chief of Staff of the Army General Staff

Chapter 2

How I Came to Fly

By Hans Buddecke

'Oh,' said my young female cousin from America, as I showed her the Victory Column,[5] 'Oh, Häns, you ought to come to us in America, you'd have a very fine time.'

My cousin's 'Oh' went around in my head for a long time with the subsequent request to come to 'Ämörrikä.'[6] I was as proud as a man could be of the uniform I wore – I stood as a lieutenant in a Guard regiment – but here I had an opportunity to get out into the world and blow the wind around my ears. The decision was not made overnight, but one fine day a letter was sent to my uncle, and a few weeks later I stood at the train station in Indianapolis.

The first days were very pleasant and merry; it was, as my cousin had said, 'a very fine time.' But I hadn't come over for that. So I went to my uncle to discuss the matter with him. As if in one fell swoop, as soon as the conversation turned to business, he was no longer the relative who had welcomed me with open arms but a sober American businessman, interested only in the numbers.[7]

'Well, what can you do?'

What could I do? My cadet education and lieutenant's training had not weighed me down with too much practical knowledge. Giving commands, tying a knot in a necktie, those kinds of things perhaps, but otherwise …

So I was silent.

'You have technical knowledge, don't you? In particular, do you understand anything about automobiles?'

Hold on, that was something I could answer. Did I know anything about automobiles? Well, I was interested in them. Although previously, cars had only attracted my attention as a means of transport, that was, after all, also a technical interest. So I said 'yes.'

My uncle liked me very much – I had figured that much out on the first day. He took my 'yes' as an affirmation to carry out the plans he already had for me and quickly got me a job in a factory. Now I had what I had aspired to: I stood on my own two feet. But how and where?

Ten hours a day, sometimes even on Sundays, working a vise. My hands became rough and calloused. None of the men around me with whom I could have spoken a reasonable word took the slightest interest in me. The youngest and most useless of them was my supervisor, and even he could teach me something. Anything would have been better, but I gritted my teeth and persevered. At noon I would eat next to my vise, unpacking the sandwiches and bananas that my landlady had given me. Next to me, an old man chewed and slurped, spat artfully and then returned to his feeding, so that I almost lost my appetite. Poor people – dear people who had spent their whole lives here.

That's how I got to know the country and the people at the bottom, not dressed as a cavalier, but as a real journeyman, for weeks, months. The will to stand out from the dull mass around me grew stronger and stronger, but how?

Sometimes – it didn't happen too often – I was invited to my uncle's house. I would slip into my evening clothes after work, and after dinner I would sit next to the piano where the little dollar princess[8] played and sang – she liked to sing 'Mignon'[9] – and look at my crushed, smashed hands and consider, as beside me rang out the tones of 'Know'st Thou the Land Where the Lemon-trees Bloom?', the means by which I might better my station.

Soon thereafter I began to decline all invitations and buried myself in books and calculations, logarithms and drawings, until late at night. This went on for nine months or so, until the morning came when

I left my vise and told the foreman I was going to use the telephone for a moment.

'Hello, is that Mr. Morris's department store? I'd like to speak to Mr. Morris himself...

'Hello, Mr. Morris? This is Mr. Buddecke, N.N.'s nephew. I would like to present you with a project, the creation of a company for the construction of aircraft. May I come see you?'

All I heard was a quiet hum, then his voice sounded back: 'Come at three o'clock.'

I waited in his vestibule from 3:00 to 4:00, and the minutes crept by slowly. Again and again, I was told, 'Mister Morris is busy.' Finally, I stood before him, a smooth face, sober, slightly protruding eyes, thin lips; not very sympathetic, but I wasn't asking for sympathy. I explained my plans to him and summarized my calculations. He listened to me calmly, expressed neither consent nor concern, and ordered me to come back to his apartment in three days.

Punctually at the appointed hour I found myself again with him. I talked with him for a while and he gave me a thick cigar. A few minutes later, several people came in who I only knew were the richest and most respected merchants in the city. When everyone had taken a seat around the circular table, I spread out before me the results of all those nights' work and began to speak. It was, as I said, the creation of a company to build all kinds of aircraft for advertising, transportation, sports, and military purposes. At first my voice shook a little, but I soon warmed to the task and became more confident. I still remember clearly that I was looking for any sign of approval in the faces around me, but saw only the cool faces from which nothing could be read, except one that sat opposite me. He sometimes nodded kindly to me and I even heard him utter a benevolent sentence that went something like: 'Yes, yes, the Germans. It is impossible to believe what fear they have in England of these damned German professors.'[10] No decision was taken, and the decision was postponed. All my calculations were correct, everything was clear and elegant. Only one thing was missing, which I could not put on the table in front of these older men like I had spread my plans: the proof that I was really an expert.

The next morning I slunk into the factory again, slipped into my work gear, and started tinkering with my vise. A coincidence came to my aid. Some kind of crisis broke out, and my factory stopped working. I was not alone in America, as I mentioned earlier. I was sponsored by my uncle, who owned several factories there. He had let me start downstairs on the factory floor, as you do with all the strangers over there, to see if I could work independently and get settled in. Now that my factory had to close, he offered me a commercial position with him. I jumped at the opportunity and travelled across the country for two months. At the end of that time, I came before him again. I was worried as he looked at me. He knew what plans I was formulating, he liked me, and he knew what was coming. I wanted to fly instead of sitting in a musty car all day. Reluctantly, he consented and provided me with the necessary means.

A few days later, in Chicago, I bought a small monoplane from Messrs Orr & Linn, which was to serve as evidence that I was indeed an expert and qualified to go from worker to director. One thing, however, I couldn't do – the exact thing that my people expected of me – was fly. In Germany I had arguably seen how to fly; indeed, a comrade had taken me once and thrown me into the dirt, but that was my whole practice. Mr. Orr took me in his car to the Chicago airfield[11] and showed me two small Nieuport monoplanes that had already been stored in their shed for a year. Before I continue, I would like to say a few words about these two Americans.

After they finished college, Orr and his friend Linn had packed their golf clubs and tennis rackets in their car, loaded their vehicle onto a ship, and sailed to Europe, which they crossed from west to east. Then they came back to America, where they soon became dreadfully bored of their money, and they were constantly wondering what to do next. That's how they got into flying. It was the latest thing and would bring them some variety. They decided to build airplanes, which only Wright and Curtiss were doing over there at the time, but they couldn't get past a certain initial stage. They then bought a tiny Nieuport in Paris and copied it faithfully in Chicago, proceeding with great diligence. To get strong wing spars, they bought wood from a tree that had to meet the most incredible requirements. It must not be too thick and not too thin, must not have grown too close to another thick tree, and must have grown on the southern or northern slopes of a low mountain. Another condition was that it had to have been cut down at a very particular time of year during the night, and similar nonsense. When the copy of the Nieuport was finished, it had only cost seven times as much as the original. Orr and Linn therefore realized that it was not worth building planes, and changed their plan. They bought some more machines, recruited pilots, and set up a travelling airshow. In winter they moved south, in the summer they went north, from one fair to another, to show people the new miracle. Of course, they did not fly themselves; they had promised each other that.

I spent a lot of time with the two of them in the beautiful Blackstone Hotel[12] on the lake, where Orr told cheerful stories about the group's adventures. Before long, though, the show flying was no longer worthwhile. They sold their winged darlings and now made airplane lacquer and turnbuckles in order to have some kind of occupation.

I liked the two little monoplanes. I couldn't find any better, so I decided to buy the copy because of her strength. She had a 35-hp engine, but couldn't run for more than an hour. Now that I was thinking of flying for at least three hours – I was not modest in my plans – I bought a 50-hp Gnome[13] which, if things went reasonably well, I intended to install after the first test flights. I also bought a second pair of wings; safe is safe. Our contract stipulated that the engine had to run flawlessly. To try it out, we went out to the airfield.

With a connoisseur's appraising eyes I walked around the machine. Damn, it was small! On each wing just a few wires. I didn't show any reaction; I just climbed into the cockpit with the feeling of one climbing to the guillotine for trial. I got a brief explanation of the levers, and a mechanic started the engine. I took in everything so that I could thoroughly digest it later, when I was alone. My face remained serious and indifferent, so that Orr assured me he could recognize that I was a pilot of great experience. If he had only known! … I took over the little bird and lovingly placed it in a shed next door. A 16-year-old boy served me as an auxiliary mechanic; the main work I took care of myself. Until the sun dried up the field, still under water from winter, I had plenty of time to learn about my neighbors. But I tried for quite a long time to remain Mr. Unknown, the mysterious one, so as not to be demoted to 'Hans' or 'Boy' as always before. The twelve small sheds which adorned one side of the square airfield, which was beautifully surrounded by high poplars, in the middle of a sea of houses, contained many interesting things.

In an annex of the shed, an Italian porter maintained the canteen. On Sundays his whole family enjoyed the warm sun outside and held a war council; at least that's what their chitchat sounded like to me. If their conversation had gotten just a little more lively, one would have had the impression that they were going to fight the next moment. I remember one day when I was frightened by their noise and ran over to make peace, they were talking about bread and butter.

Shed 2 belonged to Miss Stinsson.[14] She was a nice, not exactly pretty, girl and happy owner of a Wright crate. One day, she wanted to fly to a suffragette meeting, advertised that it would be held on the shores of Lake Michigan, in the pouring rain; but the poor thing had bad luck. Despite various forms of aid the thing couldn't get off the ground; and in the end, before she could fly the bird to safety, it was seized by the marshals because she had a beautiful blue dress she hadn't paid for. The next few days should have brought her sunshine and happiness. She was a splendid, dashing thing who flew in any weather and was nothing more than a 17-year-old child. Maybe that's why I'm here.

Shed 3 was occupied by another pilot. This nobleman had found the wing and fuselage of a plane somewhere, signed a contract with a carnival director, and was now due to complete a flying lap on National Day, July 4, for which he would receive $400.[15] He had arranged to get a motor for his airplane. So far everything was all right – only the tension wires and the clamping locks were missing. But that did not bother this great spirit. Who needed clamping locks? He could tighten, bend, and wrap the wire so that he wouldn't need locks. But where to get the wire? He solved that question brilliantly as well. One dark night, far outside the city, he 'found' about 500 meters of telephone line. So the next night he was able to complete his flying lap at the carnival. He circled the place at a height of five meters, but unfortunately his elevator broke right down the middle. However, because the wire was very good, he still managed to land smoothly. As soon as he had completed the lap according to his contract, he crashed his apparatus. He sent the engine back to the gracious dealer; the rest of the plane served as a source of souvenirs for the enthusiastic crowd, who bought pieces of the remains just as eagerly as they bought the image of the bold man on postcards. He smiled, pocketed the money, and the world appeared to him in the rosiest light.

Shed 4 contained a larger-than-life model ichthyosaurus with bat wings. Every Sunday afternoon, the builder appeared to revel in the glorious sight of his invention, and tried to arouse similar feelings in other naive viewers through great speeches. He found no one to rejoice with him nor to make a donation towards the purchase of the missing engine. People reasoned that if the man wanted to commit suicide in that crate, he should do it at his own expense.

Shed 5 was Mr. Partridge's factory.[16] There, he constructed a biplane from scratch. He had drawn the surface curve according to an aesthetic sense of beauty and became more grave and earnest every day that brought him closer to the completion of his work. He was a model of diligence. From early morning to night he worked on his machine, acting as both manager and errand boy.

Now to shed 8. It contained a monoplane with an unbelievable number of wires and a device that, even today, despite the enormous advances in technology, has remained new: a stabilizer. The wings had two large windows that could be opened and closed from the fuselage through sliding doors. If the plane tipped over to one side or if there was a danger of that happening, the window on the other side opened. The air flowed through, and the plane tipped back the other way until it was horizontal again, after which the windows would close. A pilot was found who was willing to try it; however, he got his payment before the trial flight, so it was no wonder that the trial never took place.

Shed 9 contained an authentic, proper aviator, Mr. Mackly. In the front part of the shed, Mackly showed me his dirty white monoplane, which had a fuselage and a propeller hood like Weddrin's plane. The personality of this lucky owner, who was both a pilot and the proprietor at the same time, had something infinitely dignified. Even his beautiful leather flying suit was a rarity, because at that time you didn't wear a sports suit at the airfield, but just whatever you had. We saw him in this aristocratic get-up day and night.

A fur-lined leather hood offered suitable protection from sunburn. The noble aviator wore spectacles, had studied in France, and could of course also speak perfect French. Unfortunately, he had forgotten everything about flying. In his monoplane sat a brand new engine, which only ran when the plane was connected to a post in front of its shed. How it behaved in the air was not determined during his two years of service. But that wasn't the most interesting thing about Mr. Mackly's shed. There was a ship behind the monoplane. Not for sailing; you couldn't really tell what it was. Maybe some junk or something like that. Ten meters long, three wide, covered and well painted. Quietly, shaken by awe, one asks what it is. The Transatlantic Flyer. One is amazed. Who wouldn't be amazed? One laughs at the sight of the wings, which are as wide as the shed, and the struts made of steel rails. I dared the shy question of what the great inventor thought it would use as an engine. A contemptuous shrug answered me, an astonishment expressed in his face, how I could be so naive not to come to the solution myself.

'A locomotive,' Mackly replied in an off-hand tone. 'I'm already negotiating with the Pennsylvania Railroad,' he said.

I gazed upon the great man in awe, for it became clear to me that he was at least fifty years ahead of his miserable contemporaries.

This neighborhood depressed me a little, but I tried not to think about it. In front of me was my task, which I had to solve out of nowhere and which demanded undisturbed will. So that's how I started. At home I had figured out what to do, had memorized the sensations I had with the engine running a hundred times, and now it was time. I lit my pipe and went over to the shed. There I fed myself into my bird and practised steering movements for two hours; then I went to sleep. Another time I imitated the start by lifting the tail. That's how I had seen planes take off in Germany and in the cinemas. Then I imagined myself flying up, down, to the right and to the left, gliding and landing, cautiously feeling my way back down to the approaching Earth – all this, of course, in my imagination – then I slept again.

I flew at any time of the day or night, while eating, in bed, at home. A rocking chair and my walking stick served as a training plane until my landlady rushed out and asked me if I had a screw loose. But all this was just a stopgap. The main preliminary exercise I did in Chicago's Luna Park[17] on the roller coaster. I'm afraid the people there also thought I was crazy.

I immediately took ten tickets, climbed into the front car, put my walking stick in front of me, made believe that it was now my joystick, and that it controlled all the movements. I did that for a few days, hours each day. The exercise was good. I got the feeling for up and down, for horizontal position, for ground level; and I overcame the fear of speed. While girls and boys cheered and screamed behind me, I sat very calmly and determinedly in front and made mystical movements with my walking stick.

Chapter 3

I Fly

By Hans Buddecke

The big day of the first outing was approaching. There were only a few puddles left on the field and I was able to roll the plane along the ground with the help of the engine. Dawn was just starting to break when at five o'clock in the morning I silently took the bird out with my boy, in the quiet hope that no one would come to marvel at my undignified maneuvers. The boy started the motor and with one-quarter power I drove through dirt and muck around the big square field. As I was sitting in the rattling thing, I thought: you will never learn to fly. After the first circuit, though, ambition spurred me on and I made another one. A little faster this time. But lo and behold, the first, apparently insurmountable obstacle appeared: the bird didn't want to do as I did. If I had straight ahead in mind, it stubbornly walked left and made a beautiful Telemark ski jump. Thank God, the wings were strong enough, otherwise they would have burst into a thousand shards in their eager efforts to drill themselves into the dirt again and again. My heart was pounding. We changed the tension of the landing gear – futile. If I continued my exercises on the ground, then it was only a matter of time before the catastrophe had to occur. Sad but unfazed, I dragged my bird back to its nest. This then was the first day.

The pilot who had flown the machine before me could not be found. Nobody could tell me how to fly the apparatus, or even how to fly at all. So I gathered my wits and thought. Around noon I struggled to make up my mind: tomorrow morning I would give it full power and steer with all my might. So far I had only dared very small movements with this mysterious and deadly device. Morning came and found me trying again. Full power. No sooner did my beast want to turn left, than I was already throwing the rudder firmly to the right, and behold, she came back, stayed straight. The tail lifted. I got scared and quickly turned off the engine, thinking that the maneuver was over. But oh, innocent and naive, while I was still rolling, I had pulled the yoke back to my stomach and suddenly saw myself in the air. But before I could react to it, I had already fallen back to Earth, hard, and come to a halt. I got hold of myself, climbed out, and spent a quarter of an hour thinking hard. I said to myself: keep firm control at the beginning, full power, everything else the beast will do itself if you just watch and keep still. So I positioned the bird again at one end of the diagonal of the square airfield that served as a runway, then got going.

The tail lifted. A wonderful feeling of speed came over me, and the uncertainty had completely disappeared. I felt the air pressure in the control surfaces, noticed that there were no more impacts from the ground and knew I was flying. But I didn't let my device go higher than 2 meters, and landed back on the flat ground pretty quickly. A quarter of an hour after that, I was off again. By now I felt so comfortable that I was already pulling curves. It worked, so I did two laps at a height of 5 meters and landed. In the evening I flew again in front of a handful of people who had come out of curiosity, and since I wanted them to get their money's worth, I went higher this time. Everything worked. After I had gone around twice, I dipped my nose forward, turned off the engine, and drove flat on the ground again.

My boy told me that my neighbors were grumbling about me something awful. I would have fooled them by saying that I came straight from Johannisthal and that there my flight demonstration would have been considered amateur.

That was the second day. So I was able to fly. When my machine first detached itself from the earth, I asked myself: Who is actually flying here? You or the bird? Most assuredly the bird flew with me, and more or less I felt completely helpless, and I kept still, let myself be carried, until we had gone far enough; then I returned us to Earth. I was in no way clear about the use of the rudder for banking – a gap in my knowledge that was very nearly fatal to me a week later. Again, I was flying early in the morning and came to the famous corner where the gasometers stood. My bird had always shown a tendency when banking to tilt too far, and this time was no exception. It was very gusty, and my bird was banking, more and more. All my efforts to counteract the tilting were in vain. Now the wing was perpendicular to the ground, and I involuntarily reached for the side wall with my left hand in order to hold on. I had done everything I thought I could do. Naturally, I didn't know that there were all sorts of other things I could have done.

The moment I hung there seemed like an eternity. I gave up. I think I was screaming, and I thought about my parents' grief. If my machine slipped another hair sideways, then I would fall out … and there was no reason for her not to slip. But she didn't slip. I still don't know what I was doing in my desperation at that time, only that my machine was suddenly horizontal in the air again. I turned off the gas and landed quickly. I was congratulated below; such a plane had never been to Chicago! The curves I had just made were wonderful! I kept a straight face; I didn't feel like it at all. Later, however, I found out what had caused this incident.

The next day I ripped out the small engine to install the Gnome. After four weeks I was done. My boy and I had done everything on our own. In the sunshine, my bird stood in front of the shed. He[18] looked quite smart: he had a new coat of paint, and the gyro engine was three-quarters covered by a wonderful silver cowling. I was just putting on the finishing touches when Mr. Robinson,[19] who had been the mechanic for my beast years ago, came along the way and saw his old friend. He turned to me: 'Do you want to fly like this?'

'Why not?' I replied.

'Your wings are hanging down.'

'Yes,' I nodded, 'of course. That's how I got it and that's how I flew.'

At first he looked at me in disbelief, then he told me that thick rings between the fuselage and the wing had been forgotten. When I got them later and installed them, the wings lifted up. Again came a big moment. After that conversion everything about the plane had changed, balance as well as strength, and again I was faced with a moment that was to decide everything.

Monday evening – at that time I didn't know that I am always unlucky on Mondays – the shed opened, and 'He' emerged. Everything checked out. The engine was running. Let's go! He flew amazingly beautifully. After a simple straight-line flight, I landed and thought I knew everything. I wanted to do another straight line. No sooner was I off the ground when I felt as comfortable as the donkey that deliberately decided to go dancing on the ice. So I stayed in the air. Curve. The apparatus had become considerably faster, and within a short time I was on the border of the square airfield opposite the Finnish poplars. The thoughts quickly ran through my head. Over them? No, not over the city. If the engine stopped there, then everything is over. So land quickly. I rolled towards the poplars … For God's sake, I'm going to run into them … Get altitude … Bank. At a height of one meter I wanted to make a curve … Slowly and surely, the left wing tip approached the grass … Yes, if I had known how to make a curve! Again, in my naivety, I thought I had done everything, and now I calmly watched the wing tip approach the ground … until it crashed around me and I found myself in the green. The Italian called everyone together and assured them that I was dead. It was good that he did this – at least I had people who wanted to carry the wreckage home. But it wasn't as bad as it looked. The wings, unsurprisingly, were broken. I had a reserve pair. But the engine screw, my pride, was whole. The propeller, however, was done, the engine cowling cracked, and the prop shaft bent. That was the worst. The cowling cost $50 and was quickly refabricated. A new propeller was made by a Swede who had taken up this craft without any prior training. Only the prop shaft remained. A man who had travelled the world with Latham promised to get me a new one. In fact, he intended to break into a neighboring shed, where he knew there was an airplane with the same engine, and just swap the shaft with mine. However, I only considered this aid as a last resort. In the meantime, I noticed that the engine was also able to run quite well with the crooked shaft. It sat awkwardly in the apparatus and pulled a bit to one side, a flaw that I was able to compensate for by using the rudder. I had more serious concerns about the new propeller. It seemed to me that it wasn't doing enough revolutions. I didn't have an RPM counter in my machine; that would have been luxury. I informed the Swede of my fears, but he believed in his work as firmly as I believed in mine. He fetched an instrument and stood close to the running propeller, stopwatch in one hand and the fabulous instrument in the other. He checked for one minute and then told me that everything was fine. He was a good honest man.

I started again the next morning. I let my bird fly dead straight just above the ground, then I landed with a lot of hops and jumps. It went. A stone fell from my heart; I hardly dared to believe in the success. I took off three more times, flew, landed and repeated this for a whole week. On a clear evening, I set a course for the endless sea of houses, the parallel streets of which seemed to meet at one point in the haze, beyond the lake. Bluish mists swam around the lakeshore, the skyscrapers below me rose irregularly out of the darkness like pillars of basalt. That's when I felt for the first time that flying could be beautiful. I packed up, went back to Indianapolis, my starting point, and flew over the heads of many people who envied me. I flew because the train ride was too hot for me.

The next day, the company to which I had submitted my plans weeks before met to sign a paper, with my own name written above all the others. I had provided proof that I was an expert. Letters flew in all directions, material was procured. I had learned during those bygone winter nights what things were needed to set up and operate my factory.

Then came the war and brought new experiences.

Chapter 4

Homecoming

By Hans Buddecke

When I heard the news of the opening of hostilities, I packed my suitcase with two shirts, six collars, toilet articles, and technical magazines. I also didn't forget my good old work suit. Before I took off, I met a young lady with whom my cousin and I had been canoeing a lot. She was completely indifferent to the war. She had bought a new hat that fully occupied all her thoughts. This is probably why she said to me, as a form of farewell:

'Well, have a good time!'

What did these people know about war? In their Spanish conflict they had thrown stones, and their Mexican adventure was a classic example of military caution.

Another prophesied to me:

'Oh, you'll come back with all kinds of crosses and medals.'

That was the most important thing for him, that there would be awards and medals.

Twice before, I had been interested in military ventures. The first time was when I wanted to set up a volunteer machine gun unit with some acquaintances and go kill Mexicans. The other revolved around an island on the Mexican coast that belonged to a Chicago family. The Mexicans had occupied and looted this patch of earth. When diplomacy failed, the family set about trying to raise a private force to exact some justice. But nothing came of it.

The American is a courageous, intrepid man; he is tempted by danger. On the other hand, it seems incomprehensible to him, who only has a sense for his family, that there are noble families in Germany whose sons are aviators or who drive torpedo boats, although they don't need to put themselves in that danger. The first folk song the Americans came out with during the war was 'I Didn't Raise My Boy to Be a Soldier.'[20]

In Indianapolis, all the Germans had gathered in a large hall, shouting three cheers for the Kaiser and the homeland. Then we discussed among ourselves how to get over there. Money was available to us from the older German-Americans in any amount. I was the first to go to New York. If I had found a safe opportunity, the others would follow. I believe, however, that despite my great efforts, I remained one of the few who got through.

The Gotham Hotel's express lift quickly took me from the 19th floor to the flat ground. I stepped out of the luxuriously appointed hall and slowly strolled up Broadway, the Grand Canyon of the East, pondering everything that was now behind me. I had already sent the telegram explaining how to get home to the Germans still in Indianapolis. I had been to our consulate. Unfortunately, the officer had rejected my plan to book passage on a French carrier and advised me to go home in a somewhat more innocuous way. So I modestly visited the office of a Greek steamship line, called myself Morice Adolph, and asked for a ticket. The young lady clerk laughed when I hesitantly wrote down the unfamiliar name; she didn't seem to quite believe me.

The letter telling my relatives at home that I was on my way had also been sent. It said that my doctor was sending me to Palermo, where I would restore my health, and that I would be sailing on the *Athena*.

The whole dazzling life of New York surged around me. Wherever you looked, newspapers were offered that outperformed one another in the craziest news. Right at the top of the stack, for example. Simply fabulous what this French aviator Garros[21] has done. Flies into a zeppelin near Luxembourg and crashes with it. Of course, there just happened to be a draftsman nearby who immediately recorded the event for posterity. I could see all the details clearly in the blurred picture. Uh-huh …

I slowly approached a crowd of hundreds of people who had gathered in the spacious square in front of a brightly lit shop window on the first floor. This is where the *New York Herald* posted its latest news. Of course, *à la* Garros. In the top left corner it was emblazoned in black and white that the English Admiralty had given the Royal Fleet the order to sail, with the mission 'capture or distroy [*sic*] the enemy.'

Aha … ghosts of Nelson's 'England expects' … still in the heads of these chaps. But there were other beautiful pearls. In the middle, a naval battle fought on the American coast; at the very bottom, German Uhlans galloping around in Luxembourg.

My attention turned to the crowd around me. There they all stood, shoulder to shoulder, who were mortal enemies on the other side of the great water. It was very quiet, only whispers; German, French, and Russian sounds came softly to my ear.

The next evening at seven o'clock I boarded the *Athena*, my dark appearance and American clothes completely covering my Germanness. At first glance, anyone would conclude that I was a Frenchman or something like that. After bringing my little suitcase into the cabin, which I was supposed to share with Mr. Haas, a Swiss, I walked up and down the deck and sniffed around. There were very good-looking young and older people on board. Among other things, I saw a lanky brunette and a not-so-big flaxen-haired man wrestle their suitcases, one of which bore the Russian colors, down the aisle. I memorized the people. As I walked up and down the Promenade Deck, I noticed that I was being watched from different angles; the faces of the gentlemen did not seem too friendly to me. Every quarter of an hour or so I returned to my cabin to make sure my suitcase was still there. I also met Mr. Haas. We spoke English because he couldn't speak French, thank God!

We passed the Statue of Liberty with its crown of thorns, then slowly the lights of the skyscrapers were lost in the dark. To the right and left the passengers – almost all young men – leaned over the railing and watched the fading, majestic backdrop, on the other side of which each one of us had fought a battle to get here … and right and left, whichever way I listened, they were all speaking German. I couldn't stand it any longer and turned to my neighbor on the right, whom I had noticed earlier with the Russian, but whom I now heard speaking German quite well. He had bright, clear eyes and an open face that seemed to deserve trust. Within five minutes I realized that I knew his sister, who had married a regimental comrade of mine, and that he was the son of one of our colonel generals. A stone fell from his heart, like the others who were gradually gathering around us when they learned that I was not French, as they had originally assumed. We were looking at spending three weeks together on this voyage, or maybe months, years in Gibraltar.[22]

The tall Russian – who turned out to be a Bonn Hussar[23] – the blonde, and I formed a circle. Besides ourselves there were five Germans, two Austrians, a Polish prince, and Mr. Haas. We stayed away from the other society, which consisted of Greeks and Italians, but we got on very well with an Armenian Turk who was constantly playing with a beautiful amber chain, and who had the same name as the former minister, Noradungian.[24]

It was very sultry on the Atlantic. All you did was play poker and wait for messages from the wireless station operated by two young Danes. There was no love lost between these two gentlemen and ourselves, so we did not learn anything in the first days. Then odd rumors started circulating, no telling where they came from. There was talk of German defeats. We inquired. Oh, it wasn't so bad; they'd rather not tell us at all. A very insignificant story. We had lost only one huge battle in Belgium – 80,000 had been killed, the crown prince had fallen, and the Guard had been destroyed.

We sat in our dark corner, where we had been playing poker, and the tears were in our eyes. Until now, we had not hated the enemy, because a declaration of war in itself seemed to us to be the reason for the war. But now the lumps came up in our throats, thick as a fist, and strangled us. Now we hated these black skulls around us, now we felt exalted over them. The difference between the strong, straight people of our homeland and those marketplace barkers was too obvious. If we hadn't known why the fight was being fought, now it became clear to us: envy.

Three weeks of travelling gave me enough time to study the company on board. To my dining table were assigned the two Austrians, Mr. Haas, and myself. Herr Haas from Switzerland knew incredibly little about his country, as he himself had to admit to me. One day at noon he suddenly claimed that his emperor[25] was 57 years old. Just think! Another time: 'Our fleet has nineteen ships of the line.' My neighbor whispered to me: 'Just imagine the wonderful picture, the mighty ships on Lake Lucerne.'

We could hardly suppress our laughter, but Mr. Haas, who in reality was a reserve officer in a Berlin regiment, did not seem to be able to explain our uproar. He was the only one of us who, apart from these small infidelities, played his role – even to us – until the last day.

The Polish prince intended to have a real prince's suit and boots made in Italy for the time being, and he would play it by ear from then on. For the time being, all his income came from the money he took from Mr. Noradungian at poker, as he told me two years later at a club in Smyrna, where he suddenly sat down across from me at my table one fine evening.

One morning we found ourselves in the Strait of Gibraltar, and approached the Rock where so many good Germans had already met their fate. The hussar had kept three beautiful long Coronas. He took these out and gave one to each of us.

We stood on deck, forced ourselves to smoke the heavy cigars, and looked out across the water, on which one black torpedo boat after another with the red-striped Union Jack passed the *Athena*. Each time the feeling twitched through us: this one will be the one.

We had already anticipated that English officers would come on board and search our ship. If they really came, it was time to act immediately. All my German papers were hidden, buried in the plush sofas of the smoking parlor, as was my pistol. The evening before I had thrown my pair of field-gray breeches into the sea. My factory worker's outfit from America was ready; in my pocket I had a handful of shiny twenty dollar pieces.

There are often stowaways on the big ships who stay on board for weeks without anyone being able to catch them. Why shouldn't I do that too, if it came to that? I knew the ship from the keel to the bridge. So I watched like a hawk. What if they did get hold of me? I was an Alsatian, why shouldn't I become a soldier with Joffre? But I would find a way to avoid that somehow. There was no reason for me to get involved in an investigation. My English was okay. But by the same token I shouldn't underestimate my opponent, expecting him not to recognize my German accent and mannerisms. In any case, I had invented and rehearsed a French dialect that no one could have distinguished from Chinese.

The excitement was great. Under other circumstances the passage would have been most edifying. One could have counted the tanks in the port of Gibraltar, admired the area. But as it was, one stared only fixedly at the little black dogs of Hell, which were coming closer and closer. As if nothing was happening, the blue and white flag of Greece fluttered at the stern so merrily, and unintentionally kept the English gentlemen off us.

Unintentionally. We knew for sure that the ship's officers had drawn up a blacklist and were ready to sell us out. The English, however, thought it better to use us as catspaws because they thought the Greeks would join the war at their side at any moment.

Ahead of the ship the land disappeared again; the Coronas were already beginning to burn our fingertips. We clenched our fists in our pockets; you had to grit your teeth in order not to cheer out 'Aha!' But wait, don't go crazy with joy, stay calm. We pulled ourselves together and went below deck with indifferent faces.

Our eyes shone. This obstacle was bypassed by God knows what chance. The black devils with their red handkerchiefs were behind us. Behind us also were the nightmarish fears of imprisonment, in which our only prospect was to play cards, day and night; in which one only had to say: 'Joke number 301,' and everyone would laugh because they already knew all the jokes by heart.

The next morning a steamer carrying the Tricolore crossed our course so closely that we thought it was going to ram us. Hard by us he let his siren howl violently, and the Greeks roared hurray until they could no longer shout.

The long sea voyage had made us a little discouraged. But the more we saw of the enemy, the more we believed in our strength again. When we arrived in Palermo, we hurriedly jumped into the boats that were bringing us to shore. We immediately grabbed the newspapers in the hotel and puzzled out from the Italian accounts what we wanted to know. Again and again the headlines read: 'Paris Nuova vittoria,' (Paris claims new victories) but below: 'Berlin denies.' This told us all we needed to know about our former allies, the Italians, before we had even spoken a word with them. Our consul told us that nothing had been lost, but…

In Rome we got our hands on a German newspaper for the first time, which, to our amazement, was teeming with news of our victories. The patriotism of our Bonn Hussar found few friends in Italy. Here and there he crowed a 'Three cheers for the Triple Alliance!'[26] for the porters, but the expressions they returned to him were still quite cool. He acknowledged this fact when we had approached the Monastery of the Dead in Palermo, with the monks' skeletons nailed to the walls,[27] with the dry words: 'Enh, I prefer my royal Prussian mass grave.'

From Rome we travelled on to Upper Italy. The further north we got, the more it was teeming with soldiers. By the time we got to Verona, the crowds of them had become so large that we seriously asked ourselves: is this a general mobilization here, or are these boys planning a theatrical performance?

The overcrowded train brought us at a snail's pace over the Brenner Pass to Munich. It was wonderful to finally hear the truth here, to finally enter the homeland. One would have loved to hug every telephone pole, every tree, and the lovely people who laughed at me because of my incredibly beautiful straw hat from Chicago. Yes, yes, you could see that we had come a long way. A handshake, a goodbye, worried eyes in laughing faces, so we shipmates parted and headed off in all directions; sure that we would never forget each other.

Somewhat anxiously, I bade the young lady at the 'Franfkfurter Hof': 'Put me through to Major Buddecke.' On the off chance of getting some news, I wanted to call my uncle's house and ask about my relatives. Surely the men were all already abroad on assignment. What would I hear? Had any of them been killed? And who?

"Hello, this is Hans Joachim Buddecke. To whom am I speaking?"

"Your mother."

We hadn't seen each other for two years —

Chapter 5

Indianapolis, 1913–1914

Hans Buddecke arrived in the United States sometime in late 1913 or early 1914.[28] It didn't take him long to make a splash in Indianapolis' social circles. The first article about him in the *Indianapolis Star* appeared on 22 February 1914, entitled "Ring of Fencing Foils Soon May Resound in Homes of Indianapolis Society Folks." It described how Buddecke, "formerly fencing instructor of the Royal Cadets Corporations in Prussia and an aviator in Emperor William's army" was hoping to spark an interest in fencing among Americans and hinting that he might even become a paid instructor for the wealthy. Also mentioned is how:

> Buddecke also will be an assistant to Capt. G.L. Bumbaugh in his flying machine and airship enterprises and will be engineer for the dirigible which Capt. Bumbaugh proposes to build. Buddecke's four years of experience as a pilot of flying machines in the German Army and his study of motor mechanics at the National automobile factory and experience as a machinist at the Atlas Engine Works have given him a fund of mechanical information upon which to draw.

This is a very odd article. It is hard to determine if the national fencing school was an earlier business effort, a hobby, or a simply an excuse to get into newspapers so as to advertise his flying. The article does include three pictures of Hans Buddecke engaged in sword play.

If fencing instruction was his idea for a business, it was not a particularly good idea. The fact that some young 23-year-old German who had been in country for only a short while had gotten a front-page article in the *Indianapolis Star* was either extremely fortuitous, or shows the influence and connections of his American uncle. It was likely the latter. The idea of a recently transplanted German suddenly deciding that Americans – in a country with widespread gun ownership – needed to understand and appreciate the fine art of sword fighting, would have been very naive. The article was probably for the purpose of generating some interest for his flying business.

As Buddecke notes in his book: "My cadet education and lieutenant's training had not weighed me down with too much practical knowledge. Giving commands, tying a knot in a necktie, those kinds of things perhaps, but otherwise …." Was this a case of him attempting to use what he did know for the sake of establishing a business or purpose in the United States? He never discusses the fencing idea in his memoir. He describes working as a machinist and then moves immediately to his aircraft business idea. This may have been for the sake of the narrative or because he preferred to sweep the failed fencing idea under the rug, or because the real purpose of the article was to advertise his flying business plans. In light of future business arrangements with Captain G.L. Bumbaugh, we suspect it was the latter.

Of more interest are the references in the article to aviation. It specifically states that he had four years of flying experience as a pilot in the German Army. We know from his own account that this is not true, and we assume that his American uncle also knew this. Yet, here is Hans Buddecke introduced to Indianapolis as a flying expert, despite never having flown a plane – a bold and outrageous lie. Having made such a public claim in print in February 1914, it is clear that his own plans and schemes for some business and career in aviation were firmly set.

There may be a second lie in the article, which is a claim that he studied motor mechanics at the "National automobile factory." There was no such organization in the United States, though the reference may be to some organization in Germany. Buddecke's memoir makes no mention of this either, and emphasizes that he actually did not have any 'practical knowledge'. The purpose of the article appears to have been to create a falsified résumé for Buddecke, probably in cooperation with his uncle.

Still, the article clearly establishes that he was working with Captain G.L. Bumbaugh, that his uncle was Albert Lieber, and that he was working at the Atlas Engine Works.

Buddecke's family:

Hans Buddecke's father, Albert Buddecke, was born 14 or 16 August 1858.[29] On 22 August 1890 he was made a lieutenant in the 1st Grand Ducal Hessian Infantry (Life Guard) Regiment No. 115 and later held a command at the War Academy in Berlin. In 1908 he was a captain attached to the General Staff. During his career he wrote several studies for the German Army.[30] He was appointed head of the library of the High General Staff in 1909. At the start of the Great War he served for two months on the Western Front, but returned to the General Staff from December 1914 to October 1918.[31]

By the spring of 1918 the elder Buddecke was a Lieutenant Colonel serving as the Deputy Chief of Staff of the German Army General Staff. The General Staff tended to attract some of the brighter, more forward-thinking officers in the German Army. It was far more than just an administrative function.[32] He rose to the rank of colonel and passed away in Jena on 24 October 1931 at the age of 73.

Albert was married to Anna Herber (1864–1950) and they had three sons. The eldest was Werner (1887–1967) who was wounded in France during the early part of the war.[33] He then served in the Army Command's central library (perhaps indicating that he had a long-term disability, or he could have been working with his father). Their second son was Hartmut[34] (1888–1945) who commanded the torpedo boat SMS *V27*. He was a senior lieutenant at that time and his was the lead boat of the 17th Half-flotilla. The boat, which was the size of a destroyer, was over 250 ft long with a displacement of almost 1,000 tons. It was armed with three 3.5 in guns, six torpedo tubes, eight torpedoes, and could carry up to twenty-four mines. It had a speed of 33.5 knots (38.6 mph) and a crew of eighty-three. It was sunk during the Battle of Jutland on 31 May 1916. The SMS *V27* took part in a torpedo attack on the British battlecruisers at around 17:26 CET (16:26 MGT). The attack by the 17th Half-flotilla was disrupted by British destroyers and *V27* was immobilized by two 4-inch shell hits. Her crew was taken off by a sister ship, which then scuttled *V27* with gunfire. Three crew had been wounded. Hartmut does not appear to have been seriously injured as he later appears in photographs with his younger brother Hans in October 1916. Hartmut also later patented a fire extinguisher in several countries.[35]

Adolf August Hans-Joachim Buddecke was their youngest son, born in Berlin on 22 August 1890.[36] He went to school in Potsdam, Strasbourg, and Charlottenburg, the result of the peripatetic life as a military dependent. He entered the Cadet Corps in spring 1904 at age 13, and was admitted to Selekta, a special cadet course for preparation to the War Academy and eventual service with the General Staff, on which his father ended up serving. He passed his final exam in 1910 and now-Lieutenant Buddecke was assigned to his father's former unit, the 1st Grand Ducal Hessian Infantry (Life Guard) Regiment No. 115.[37]

It is clear that the Buddecke family were an intelligent group – his father was a soldier-scholar and there was a long tradition of military service in the family. This is reflected by Hans Buddecke, who also appears to have been a talented man and a decent writer. Talented writers also appear with his American family, as noted below.

Albert Lieber (uncle):

Hans Buddecke's uncle on his mother's side, Albert Lieber, was born on 16 August 1863 in Indianapolis, Indiana, according to some sources.[38]

Albert's father, Peter Lieber (1832–1915), was born in Düsseldorf, lived in Indianapolis, and died in Düsseldorf. His mother, Sophia St. André (born 16 August 1839 in Freiburg, Germany) was reported to be living in Düsseldorf at the age of 78 in a newspaper article published in November 1914.[39] Albert Lieber's parents moved to Indianapolis sometime around 1860, three years before Albert's birth.

Peter Lieber immigrated to the United States around 1850 when he was 18. He lived in Cincinnati, Ohio, and then New Ulm, Minnesota. He enlisted in the Union Army during the Civil War and became the private secretary to Oliver P. Morton (1823–1877), the very pro-Union Republican governor of Indiana. He is described in the Vonnegut family history as a 'limping war veteran'.

In 1863 Peter, his older brother Herman, and Charles Mayer, bought Gack & Biser brewery, founded in 1859 in Indianapolis. It was renamed the P. Lieber Brewing Company. In 1879 the brewery sold about 15,000 barrels of beer. Mayer retired in the 1870s and Peter Lieber bought his shares. Herman sold his interest in 1880 to William Schrever and the business was reincorporated with Joseph Gies as the head brewer.[40]

Peter Lieber retired in 1887 due to ill health and returned to Düsseldorf. He and his wife are not listed in the 1910 or subsequent U.S. censuses. Peter left his son Albert in charge of the brewing business. In 1893 U.S. President Grover Cleveland appointed Peter Lieber the American Consul to Germany, a post he held until shortly before the Great War started.

Albert Lieber remained in Indiana and continued building up the brewing business and becoming the president of the largest brewery in the Indianapolis area, the Indianapolis Brewing Company, which was created by the merger of three brewing companies, of which Albert was the director, treasurer, and manager of all three brewing arms. The capital stock of the corporation in 1890 was $800,000, which would be well over $10 million in today's dollars.[41]

The family history continues with a rather unflattering description of Albert Lieber. For purposes of illustrating the kind of man Buddecke's mentor was, the account says:[42]

> He was often in London on business when he was young. He had his clothes tailored in Savile Row and was the very model of Victorian sartorial elegance; broadcloth Prince Albert coats, silk hats, Scotch tweeds, starched shirts and collars, and handmade boots. He was handsome, friendly, and highly sociable. He loved parties, good eating, and fine wines. He was always much involved in a series of love affairs, passing feminine attachments, and ribald entertainment.
>
> The brewery was under the general supervision of a retired British Army officer – Colonel Thompson – who visited Indianapolis every year or two to look things over and report back to London. He and Albert between them milked the local operation of most of the profits of the brewery through padded expense accounts, sales promotion schemes, public relations departments, political contributions and other devices to skim the cream off the profits. The syndicate demanded a five per cent return upon its investment and got it. Albert and his cohorts lined their pockets.
>
> In contrast to his father, who was conservative, retiring, and extremely modest and unassuming, Albert was extroverted, flamboyant, sociable, and a big spender. He always lived on a very lavish scale in various large houses with lots of servants, horses, and carriages and later the earliest and finest motor cars. In his heyday he always had an English butler and a footman in livery. He entertained his friends without thought of cost: the choicest viands, rare wines, flowers, the whitest linens, and choicest porcelain chinaware.
>
> He soon acquired the reputation of a millionaire who counted the cost of nothing. He became a jolly companion of

> the town's 'fun boys' who consisted of other rich men's sons, among them Booth Tarkington. They gave fabulous parties. One of them owned the English Hotel on Monument Circle and English's Opera House where all the principal traveling shows played. He had a stage box reserved for his use on the right side of the house where he had a door which connected to the stage. This gave him and his cronies access to the stage and easy opportunity to meet actresses and particularly the chorus girls with musical comedies.
>
> At other times they would take over for the night the leading bagnio of the town – facetiously known as the University Club Annex – which was situated on the east side of New Jersey Street about two blocks north of Washington Street. No cash changed hands to sully the dignified atmosphere of the Annex. Each month its devotees were billed discreetly for their share of maintenance. Here the local 'fun boys' would stage real bacchanalian orgies which provided choice and juicy gossip for the staid community. But they always committed their indiscretions, with due respect for the Victorian proprieties, in privacy behind doors – which is what doors are for.

Booth Tarkington (1869–1946) was an American novelist and playwright who in the 1910s and 1920s was considered by some to be America's greatest living author. He won the Pulitzer Prize for Fiction two times, in 1919 and 1922.

At this time, Albert Lieber had one daughter, Edith Sophia Lieber (see below), and two sons: Peter Lieber, born in 1891, and Rudolf Lieber, born in 1896. Albert's first marriage was to Alice Sophia (Barus) Lieber. The mother of his three children, she is described in the Vonnegut family history as 'beautiful and musical'. She was born around 1868. They married in 1885 and she passed away in Indianapolis on 10 December 1897, at only around 31 years old.

According to the Vonnegut family history, she died of pneumonia when Edith was around 9.

His second marriage was to Ora D. Lane, born around 1865 according to some sources, but the 1910 census lists her age as 36 (born around 1874). She is described in the Vonnegut family history as:

> very attractive but extremely eccentric woman, who was never accepted by Albert's family or close friends … She was an accomplished violinist and came from Zanesville, Ohio. She was familiarly known as "O.D." but most people referred to her as "Odious." She became a sort of storybook stepmother to Albert's children. She terrorized Albert as well, threatened his life, slept with a pistol under her pillow, and was a perfect demon and termagant. Kindly, gentle Albert stood it as long as he could and then divorced her but he was obliged to settle a large alimony upon her which depleted his capital, which was not large. He had never been an accumulator and had spent freely, relying on the brewery to carry him as usual with a large annual income.

Albert was married a third time to Meda (Langtry) Lieber, listed as age 32 in the 1920 census, which would have made her about 25 at the time of Buddecke's soujourn in Indianapolis. (Albert would have been 50.) She was described in the Vonnegut family history as "a nondescript widow … who had a daughter whom Albert adopted and renamed Alberta." There was a second young daughter named Lillian.

Edith Sophia Lieber (his cousin, the "dollar princess"):

The cousin that Buddecke mentions in his book was Albert Lieber's oldest daughter, Edith Sophia Lieber, born in Indianapolis on 26 August 1888.[43] She married Kurt Vonnegut on 22 November 1913.

She is described in the Vonnegut family history as "a rather tall woman, about five feet eight inches, with a fine graceful figure. She was auburn-haired, not quite red, with a very fair clear skin, finely modeled features, and blue-green eyes. She was stately and dignified in bearing. She had a lively sense of humor and laughed easily."

The Vonnegut family history suggests that she was emotionally scarred. As it notes:[44]

> Edith Lieber's mother Alice Barus died of pneumonia when Edith was 6 [most likely she was 9]. Soon afterward, her father Albert married a very attractive but extremely eccentric woman, Ora D. Lane, who was never accepted by Albert's family or close friends. She became a sort of storybook stepmother to Albert's children. She chastised and ill-treated them in subtle ways. She seemed to resent them and abused them so that they all suffered a distinctive psychic trauma from which they never fully recovered. Where formerly they had known nothing but loving and tender care, now they were subjected to every sort of indignity, humiliation, and neglect … [Edith's] adolescent years had been difficult with her odious stepmother, but she was strong enough in spirit and courage to endure her ordeal, although the scars were there.

Edith was married at the age of 25 on 22 November 1913. Buddecke was probably not yet in Indianapolis at that time. Her life before that is described in the Vonnegut family history:

> As a young woman, Edith had been engaged to other men but had each time broken her engagement. These suitors were all Europeans; for in the years from 1907 to 1913 [when she was between 19 and 25 years old] Edith lived mostly abroad. As an extremely handsome woman and the daughter of an American millionaire she was much courted.

She first became engaged to Kenneth Doulton, an Englishman, a grandson of Sir Henry Doulton, and a scion of the family who for generations had owned the world famous Royal Doulton Porcelain Works in Lambeth. She met him while visiting London for the social season of 1908. Doulton was an attractive member of the upper-middle class with connections in the aristocracy. He was a charming idler and of course expected Albert to supply a suitable settlement as a dowry upon his lovely daughter. Albert enjoyed a large income at that time but was not enthusiastic to part with his modest capital. And Doulton was not about to go into the brewery business in Indianapolis. He wanted to marry Edith, have her father buy them a country place and a little house in Mayfair, and remain in old England. Edith demurred and the engagement was broken. In the Great War, Doulton, as a junior officer in a Guards regiment, lost his life while serving in the first British Expeditionary Force in the first months of the war.

Edith then forsook merrie England and shifted her European base of operations from London to Düsseldorf. From 1909 to 1913 she spent most of each year staying with her grandfather, Peter, then past 80, and her maiden aunt Laura, in the old man's Schloss on the Rhine. He was no longer Consul General of the United States but he kept the Stars and Stripes flying over his palace and retained his American citizenship to the end. But his three children, Laura, Emily, and Rudolph, became German citizens. Rudolph adopted a military career, went through the Cadet School and became lieutenant colonel of a regiment of cavalry – the Uhlans – garrisoned in the area of Düsseldorf. Emily married a German Army officer. Edith was thus thrown into the company of subalterns in her uncle's famous regiment. At the time the Kaiser's army officers constituted a sort of elite social group with many privileges and much prestige. The Kaiser's pay and allowances to his officers were extremely meager. If an officer did not have substantial means to supplement his pay and maintain the position required of him, he was expected to marry a rich wife. In fact, he could not marry except with the consent of the colonel of his regiment; and the consent was withheld until the social position, reputability, and dowry of the bride were officially approved.

Edith's first serious German suitor was Lieutenant Paul Genth of the Uhlans. She gave him the go-by after a brief courtship. Shortly afterward Captain Otto Voigt of the regiment proposed to her, and after a spirited courtship was accepted by her with the consent of her family and of his commanding officer. The captain was a dashing figure in his colorful dress uniform with shako and 'Merry Widow' accoutrements. But here again the course of true love did not run true and smooth. There were difficulties about the dowry, and the prospect for Edith of a career as an army wife in the highly artificial and regulated life of the imperial army palled upon her. Captain Voigt was one of those heel-clicking Prussian-type officers who looked good in his uniform in command of his squadron of cavalry but was quite different from the easygoing, indulgent, and deferential American husbands of Edith's experience. She wavered. But Albert gave her carte blanche to buy a trousseau and she proceeded to do so. All of the linens were duly embroidered "L-V." The Liebers of the German branch thought it was a great match. But Edith began to have misgivings. So did Albert, who never liked dowries anyway. And Edith did not want to make her permanent home in Germany. The captain was likewise not an enthusiastic candidate for a job in the brewery. At all events, the engagement was broken by mutual consent.

Edith Lieber got along well enough with her father and his third wife Meda and their two young children, so returned to Indianapolis. Albert Lieber was then in the full tide of success as one of the town's rich men. He resided on a beautiful estate of

> some hundred acres just to the northwest of the city, in a large residence which he had recently constructed. He built for her a small cottage on his estate very attractively situated on a bluff overlooking White River. It was furnished to her taste; had a grand piano in the living room, a fireplace, comfortable lounge chairs and couches; and it was her own retreat when she wanted privacy – which was most of the time.

Bear in mind that real millionaire families were rare at this time; one estimate states that in 1914 in the United States there were 7,000 millionaires.[45] Edith's height of 5 ft 8 in was similarly rare; at the time, the average height of men was 5 ft 8 in or less, 1 or 2 inches lower than it is today.[46] At 5 ft 8 in, Edith was taller than many men.

So, this was the life of the "dollar princess," as Hans Buddecke rather caustically refers to her. As the Vonnegut family history notes:

> Edith, a very beautiful woman, tall and statuesque, resumed contact with her old friends, went about in the social life of the city, and had plenty of suitors. Kurt always admired her beauty and was very proud of her. They fell in love, became engaged, and were married on November 22, 1913.

The engagement between Kurt Vonnegut and Edith Lieber was announced in the 15 October 1913 edition of *The Indianapolis Star.* As the paper notes: "The marriage of Miss Lieber and Mr. Vonnegut will connect two of the oldest and most prominent German families of Indianapolis. Miss Lieber has spent much of her time abroad with her grandparents, Mr. and Mrs. Peter Lieber, at Düsseldorf, Germany."

This last statement is interesting as Buddecke in his book makes fun of her accent. One could also assume from her time spent in Germany that Edith and Hans were well acquainted, although this is not clear from Buddecke's account.

The 6 November 1913 issue of *The Indianapolis News* states: "Albert Lieber has issued invitations for the marriage of his daughter Edith to Kurt Vonnegut, to take place Saturday evening, November 22, at All Souls' church." In the 16 November edition of *The Indianapolis Star* it states:

> The marriage of Miss Edith Lieber, only daughter of Albert Lieber, and Kurt Vonnegut, son of Mrs. Bernard Vonnegut, will be celebrated Saturday evening at All Souls' Unitarian Church and will be one of the interesting and most brilliant nuptials of the season. Following the ceremony, a reception will be held at the Claypool Hotel, which will be followed by an exquisitely appointed dinner. The attendants will be Mrs. Robert Blee Rhoads, a recent bride and formerly Miss Erna Francke, who will attend her cousin as matron of honor. Miss Irma Vonnegut, a sister of Mr. Vonnegut, comes from Boston this week, where she is attending Simmons College, to serve as maid of honor; Miss Rave Dryer, Miss Marie Lieber, Miss Bertha Schnull and Miss Monica Sheerin will be bridesmaids. Peter Lieber, the bride's brother, will attend Mr. Vonnegut, and the groomsmen will be Herman Kothe, Harry Glossbrenner, Harry Bentley of Chicago, Robert Blee Rhoads and Dr. Herbert T. Wagner. Miss Lieber will give a luncheon Thursday at the Lieber country place, "Wildflower Glen," New Augusta, for her attendants, and Friday evening Mrs. Bernard Vonnegut will give a bridal dinner.

This illustrates the life of this "dollar princess." Most of the attendants listed have German last names. It is possible that Hans Buddecke may have come over to the United States at this time to attend the wedding, although there is no documentation one way or the other.

There are multiple references to the nuptials in the papers under the Vonnegut name. The most interesting is in *The Indianapolis News* of 22 November 1913 where it says in part:

> A beautiful wedding will take place this evening at All Souls' church … Mr. Vonnegut and his bride will leave later for a wedding trip, and they will be at home at The Farm, New Augusta, after January 1. Albert Lieber, father of the bride, will leave tomorrow for New York, and will sail for Europe to visit his parents, Mr. and Mrs. Peter Lieber, in Dusseldorf, Germany.

It is perhaps during the return from this trip to Europe that Albert Lieber brought his nephew Hans Buddecke to America.

As the Vonnegut family history notes:

> They [Kurt and Edith] were a charming and extremely attractive couple. The marriage was approved by both families; but the Schnull-Vonnegut clan was slightly condescending. In the pecking order in the social hierarchy of the community, and particularly in the German group it was generally understood that the Schnull-Vonnegut clan ranked ahead of the Lieber-Barus clan. Edith and Kurt's wedding celebration was one long remembered in Indianapolis.

It was probably the biggest and most costly party the town had ever seen, or was likely to witness again soon because by the next year came the Great War and then Prohibition. The curtain fell on such extravagance.

Edith Vonnegut had three children with Kurt. Her eldest son was Bernard Vonnegut, born 29 August 1914 in Indianapolis. He became an atmospheric scientist and is credited with discovering that silver iodide could be used to seed clouds in order to produce rain and snow. Her youngest son, Kurt Vonnegut Jr., was born 11 November 1922 in Indianapolis. Kurt Jr. later became famous as the author of such novels as *Cat's Cradle* (1963), *Slaughterhouse-Five* (1969) and *Breakfast of Champions* (1973).

As Edith Vonnegut was the mother of a famous writer, it is perhaps appropriate to get a description of the dollar princess' sad later life from her son's autobiography:

> our mother … was going insane. Late at night, and always in the privacy of our own home, and never with guests present, she expressed hatred for father as corrosive as hydrofluoric acid … I made the suggestion in *Palm Sunday* that my mother's untreated, unacknowledged insanity was caused by bad chemicals she swallowed rather than created within herself, principally alcohol and unlimited quantities of prescribed barbiturates. I am willing to believe that her ailment was hereditary, but I have no American ancestors (fully accounted for in *Palm Sunday*) who were clinically crazy …
>
> So when my mother went crazy, long before my son went crazy, long before I had a son, and finally killed herself, I blamed chemicals, and I still do, although she had a terrible childhood. I can even name two of the chemicals, phenobarbital and booze. Those came from the outside, of course, the phenobarbs from our family doctor, who was trying to do something about sleeplessness. When she died, I was a soldier, and my division was about to go overseas [the 106th Infantry Division in late 1944].
>
> We were able to keep her insanity a secret, since it became really elaborate only at home and between midnight and dawn. We were able to keep her suicide a secret thanks to a compassionate and possibly politically ambitious coroner.
>
> When my mother went off her rocker late at night, the hatred and contempt she sprayed on my father, as gentle and innocent a man as ever lived, was without limit and pure, untainted by ideas and information … she died on Mother's Day in 1944 (about a month before D Day) … My mother never saw any of her one dozen grandchildren, although my sister Alice was pregnant with

her first one, Jim, when Alice and I found Mother dead. (No prospect of good news, obviously, could rescue Mother …).[47]

Captain George L. Bumbaugh:

Captain George L. Bumbaugh was one of the leading aviators of his day, specializing in balloons and later heavier than air machines. He was born 7 January 1876 in New Castle, Pennsylvania, and began flying balloons and making parachute jumps in 1898. In 1905 Bumbaugh founded the West Virginia Aerial Navigation Company with thirteen other Charleston shareholders. They had raised enough money to build several of the airships designed by Bumbaugh. Their first flights were in 1906, and in June he flew an airship at Cincinnati's Coney Island amusement park. The ship rose 600 ft and circled the park several times. The flight was brought to a premature end when vibrations from the airship's one-cylinder engine knocked loose a copper gasoline line. Bumbaugh switched to using rubber fuel hoses, solving this problem. He then purchased advertisements in the *Charleston Daily Gazette* announcing demonstration flights on Independence Day, July 4, 1906. These were staged at the city's baseball park. He charged 25 cents (around $7.00 in 2023) for admission and nearly 2,000 people attended. This effort failed, though, as the platform that carried the blimp's motor, controls, and pilot had not yet been attached to the underside of the gas-filled balloon by the 4 p.m. flight time that had been announced. The disappointed and restless crowd ended up dispersing, but no refund was offered, which led to "symptoms of an incipient riot." As sunset approached, the airship named the *Comet* was finally ready for flight. It took off and circled the baseball park several times before having to land for a rudder repair.

Bumbaugh moved to Indianapolis in 1908, and between then and 1914 he was one of the most prominent pioneering balloonists in America, setting many records and winning many championships. In 1914 Bumbaugh signed up as the President and one of the five directors of the Aerial Advertising Company of America, along with Hans Buddecke, and eventually moved to flying and working with airplanes. In 1916 he designed and built several airplanes at his machine shop, which was adjacent to the Indianapolis Motor Speedway. He later founded the G.L. Bumbaugh Airship and Balloon Construction Co. in St. Louis, Missouri, and from 1917–20 built balloons and airships for the U.S. Army and the U.S. Navy. Bumbaugh died near Chicago in Hickory Hills, Illinois in 1955.[48]

It is odd, considering his national reputation, that Buddecke did not mention Bumbaugh in his book. His account makes it appear as though the aircraft company he was establishing was all his doing, when in fact there were five people listed as directors, including the vastly more established, experienced, and well-known Captain Bumbaugh. Possibly Buddecke was once again using his memoir to burnish his reputation by taking sole credit for what appears to be a shared effort.

Lyons-Atlas Company and Atlas Engine Works:

According to his account, Hans Buddecke worked for a while as a laborer at the Lyons-Atlas Company, previously known as the Atlas Engine Works. The factory was not identified in his memoir, but was mentioned in the newspaper article quoted above.

The Atlas Engine Works was a large industrial complex covering multiple blocks located on Ninth Street and Martindale Street in Indianapolis (now 19th Street and Andrew J. Brown Drive). It had been in existence since 1872 as the Indianapolis Car Works, manufacturing railcars. That business soon failed, and the industrial complex became the Atlas Works in 1874 and then in 1878 the Atlas Engine Works. They were by then a major manufacturer of steam engines and boilers.

In 1897 they expanded their production into gas engines. By around 1900 the factory had roughly 2,000 employees and was one of the largest engine manufacturers in the United States.

On 16 October 1912 the company was purchased by James W. Lyons, a Chicago businessman, and several associates. This sale included the diesel and automobile engine lines, including the Knight sleeve-valve engine for automobiles. The new company was renamed the Lyons-Atlas Company and incorporated for a capital stock of $500,000 (over $13 million in 2023). This is probably when Albert Lieber purchased an interest in the company.[49]

The Aerial Advertising Company:

On 6 March 1914, *The Indianapolis News* reported that the Aerial Advertising Company of America had filed articles of incorporation in Indianapolis, with operating capital of $300,000, to "operate air craft of all types, to carry passengers and freight and to display advertising from air craft." The directors were listed as G. I. [*sic*] Bumbaugh, H. R. Fletcher, and H. I. [*sic*] Buddecke.

The Indianapolis Star on Saturday, 7 March 1914 had a more extensive article on the subject:

Balloon Publicity Company Launched

Local Men Interested in Concern Which Proposes to Establish Fleet of Dirigibles for Operations Day and Night

Advertising by balloon is the latest idea in publicity, and, according to information given out yesterday, the recently incorporated Aerial Advertising Company of America, which has filed articles of incorporation with the secretary of state, will begin operations immediately. Capt. George L. Bumbaugh, the Indianapolis aviator, is president of the company. He and H. Ioachim [*sic*] Buddecke, formerly of the aviation corps of

> the German Army, and H. R. Fletcher of Indianapolis are the incorporators.
>
> The directors are: Mr. Bumbaugh, Mr. Buddecke, Mr. Fletcher, Albert Lieber and Harry B. Wilson. George M. Conner is the business manager and Charles W. Miller is the legal counsel. The company will have offices at 538 American Central Life Building.
>
> It is the plan of the company to manufacture dirigible balloons for the purpose of displaying advertising. The officers assert they have patents pending for a system of illuminating the sides of the balloons so that the advertising may be read as the balloons pass through the skies at night.
>
> "The company plans to build a fleet of dirigible airships to be located in different districts of the country to specialize in commercial advertising, with the large national advertisers, making both day and night flights," says a statement issued by the company.
>
> "The company expects to complete its first dirigible in time for the Speedway races. In addition to Capt. Bumbaugh and Lieut. Buddecke the company is negotiating with the best talent available as operators for its fleet of airships."

Clearly Hans Buddecke was the youngest member of this team, but one with the family connections that allowed him to finance such an operation as his uncle Albert Lieber was also one of the directors. The capital amount of $300,000 was substantial – almost $8 million in 2023 dollars. In his book, Buddecke mentions a Mr. Morris of Mr. Morris' department store. No evidence of such a person has been found.

According to one source, Buddecke purchased his airplane at Chicago's Cicero Flying Field on 20 May 1914.[50] He stayed at Cicero for a few weeks, and was first reported back in Indianapolis, flying, in mid-July 1914.[51] His account states:

I packed up, went back to Indianapolis, my starting point, and flew over the heads of many people who envied me … The next day, the company to which I had submitted my plans weeks before met to sign a paper, with my own name written above all the others. I had provided proof that I was an expert. Letters flew in all directions, material was procured. I had learned during those bygone winter nights what things were needed to set up and operate my factory.

Then came the war and brought new experiences.

From this narrative, it seems "the next day" would be mid-July. Yet it is clear that the company was founded in March 1914 with Buddecke as one of the directors. It was founded before he learned to fly. So, either the story plays somewhat with the timeline of the narrative, or Buddecke founded a second business for which he was a director. It is almost certainly the former.

The business tie-in of the Aerial Advertising Company of America with Hans Buddecke's uncle, Albert Lieber, is repeated by an article in *The Indianapolis News* on Monday, 25 May 1914. It states:

Brewery Buys Aeroplane

For some time a number of brewers and brewers' agents in this city have had vague intimations that Albert Lieber, president of the Indianapolis Brewing Company was about to spring something new. What that something is was disclosed yesterday at a picnic when a new keg was being put on tap. It seems the company has bought an aeroplane of French make, latest type, which, for advertising purposes, it will fly in various cities and towns in Indiana, chiefly in Indianapolis. The pilot will be Captain Hans Buddecke who until recently was a captain in the Royal Guards of Berlin and is credited with a large experience

> in aeroplanes in Germany. The captain is a relative of Mr. Lieber by marriage. Altogether the aeroplane venture will be an international affair – made in France, piloted by a German, to fly in America. The date of the first flight in this city is not given, but will be, it is understood, in a few days.

Again we read the claims of Buddecke having flying experience in Germany and now he has been promoted to captain and was with the "Royal Guards of Berlin." The article says the brewing company purchased the plane, clearly indicating Lieber's involvement in this business. Presumably the paper's reporter gathered all this information directly from either Albert Lieber or Hans Buddecke while at the aforementioned picnic.

The next time Buddecke appeared in the Indianapolis papers, in this case the *Indianapolis Star* on 22 July 1914, was a week and half before he headed to war in Europe. The article reads:

Amateurs in Weak Machines Principal Toll of Aviation, Declared German Flying Here: Aeroplaning Really is Safe, Says Hans Buddecke, After Making Trial Flight at Speedway

> According to Hans Johann [*sic*] Buddecke, a young German aviator who has just come to Indianapolis and who intends making some spectacular flights over the city within the next week or two, the reason for the alarming frequency of accidents among aviators is easy to explain.
>
> "Most of the men who are hurt or killed in aeroplane accidents," said Mr. Buddecke, "are amateur flyers – they are lazy fellows who don't want to work and who think they see a chance for 'easy money' in aviation. They buy a cheap aeroplane after getting backing from some company and decide to make the money on taking a few risks. They get this cheap aeroplane

with a bad motor and give 'exhibition flights' at state fairs and places of that sort, and, not thoroughly understanding aviation they smash the 'planes and themselves to [bits].

"Aviation is really one of the safest things in the world. If the aeroplane is right and the aviator knows his business, there should be no accidents. Accidents occur because of a badly built 'plane, or because the aviator loses his head."

Buddecke, while not 25 years old, has been an airman for five years. He acted as "locator" for Euler, the famous German aviator, who was the first man in Germany to take an aviator's license. The "locator" handles the charts and maps and routing, while the pilot steers the plane. He has made numerous long cross-country flights in Germany and this country and given flights in Berlin, his home city. He has been in America a year and arrived in Indianapolis about a week ago, staying at 2209 Central Avenue. He is the nephew of Albert Lieber.

Buddecke made a brief trial flight at the Speedway yesterday afternoon, his aeroplane having arrived from Chicago only a day or two ago. While opposed to "stunts" in flying, such as "looping the loop," and flying upside down, on the grounds that they are not really of any use in the art of flying, he proposes to rise to a height of 8,000 feet directly over the monument, stop his motor and volplane to a landing in the Speedway – just to show how safe aviation may be.

Buddecke uses a French built aeroplane – a monoplane of the same type as that used by Garros, DeMolineaux and other famous French flyers. It is a "Nieuport" monoplane, with a fifty-horse power Gnome rotating engine, weight 800 pounds, built at a cost of $9,000. The motor is of the same make that is used by Lincoln Beachey, only Beachey's motor is eighty-horse power. Buddecke's aeroplane can "do" eighty miles an hour without an effort.

About the proposed flight of Lieut. Porte, the English aviator who plans to fly across the Atlantic, Buddecke was skeptical.

> He says the type of aircraft that Porte is using, a hydroplane, requires too much "luck" to make such a trip – that it is not dependable enough on itself.
>
> Buddecke, in the five years of his flying in all types and makes of aeroplanes, has had only two accidents – one in Darmstedt [*sic*], Germany, where the plane turned over on the ground, and once within the past year in Chicago, when he fell thirty feet, and was bruised and shaken up.
>
> He follows the profession of aviation for the sport of it. To him, the beginning of the conquest of the air is one of the greatest epochs in civilization.
>
> "I think the present time should be known in all history in all the years to come as the time that man learned to fly," he said.

This amusing article twice repeats the increasingly outrageous claim that Buddecke had five years of flying experience, creates a connection to the German flyer August Euler that did not exist, and documents an accident in Darmstadt that never occurred. The degree and chutzpah of these lies is actually fairly astounding, especially as the point of the article is that there are only accidents because of amateur flyers – Buddecke himself being the epitome of an amateur flyer who falsely claimed years of experience. He also made sure that his uncle was again mentioned.

While it is not unheard of for otherwise accomplished people to sometimes "pad their résumé" early in their careers, the nature and extent of these lies is unusual, especially as this was a former officer in the German Army who could have been expected to have a sense of honor about such things. Furthermore, these lies were published in the Indianapolis newspapers, making them public record. One can only assume that Albert Lieber was aware of this and may well have encouraged it.

Buddecke is mentioned in passing on page six of the 23 July 1914 newspaper in a series of stand-alone couplets, one which reads: "No, Herr Buddecke, flying is not dangerous. It's only the possibilities connected with alighting."

Indianapolis Motor Speedway:

The Indianapolis Motor Speedway complex initially included an aerodrome. Construction of the aerodrome began in 1909 and was completed in 1910. It was designed to house up to ten airplanes and two fully-inflated balloons. The hangar was 300 ft long, 60 ft wide, and 100 ft high. There were large doors at both ends of the hangar to allow dirigibles to fly in and out. The balloons stored there belonged to George Bumbaugh.

Starting around mid-July of 1914, Buddecke kept his airplane at this airfield. It was claimed in *The Indianapolis News* a year later that one week after Buddecke left Indianapolis for Germany the aerodrome at the Speedway burned, destroying his aeroplane as well as some flyers of Captain Bumbaugh.

Racing was halted for 1917 and 1918 because of the Great War, and instead the speedway served as the Speedway Aviation Repair Depot, which continued operation until late 1920. At least one test pilot was fatally injured in a plane crash at the track.

August Euler:

August Euler (1868–1957) was a pioneer German aviator and aircraft constructor. In 1908 he started the first German company for building engine-powered aircraft near Darmstadt. The firm originally built French Voisin aircraft under license. Euler also opened an airfield in Frankfurt. On 31 December 1909 he was issued the first German pilot's license. As we have seen, in 1914 Buddecke claimed to have worked with him for five years.

Lincoln Beachey:

Lincoln Beachey (1887–1915) was an early American aviator who gained fame and fortune for his flying exhibitions, aerial stunts, and aviation records. In 1911 he became the first person to fly over Niagara Falls. In late 1913, he was one of the first Americans to have executed a loop. In 1914 he "dive-bombed" the White House and Congress in a mock attack to demonstrate how the U.S. was not prepared to defend against modern aircraft. He died in a crash in San Francisco Bay in 1915 while flying inverted. He drowned in the crash.

The 80-hp rotary engine from his plane was recovered in working condition and used by aviatrix Katherine Stinson, Buddecke's acquaintance from Cicero, on her tour of the Orient.

Roland Garros:

Martinque-born Roland Garros was one of the most famous aviators in France before the Great War, thanks to his non-stop flight from France to Tunis in September 1913. He was awarded the Legion of Honor medal (*Chevalier de la légion d'honneur*) by the President of France on 15 October 1913. Before that he had set several altitude records and had conducted an extended tour of flying demonstrations across the United States in 1912.

He joined the French Army at the start of the war and went into the air service, being commissioned a lieutenant. He then secured his place in aviation history, not by the sensational but false story of his death by crashing into an observation balloon, but by developing, with Raymond Saulnier, bullet deflectors on the propeller of a plane that allowed him to mount a forward-firing machine gun on the cowl of a scout plane, creating the first real fighter plane. He shot down three German aircraft in April of 1915 before mechanical problems forced him down behind German lines.[52] He and his partially burned plane were captured. The German capture of this innovative firing system helped Anthony Fokker sell his interrupter system to the German Army. It was a system that he was already developing for his planes. It gave the Germans their first effective fighter planes and started the "Fokker Scourge" of 1915–16 that took the lives of so many Allied pilots.

One of the odder stories early in the war, and which is referenced in Chapter 4 of Buddecke's account, is that Roland Garros rammed and took down a Zeppelin. Most versions of this story say he died in the attack. This supposedly occurred in August 1914 and was published in a number of newspapers.[53] Needless to say, this story was entirely fictional and Roland Garros was still quite alive. It is unknown how such a completely false story could be published or what the source of it was.

Garros escaped from captivity in February 1918 and returned to flying, scoring one more confirmed victory before being shot down. Though often considered the first ace (five victories), he was never officially credited with shooting down five planes. He could certainly be credited with being the first fighter pilot. The honor of being the first official ace belongs to fellow Frenchman Adolphe Pegoud, to whom the word "l'as" was first applied.[54]

Lieut. Porte:

Buddecke's reference to "Lieut. Porte" in the *Indianapolis Star* article is certainly Colonel John Cyril Porte (1884–1919), a British flying boat pioneer. Irish by birth, he joined the Royal Navy in 1898 and designed and flew his first glider in 1908–9. Contracting tuberculosis, he retired from the navy with a rank of lieutenant, RN. He began flying powered airplanes in 1910 and got his flying certificate in 1911 in France. He then became a test pilot for the British Deperdussin Company in 1912, which went bankrupt the following year.

Working with famous American pilot Glenn Curtiss, they developed a prototype flying boat for crossing the North Atlantic for a cash prize of $55,000. The trip was originally to start on 20 July

1914 in St. Johns, Newfoundland, and from there go to the Azores, Vigo in northern Spain, and finally to Plymouth for a 1,198 mile trip. The contest was cancelled when the United Kingdom declared war on Germany on 4 August 1914.

With the start of the war, Lieutenant Porte joined the Royal Naval Air Service, for whom he operated and further developed flying boats and seaplanes. In 1917 he was disgraced in a scandal about his accepting money, allegedly £48,000 (over £1 million in 2023), for the sale of Curtiss aircraft to the Royal Naval Air Service. An associate admitted guilt, but charges were dropped against Porte after he returned the money. He continued with the Air Service until the end of the war.

Ill for the latter part of his adult life, he died on 22 October 1919 at the age of 35 from pulmonary tuberculosis.

Blériots vs Nieuports:

The famous Blériot Type XI monoplane, with which Louis Blériot crossed the English Channel in 1909, was the most commonly available plane before the start of the Great War. Over 1,000 single-seat and two-seat versions were produced. In the early part of the Great War the French, British, and Italians used them in six to eight of their squadrons. The Type XI was designed by Raymond Saulnier, before he joined with the Morane brothers to form their own corporation, the *Aéroplanes Morane-Saulnier.*

The Nieuport monoplane was a similar, but much less common design. It had cloth covering running down the entire length of the fuselage. It employed a variety of engines. The various models included the Nieuport II, whose first flight was in 1910; the two-seater Nieuport III; and the Nieuport IV, whose first flight was in 1911 and which was used by Pyotr Nesterov to perform a loop on 9 September 1913 (less than two weeks before Pegoud did it in a Blériot XI). There was also the Nieuport VI, a three-seat sport monoplane first flown in 1913, and the Nieuport VIII, a variant for Turkey. The company switched to producing biplanes in 1914.

The military version of the Blériot XI originally used the 50-hp Gnome rotary engine and later used the 70-hp Gnome 7 Gamma rotary engine. The Nieuport IV used the same engines. Buddecke writes that he used the 50-hp engine in his first plane.

Both Blériots and Nieuports were used in the Italo-Turkish War of 1911–12, with the Nieuport being the first plane to conduct a reconnaissance mission. That war also saw the first use of an aircraft for bombing (by an Italian German-built Etrich Taube), first night mission (by the same pilot, Giulio Gavotti, also in a Taube), and first plane shot down by ground fire.

Buddecke's Nieuport was an American-built plane modeled after the French Nieuport.

A Short History of Cicero Airfield:

Buddecke's purchase of an airplane and his desire to learn to fly brought him to Cicero Flying Field, at Cicero, Illinois, just to the west of Chicago. This was one of the early aviation airfields in the United States and hosted a number of American pioneers of flight. Some of these are described, often sarcastically, in Buddecke's book.

Cicero Flying Field was formally opened in June 1911 and abandoned in the fall 1915.[55] Its history was brief, but being located near Chicago, the second largest city in the United States, it very quickly became one of the central meeting fields for aviators across the country.

In his book, Buddecke describes six people in the twelve sheds at Cicero Field. They include 1) Shed 2: Katherine Stinson; 2) Shed 3: the "nobleman"; 3) Shed 4: "ichthyosaurus with bat wings"; 4) Shed 5: Mr. Partridge (and Mr. Keller); 5) Shed 8: "monoplane with an unbelievable number of wires and a 'stabilizer'"; and 6) Shed 9: Mackly. He also describes the two people from whom he purchased his plane, Orr and Linn, and a previous owner of the airplane named Mr. Robinson. Buddecke also had a 16-year-old boy working for him. Following are the capsule biographies of each of these people that we have been able to identify.

Katherine Stinson (shed 2):

Buddecke describes Katherine Stinson as:

> [A] nice, not exactly pretty, girl and happy owner of a Wright crate … She was a splendid, dashing thing who flew in any weather and was nothing more than a seventeen-year-old child.

Katherine Stinson was born 15 February 1891 in Fort Payne, Alabama. That would make her, in fact, 23 at the time Hans Buddecke met her.

Of necessity, she learned to drive a car at the age of 14, her father having left the family and she being the oldest. In 1911 she took a hot-air balloon ride in Kansas City, which sparked her interest in aviation. In 1912, at the age of 21, she became only the fourth woman in the United States to earn a pilot's certificate, having made her solo flight in a Wright B on 13 July 1912 at Cicero Field. In April 1913 she and her mother incorporated the Stinson Aviation Company to "manufacture, sell, rent or otherwise engage in the aircraft trade." In May 1913 she purchased a Wright B flyer from Max Lillie, a pilot for the Wright Brothers. She then participated in flying demonstrations across the country.

In 1915 she established the Stinson Municipal Airport near San Antonio, Texas, as well as the family-run Stinson Flying School. The Stinson Municipal Airport is the second oldest airport in continuous operation in the United States. In March of 1915 she acquired the rotary engine from Lincoln Beachey's wrecked plane and installed it in her own craft. On 18 July 1915, Stinson became the first woman to perform a loop at Cicero Field. She then accumulated a number of firsts, including first pilot ever to fly at night, first female pilot to fly a loop, first female pilot to fly for the U.S. mail service, first female to fly in Canada, China, or Japan, and she set a new American non-stop distance record in 1917 of 610 miles.

During the Great War, she briefly flew airplanes for the U.S. Postal Service, but quit after one round-trip due to issues with the organization. She then went to Paris and became an ambulance driver for the Red Cross. This ended her career in aviation. She contracted tuberculosis and moved to New Mexico, where she married, raised four adopted children, and died at the age of 86 in 1977.

Katherine Stinson was the premier American aviatrix of her day, very much preceding the much more famous Amelia Earnhardt.

Elmer Partridge and Henry Keller (shed 5):

Elmer Lee Partridge was born in 1880, making him 34 at the time Hans Buddecke met him. Henry C. 'Pop' Keller was actually a bit younger, having been born in 1881 in Pittsburg. Over the winter of 1911–12, Keller, who worked as a mechanic at Cicero, built an airplane. Later in 1912 he teamed up with Partridge to do repair and revision work on planes at the field. They then began to build planes on order in a hangar at Cicero Field. By the time Buddecke arrived, the partnership of Partridge and Keller had already built four airplanes and were working on a tractor biplane for Michael Morris. It was delivered in mid-July, and the Partridge Tractor Biplane became a staple of training and exhibition flights in 1914–15; Katherine Stinson's publicist/manager had one built for her at Partridge's factory at Cicero, powered by the engine salvaged from Lincoln Beachey's wreck. The two men continued building prototype aircraft while they ran the Partridge & Keller Aviation School at Cicero.[56]

After Cicero Flying Field was shut down in fall 1915, the wealthy aviation enthusiast Charles Dickinson purchased a plot of land on Chicago's southwest side between 79th and 87th Streets and from

Pulaski Road to Cicero Avenue. This was named Ashburn Field, and it replaced the Cicero Flying Field and continued operation until 1951.[57]

In spring of 1916, Partridge & Keller moved their operation to Ashburn at 84th and Pulaski. During the Great War, they served as aviation instructors. They continued flying and construction after the war, but no longer as business partners.

Elmer Partridge died in a plane accident in 1926 at the age of 46 while carrying the mail for a new air mail company formed by Dickinson. In 1928, Keller was killed at the age of 47 in a plane accident while training a student at Ashburn.

Shed 3, Shed 4, Shed 8, and Shed 9:

It is unclear who was occupying these hangars at this time. The identity of "Mr. Mackly" remains unknown.

Orr and Linn:

These are the two gentlemen who sold Hans Buddecke his Nieuport-type monoplane. It was an American-built plane modeled after the Nieuport design. It was previously owned by William "Billy" Robinson.

According to Buddecke's description these were two well-to-do men. Nothing further is known about them.

William "Billy" Robinson:

Billy Robinson was born in Redfield, South Dakota, on 24 September 1884, and moved with his family to Grinnell, Iowa, in 1896 at the age of 12. As an adult he, like the Wright Brothers, was a bicycle repairman who designed and built his own monoplane. He had trained at the Max Lillie school in Cicero as a mechanic and learned to fly Wright aircraft and Nieuports. In 1911, with the help of Charles Hink, he built a 60-hp radial engine for his airplane. That same year he set a record for non-stop flight, carrying mail from Des Moines, Iowa, to Kentland, Indiana. In 1913 he returned to Iowa and founded the Grinnell Aeroplane Company. That company would later build two designs, a parasol scout plane that first flew in 1915 and a biplane that first flew in 1916.

Robinson died on 11 March 1916, while trying to break the 17,000-ft altitude record. The suspected cause was hypoxia. His airplane company was dissolved after his death.

According to some accounts, Billy Robinson sold the Nieuport-like airplane to Buddecke. As Buddecke described Orr and Linn in depth, and later only cursorily mentions Robinson, it appears that Robinson sold the plane to Orr and Linn, who then sold it to Buddecke.

The Gnome Rotary Engine:

One of the commonly used engines in airplanes at this time was the Gnome Rotary Engine. This seven-cylinder engine was originally designed to pump water from mines. It was then adapted for use as an airplane engine in many of the early designs due to its light weight. It initially produced 50 hp, but before 1914, was upgraded to 70 hp (the Gnome 7 Gamma). There were also some 80-hp versions and later the 100-hp nine-cylinder Gnome Delta. A 14-cylinder, two-row variant existed called the Gnome 14 Gamma-Gamma that produced 140 hp. It was basically two seven-cylinder Gnomes lashed together.

A rotary engine had an advantage over in-line engines in that no coolant or cooling arrangements had to be made, as the rotation of the engine itself provided sufficient air cooling. This allowed for a lighter engine installation which was critical for early underpowered aircraft.

Johannisthal Airfield:

The Johannisthal Airfield that Buddecke references was an airfield constructed in a suburb just southeast of Berlin in 1909. It was

Germany's second airfield and first commercial airfield. Just outside the city limits of Berlin, it quickly became the center of German aviation. By 1914 its large number of hangars housed the factories and support facilities for plane manufacturers Aviatik, Rumpler, L.V.G., and part of Fokker until that company moved all its facilities and employees to Schwerin, around 220 miles north of Berlin, near the coast of the Baltic Sea. The site was absorbed into the expanding city of Berlin in 1920.

Johannisthal was also the home base of famous German aviators including the aviatrix Amelie "Mille" Beese and the Dutchman Anthony Fokker. The famous French flyer Adolphe Pegoud flew demonstration flights there twice, in October 1913 and March 1914.

In late July 1914 it became clear that a major European War was imminent. As the front page of *The Indianapolis News* noted on Friday, 31 July 1914: "War Situation in Europe is Desperate," and "Martial Law Decreed in Germany: Military Measures on Frontiers" and "England Waits for First Shot."

On page 14 of that issue was an article on Hans Buddecke:

BIRDMAN FLIES OVER WESTERN PART OF CITY: Lieut. Buddecke may abandon advertising scheme and go to war

> With the foreign war rumors flying thick and fast, residents in the extreme western part of the city and farmers to the north were more or less startled last evening when they saw a great bird-like aeroplane shooting gracefully around through the heavens and disappear to the north. The aeroplane was in charge of Lieutenant Johann [*sic*] Buddecke, of the Royal Guards, of Berlin, Germany. Buddecke is here on a peaceful mission, but it is not unlikely that he will soon be on his way to Germany to join his regiment if he is not assigned to the aviation corps of

the German Army. Buddecke is making practice flights at the speedway and he had promised to fly all over the city before the week is out. After several practice flights yesterday, Buddecke started on a trip late in the afternoon and made a visit to the country home of his uncle, Albert Lieber, on White River north of Fairview Park.

War Upsets Plans.

If Buddecke leaves for Germany, it will upset some elaborate advertising plans which he and Lieber had planned. Lieber is at the head of the Indianapolis Brewing Company and it was planned to have Buddecke make flights from Indianapolis to all of the company's branches throughout the state. With this in view he has been working on this flying machine for some time and his practice flights have been more than satisfactory. The speedway has proved to be an ideal place for starting and alighting.

Although only twenty-five years old Buddecke has been making flights for about five years. He has made many long cross-country flights in Germany, and has flown over Berlin, his home city, many times. After making his flight over the center of Indianapolis, Buddecke said he would reach an altitude that will enable him to volplane all the way to the speedway with his engine shut down. He estimates that his altitude will have to be about a mile and half to do this.

This article echoes others, in that it grossly overstates Buddecke's flying experience. It confirms the business plans that are discussed in his memoir about using aircraft to advertise. While those plans for building aircraft for that purpose were fairly bold, to be funded by a group of Indianapolis businessmen, what is indicated in this article was a simple advertising effort for his uncle's brewery. This may have been a start to a much more ambitious business, or Buddecke may have overstated his business plans in his memoir. But this article does confirm that he was indeed developing a business based upon using airplanes for advertising.

American news services at this time were very good at staying on top of the events in Europe and in the 4 August issue of *The Indianapolis Star* the front page included headlines such as "Great Britain May Strike Today," and "Warfare Continues on the Frontier." At this point, Germany had declared war on Russia (on 1 August) and on France (on 3 August). The Germans had marched into Luxembourg on 2 August and invaded Belgium at 8:02 a.m. (local time) on 4 August. Britain declared war on Germany later that night. Clearly, a massive European war was underway that included Serbia, Austro-Hungary, Russia, Germany, France, and the United Kingdom. Back on page six of that issue were the more detailed reports for the day, including a map labeled "Actions of the Day in War Zone." The lead article on that page stated:

GERMANS FORM WAR BODY HERE: Young men, Subject to Call to Colors, Organize to Expedite Movement in Case Services Are Required. BUDDECKE OFF FOR EAST. Aviation Corps Lieutenant Will Get in Touch with Ambassador and Supply Information to Those Left Behind.

> Indianapolis Germans who, by the military laws of their home country, may be called on for service in the European war, have perfected an organization whereby they may set in a body of offering their services should they be demanded. At the meeting attended by about twelve young Germans at the offices of the Indianapolis Brewing Company yesterday morning a

temporary organization was formed to get in direct touch with the German ambassador and to raise funds if necessary to buy passage for any Germans who might not have funds available for the purpose.

All of the young men who attended the meeting have served in the German Army and some of them are officers. Lieut. Hans Buddecke of the German aviation corps, who has been the guest here of his uncle, Albert Lieber, led in forming the organization. He departed last night for New York to get in direct communication with the German ambassador, and if an immediate call is issued for Germans residing here, he will get in touch with the officers of the organization elected yesterday.

Officers are Elected.

Ernest F. Paepper was elected president of the organization, Fritz Schaefer, vice president, and Leopold Rassow secretary. It was said that several German business men who are known in financial circles may be asked to serve on a committee to receive funds if it becomes necessary to raise money to procure passage for any of the local Germans. The organization will have its headquarters at the German House.

Plans for embarking for Germany were discussed by the young men as calmly as if they had been planning some kind of pleasure trip. Plans for joining the German forces were discussed as if a business proposition were under consideration.

Lieut. Buddecke has been active as an officer in the German Army for four years. While he has been in Indianapolis he has kept an aeroplane at the Indianapolis Motor Speedway. Only a few days ago he made a spectacular flight from the Speedway over Mr. Lieber's country home. He expects to join the aviation corps upon his return to Germany.

Men Attending Meeting.

> The meeting was attended by Wilhelm Samuels, Kurt C. Volkhart, who was a relief driver for Teddy Tetzlaff in the last 500-mile race at the Speedway; Christopher Berton, Mr. Lieber, Lieut. Buddecke, Leonard Schwartz, Fritz Sehnefer, Mr. Paepper, Fritz Sieffart, Fritz Hubert, Joseph Velt, Johannes Gruner, Leo Rassow, Fritz Link, Franz Fisher.
>
> "All Europe almost has been bulldozing Germany for years," Mr. Lieber said, "and from the way that other countries have shown themselves to be hostile to Germany, the people of this country can now see why Germany should be so active recently in arming herself to the teeth."
>
> While the Germans attending the meeting said they have received no definite orders to depart for Germany, they declared that the purpose of their organization was to complete plans so that the call may be answered immediately when it is received. It is estimated that there will probably be about seventy-five Germans from there who will depart for their home country.

Again, Buddecke is said to be part of the "German aviation corps." The nice thing about all three of these articles is that they nicely verify the first four chapters of Buddecke's book. It is clear that his account is generally honest, even if some of his marketing and self-promotion efforts were not. Clearly Buddecke was instrumental in organizing this meeting and his uncle's brewing company was used for the meeting.

Lieber's quote about Germany being bullied by other European countries is telling. This is a very German-oriented political viewpoint, despite the fact that Lieber was born and raised in the United States. It is clear that he maintained strong ties to Germany, as his family regularly visited his father and mother still living in Düsseldorf, a city in the Rhineland, which was the westernmost province of the

Kingdom of Prussia before 1870 and part of Germany thereafter. (By contrast, of course, we have read how his father, the former consul, still flew the American flag over his German home.)

The article ends with a picture of "German Soldiers in Meeting Here" showing the fifteen Germans, including Albert Lieber (who, of course, was not a soldier) and Hans Buddecke.

Among the men mentioned as members of this "War Body" of which Buddecke was a member, it's interesting to take a brief look at Kurt C. Volkhart.

Kurt Volkhart was born in 1890 in Düsseldorf. He was the son and grandson of painters but became enthusiastic about automobiles and racing. He came to the United States in October 1913 to race and was still there when the war started. Volkhart was a relief driver for Teddy Tetzlaff at the 1914 Indianapolis 500.

In November 1914 he was able to get back to Europe via the Danish city of Copenhagen, helped by his German friend Hanns Heinz Ewers in New York. During the war he was employed as a driver and later as a pilot, but was injured in a crash.

The parallels to his story and Buddecke's are interesting, especially since it appears that Buddecke was not aware that another Indianapolis German made it back to Europe and ended up in the air service. Unlike Buddecke, Volkhart survived the war and stayed in Germany.

He worked as a senior engineer for the car manufacturers Steiger, Dürkoppwerke, and Opel, and continued motor racing. In 1927 he began developing a rocket-propelled car as a precursor to spacecraft. His continued development was interrupted by World War II but he continued his work after the war with support from the British occupying forces. He passed away in Germany in 1959.

The meeting of the War Body was also noted in the 4 August 1914 edition of *The Indianapolis News* with the following article:

GERMAN RESERVIST NOT ABLE TO GET STARTED: Steamship lines not booking passengers for Europe. Aviator Anxious to go.

The dozen or more German reservists in Indianapolis who have been called back to Germany for service in the army in the present war, appear to be anchored here with no prospect that they will be able to soon make even a start for the other side. Trans-Atlantic steamship companies have notified their agents in this city that they are not booking passengers for continental points in Europe. One line says, in its telegram to its agent here, that it is accepting only American and Scandinavian passengers.

Hans Buddecke, aviator, who has been here for some time as the guest of his cousin [*sic*], Albert Lieber, left the city last night for the east, hoping that he may be able to find some way to get off for Germany. He confided to some friends before he departed that he probably would try to obtain passage on the steamer to Spain and from there he would rely on his ingenuity to get into Germany. If he arrives in Germany before the close of war he will become an aviator in the German Army.

Departure Uncertain.

Otto Jahnes has not yet started for Germany, and there is no certainty as to when he will start, because of the impossibility of obtaining passage on a steamer. Mr. Jahnes served his time in the German Army, and when released from further service was placed on the reserve list. On a leave of absence he came to America. About a year ago he returned to Germany and was married. He brought his bride to Indianapolis a few months ago.

Mr. Jahnes has taken out his first papers to become an American citizen, and under the German law he could have obtained from that government a release from further service in the army for the asking, but he neglected to make the request. Therefore he is subject to call and is expected to respond. He is not yet an American citizen, because he has not taken out his full naturalization papers.

Chris Wetzel, employed at Charles Mayer & Co.'s store, is still a German citizen. He served the required time in the German Army, nineteen years ago, and was placed on the reserve list. He came to America, and a few years ago made a request to have his name stricken from the reserve list. The request was granted by the German government. Therefore, although a German citizen, never having applied for naturalization here, he is exempt from further army service.

Seeking Passage.

A number of German, Austrian and Hungarian reservists have applied to the various steamship agencies here for passage to their native countries, but no one has been able to get started. Several Servians booked here last week and started for their old homes for service in the Servian Army.

A question has arisen here as to the right of foreign army reservists now in the country to undertake any organized movement in support of any foreign army in time of war. The United States is a neutral country, and it is pointed out that under international neutrality laws such organized effort would become a violation of neutrality. It is also reported that the attention of the United States authorities has been called to the matter so that they may watch for any movement of that nature.

The significant part of this article starts with the first sentence, which notes that a dozen or more reservists have been called back to Germany. This seems to contradict the previous article, and the next. It raises the issue whether Buddecke voluntarily chose to return to Germany, or in fact was called back. In point of fact, any German in America could have ignored such a call-up if they chose to do so, as the Kaiser's government had no means to compel them. The article also raises a question as to whether efforts to organize sending reservists back to their country violated U.S. neutrality. While it does not specifically mention the War Body meeting and organizing at Albert Lieber's brewery, it is likely that this is indeed what they were referring to.

The next reference to the group of Germans was in *The Indianapolis Star*, Friday, 7 August 1914. The article states:

LOCAL TEUTONS UNABLE TO RETURN TO FIGHT: Indianapolis Germans Disappointed Because They Can Not Reach Home to Bear Arms for Fatherland in Present Crisis.

Intense disappointment is felt by the young local Germans as a result of an expedition made on Wednesday to Cincinnati to visit Oscar Metzger, the German consul. Herr Metzger told the party, which included Otto Janus [*sic*: Jahnes], Fritz Schaefer, Leopold Rassow and Ernest Paeper [*sic*: Paepper], that, since England had declared war on Germany, transporting patriotic Germans from the United States back to the Fatherland would be too hazardous an undertaking. Metzger explained that more than likely a steamer carrying Germans back to Germany would be stopped en route by British ships and that the Germans would be taken captives before they had a chance to do any fighting at all.

The local Germans, including several army officers, held a meeting at the Indianapolis Brewing Company office last Monday and discussed offering their services to the Fatherland

and raising funds to pay the passage of Germans who could not afford the expense of going back. That was before England had declared war on Germany, but, as Metzger pointed out, conditions have changed.

Many are Disappointed

"There is hardly a chance to get back to Germany now that England has declared war on Germany," said Mr. Metzger. "It would be practically useless to try to make such a trip at a time like this."

Fritz Schaefer, one of the party, admitted that the verdict of the consul was a great disappointment. There are about seventy-five Germans in Indianapolis who were eagerly awaiting a call to arms and to be forced to return to prosaic duties is irksome to them.

"We all feel as if we ought to be there," said Mr. Schaefer, "but there is no chance to go. We will, however, hold out ourselves in readiness for any future call, should conditions change so that it is possible for us to get back."

This meeting in Indianapolis appears to be the end of the Indianapolis German War Body, except for the trips of Buddecke through Italy and Volkhart through Denmark. Apparently the rest of these men remained in the United States, with Fritz Schaefer marrying Mary E. Johnson in 1923 according to *The Indianapolis Star.* The papers indicate that Leopold Rassow, who was married, also remained in the Indianapolis area during the 1920s, working as an accountant.

An article in *The Indianapolis News* of 13 June 1929 discussed a motor tour of Europe planned by eight friends, including Otto Janus [*sic*] Sr., Mrs. C. Otto Janus, Otto Janus Jr., and Alex Vonnegut (brother of Kurt Vonnegut Sr.) and Mrs. Vonnegut. This is evidence that some of the 'Teutons' remained in the United States and integrated with the local community.

The German Community in Indianapolis:

In 1914, German-Americans were the second largest ethnic group in America (after Americans of English descent). There was also a well-established German émigré community in the United States. According to the U.S. census of 1910, there were 2.3 million German-born immigrants living in the United States and 550 German newspapers in the country. This was in a nation with a population of over 92 million people.

There was likewise a large and well-established community of Germans and German-Americans in Indianapolis, including prominent families like the Liebers and the Vonneguts. As the articles above note, about seventy-five Germans from the area were expected to join the German war effort. Apparently only two – Buddecke and Volkhart – did, while most of the rest remained, integrating into American life. The population of Indianapolis according to the 1910 census was 233,650 and it was a booming city, growing to 314,194 in the 1920 census. The German community in the Indianapolis area was integrated into the business life of the city.

But the German community was not fully integrated into American society, and it tended to patriotically support the non-democratic German Empire. Therefore, the German community in Indianapolis was somewhat at odds with other parts of America, and these differences would only magnify over time until the United States declared war on Germany on 6 April 1917.

The final mention of Hans Buddecke in Indianapolis newspapers was this odd article published in the Sunday edition of *The Indianapolis Sunday Star* on 15 November 1914. It states in part:

German Boy Only 12 Years Old Writes Uncle of Part in War: Nephew of Albert Lieber Tells of Knitting Socks in Bed After Illness Prevented Hospital Duty.

"I went out in the rain and caught cold, and am now in bed, but I am still busy and doing what I can for my country. I am knitting socks for the soldiers. Grandmother taught me how."

The above is an extract from a letter just received by Albert Lieber from his 12-year-old nephew, Hans Lieber. Hans is the son of Capt. Rudolf Lieber of the Uhlans. The Liebers live in Duesseldorf, and it was concerning the prevailing conditions in the German city in war times that the lad wrote to his uncle. This letter, as well as one received by Mr. Lieber from his mother, also living in Duesseldorf, shows clearly the true German spirit, which counts no cost if it is for the "Fatherland."

According to 12-year-old Hans's letter, there is plenty for children to do when the country is at war. He writes that the school children, after hours, are mail carriers, telegraph boys, street car conductors – this latter work being done by the older ones – and are doing every variety of man's work. The schools, Hans wrote, have established depots, where clothes are given to refugees and to the poor.

Helps Care for Wounded.

He explained proudly that he, with a number of other boys, was doing hospital duty, running errands, helping the doctors and seeing the horror of war at first hand, in all its rawness. This child had helped dress the wounds of French and German soldiers and had made a study of the injuries. He said that the French soldiers' wounds were clean-cut, but that the German soldiers' bodies were torn in zig-zag fashion by the French bullets. "The wounds made by the German bullets will heal," said the boy, "but the wounds made by the French bullets are hard to heal." The letter included well-drawn diagrams of the wounds.

It was while he was doing this hospital work that he caught cold and was forced to go to bed, but even then refused to stop working for the soldiers.

Hans's father, Capt. Rudolph Lieber, is a brother of Albert Lieber. He is engaged in drilling a regiment of Uhlans. As soon as the men have been drilled, they will start for the front, to Russia or France.

Mrs. Emma Herber, Mr. Lieber's sister, is nursing her husband, Capt. Erwin Herber of the infantry. Capt. Erwin Herber and fourteen of his men are all that remain of a company of 300 soldiers who were first on the firing line at the battle of Liege. Capt. Herber, terribly wounded, lay in a trench half filled with water for five days and nights before he was discovered, his dead men piled in heaps all about him. He was barely alive when taken out, and was taken to a hospital in Liege. Mrs. Herber, with a military escort, went, almost through the firing lines, to Liege by automobile, and took her wounded husband home. He intends to return to the front as soon as he is able.

It will be interesting to the many Indianapolis people who met Lieut. Hans Johann [sic] Buddecke, the young aviator, last summer, to know that he is playing an important part in the war. A lieutenant of the aviation corps, Lieut. Buddecke has been doing scout work and is also an instructor of the corps. When he left Indianapolis for Germany, he experienced no trouble in reaching home until he got as far as Italy. Then, in order to get to Germany and report to duty, he posed as an Italian, and got to Duesseldorf.

Explains Coast Attack.

In Mr. Lieber's opinion, it is easy to see what Germany's object is in making such persistent efforts to capture Dunkirk and Calais, on the French coast.

"The German men-of-war," said Mr. Lieber, "are in the Kiel Canal, which is eighty miles long, and can take their boats from the North Sea to the Baltic Sea at will. The English fleet is in the North Sea, off the coast of Scotland, and has the advantage of being able to steam to a nearby port in case of an attack.

"The Germans can not do this. If they attack the British fleet, they can not put into port at all, for there is no porton the side toward England, and, if a ship were disabled, she could get no protection, for the only port is on the Holland coast, and Holland is neutral. England, however, can not attack the German fleet without passing the Island of Helgoland, a strong fortress.

"If the Germans take Calais or Dunkirk – both of which are strongly fortified, it will mean that they will be in a position to meet England in a naval battle in the North Sea, and it will also mean the sending of Zeppelin war balloons across the English Channel from Dunkirk to London."

A letter from Mr. Lieber's mother, Mrs. Peter Lieber, who is 78 years old, also tells, in the most graphic style, of the terrible sights, the suffering and the sorrow, but above all the love of the Germans for the Fatherland and their unshakable belief in ultimate victory.

Albert Lieber's patriotic and protective attitude towards his ancestral homeland is clear in this article.

There were international legal standards addressing warfare, predominantly the First Geneva Convention of 1864 (revised in 1906) and the Hague conventions of 1899 and 1907. The Geneva Conventions concerned treatment of the wounded and sick during war, while the Hague conventions addressed the use of weapons in war.

The Hague Convention of 1899 consisted of three treaties and three declarations. These three declarations imposed restrictions initially for five years that: 1) prohibited the discharge of projectiles and explosives from balloons or by other new analogous methods, 2) prohibited the use of projectiles with the sole object to spread asphyxiating poisonous gases, and 3) prohibited the use of bullets which can easily expand or change their form inside the human body. These three declarations were then extended and all major participants in the Great War, except the United Kingdom and the United States, signed all three treaties and all three declarations by 1900. The United Kingdom signed the second and third declarations in 1907. The United States signed the first declaration but never ratified it.

The nations of the world met again for the Second Hague Conference in 1907. It produced thirteen treaties, one of which was not ratified, and one declaration. The declaration prohibited the discharge of projectiles and explosives from balloons. It was only ratified by China, Britain, and United States among the "major powers." The third Hague conference was scheduled for 1914.

Two topics in this interview with Lieber quoted above address these conventions. First is that certain types of expanding bullets were outlawed, the so-called "dum-dum" bullets. The discussion of the differences in wound severity by German vice French bullets may simply be an observation. On the other hand, it also appears to be a manipulation of the press, as the French did not use "dum-dum" bullets.

The article also has Albert Lieber discussing Zeppelin war balloons crossing the English Channel to London. The first aerial bombing of England occurred on the night of 19–20 January 1915, when two Zeppelins dropped twenty-four 50-kg (110-lb) bombs and a collection of three-kg incendiaries on Great Yarmouth, Sheringham, King's Lynn, and other nearby Norfolk villages. Four civilians were killed and sixteen injured. The first bombing of London occurred on 30 May 1915 when Zeppelin LZ-38 dropped some 120 bombs that killed seven civilians and injured thirty-five. The declaration on balloon bombing from the Hague Convention of 1907 was not ratified by Germany.

The article notes once again that Hans Buddecke is part of the German aviation corps. This time the report is correct.

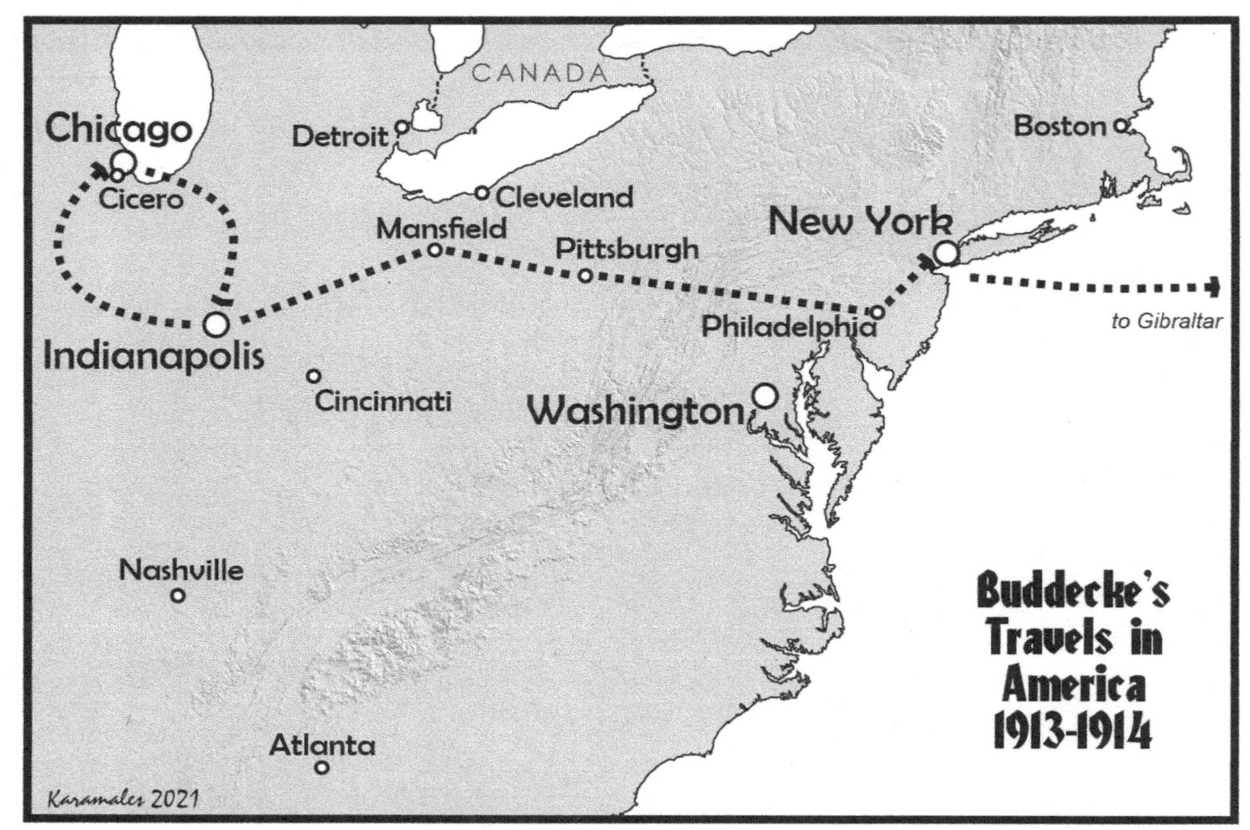

Buddecke's Travels in America, 1913–1914

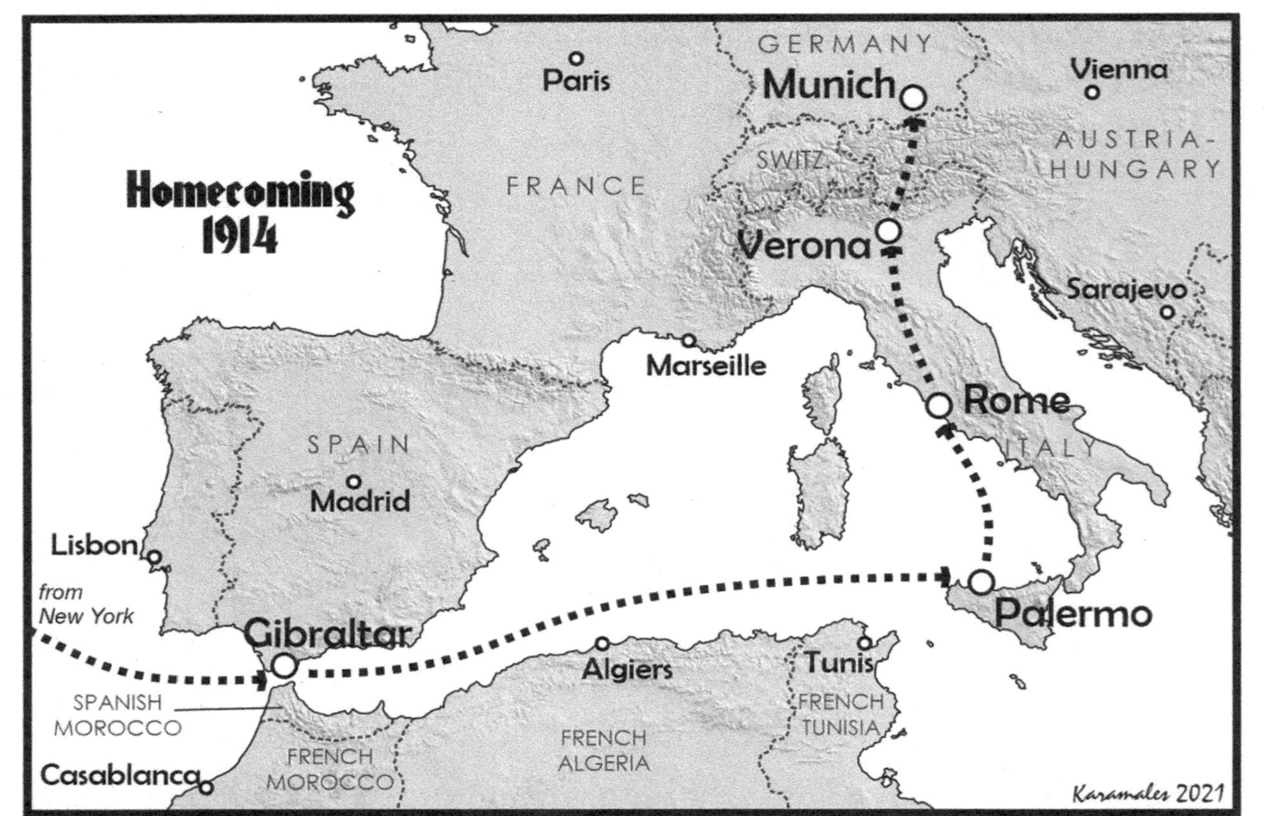

Homecoming, 1914

Chapter 6

My Fokker

By Hans Buddecke

Because of the flight skills I had acquired in America, I naturally reported to the flying service. At the replacement unit near Frankfurt, the old pilot Faller from Baden took me up three times in his double-decker. I was also planning to visit my father in Alsace on a solo flight. But after just fourteen days I was transferred to the front. I had never been asked to take any exams, and I have to admit that I was only gradually able to really control the aircraft in the aviation unit after a number of flights. But then things moved quickly. Soon my unit commander had to forbid me to turn steep curves with or without an observer, as he did not consider these kinds of maneuvers to be very necessary.

Our first fighter aircraft arrived. It had a machine gun that fired to the rear, and was greeted with joy. Finally, we were able to do "tack-tack-tack" like those gentlemen flying Farmans[58] on the other side. Our warplane should always be ready. I got the chance to be the second one to give it a test flight. I did, and lo and behold, the apparatus was so inferior in design (not all aircraft can be excellent) that it barely tolerated a steep curve and took minutes to make a half turn. When my unit leader asked me for my verdict, I did not hide my opinion from him.

Back then, everyone had his own idea of how to fight in the air. I was no exception; I saw the ideal in the small, fast-moving Fokker aircraft in which the pilot did everything on his own. My unit leader disagreed, so I requested a transfer. This does not mean, however, that

I do not still very much admire this man today – not only because he wears the *Pour le Mérite.*

I had a faithful comrade in another unit, so I went there. I had become acquainted with him in front of Reims at the beginning of September 1914. Already by then, he wore the Iron Cross 1st Class on the tunic of his Brandenburg infantry regiment, which I liked very much. But even more I respected his quiet manner, and the way he accepted me, even though I had nothing like that:

Berthold.

I had flown with him many times, and when I asked for my transfer, he asked his captain to bring me to their unit. Everything worked out nicely. I received a nice new aircraft, and flew extensive reconnaissance operations, during which I encountered Mr. Vedrines, who ignited my tracer ammunition with his machine gun while my observer was pulling out his carbine; and I finally got my Fokker, which hardly anyone else wanted to have.

There he was now. Three weeks had passed without me being able to catch an opponent, more and more it became clear that he was only a toy – then the first opponent fell after he had received 108 hits.[59]

Chapter 7

The First One

By Hans Buddecke

So far, aerial combat had really been just a lawless shootout. Chance hits may have forced one of the combatants to go down – rarely to crash. But it seemed unbelievable to us that Boelcke and Immelmann had already brought down three enemies and were still intact. It seemed natural to us that fast, maneuverable, fast-climbing planes should be able to take advantage of the weaknesses of slow and clumsy sleds, force them into defense and defeat them. But no one at the time knew anything substantive about the tactics of combat. There were no more details that anyone could give. The common saying was: just let 'em have it – the rest will take care of itself.

It was the end of September 1915 when I took my monoplane into the air at lunchtime on a Sunday from Castle Vaux,[60] where the small combat squadron of the main unit at Roupy had taken up camp, to search for the English reconnaissance aircraft that was constantly flying over Bapaume – le Château – St. Quentin – Péronne causing mischief.

I was about 2,000 meters south of St. Quentin when a yellowish-brown something appeared, growing sharper and sharper, in the bluish haze of high altitude. Was that …? The eye attached itself to it, did not let go of it, while one hand turned the lever and made the gun ready to fire. Slowly the machines moved towards each other, and the brown wings became clear.

Roundels! It looks like a red cloth.

Roundels – and with that only one feeling: him or me. In a moment I was above him… My excitement was at its peak. I had no clear thoughts, purely instinctively I made every move and turn, tipped my machine straight down, plummeted at him, aimed, fired.

Meanwhile, below me, Lieutenant Nixon awoke from his daydream. He must have been thinking of the pretty girl whose picture he carried in his breast pocket. His observer, Captain Stotts [*sic*: Stott], with his African eyes, also turned his attention from the trenches on the ground, which he had been diligently exploring, to the approaching danger above, and when he saw what was coming he probably thought: Ugh, the devil!

As a result of my dive and the forward movement of the enemy – it was a common type of biplane – I reached his altitude 200 meters behind him. I put my hand in my wire box, took aim at the silhouette in front of me, and fired. Tak-tak… tak-tak… tak… tak… tak. No result. I thought hard… Distance? … Let them get a little further ahead … aim a little to the left.

An industrious response came back … tak-tak … tak … tak … tak … tak.

Back on the ground the cook, who had just served the chicken dish, plunged into the dining hall at Roupy with the big news: "The Fokker is shooting!" Everyone dropped their knives and forks and rushed outside to watch, and to be witnesses.

Who knows where the excitement was greater, with me or with those below? With those who saw a comrade fencing with the foe, or with the French women gathered in the village road, folding their hands in prayer for the victory of their flag?

Upstairs, meanwhile, fate was fulfilled. Stott wasn't a bad shot. After a few shots, however, one of my bullets hit the mechanism of his machine-gun and stopped it. He tore his semi-automatic pistol from his pocket and fired nine rounds… The wind whistled incessantly around him. When he tried to reload his pistol, one of my rounds hit it and it was torn from his hand. Had he not lost his weapon he would have surely hit me this time, as I was now within ten meters.

His gaze fell on Nixon. He saw the pilot's head fall forward, and the whole plane tilted and plunged into the depths. Stott mustered all his strength, climbed onto the wing of the falling machine, and slung himself astride the shoulders of his dying comrade. Stott pressed his heels on Nixon's knees to work the foot controls, and snatched the steering yoke from his frozen hands.

I sat between my wings and let my machine-gun pound as much as it could. I was astonished that there was no sign of any effect over there. I was even more amazed at how steadily I was able to keep my whole machine, visor, and front sight pointed at my opponent even in the banking curves. I was within ten meters of my enemy's tail. These are the critical moments. Every shot strikes home ... Now, open both eyes ... How far? And just at that moment, when I thought I had won, Stott's God of Fortune, in the form of a gust of wind, tore the leather end of the cartridge belt out of the magazine into the open air ... my machine gun jammed.

I turned away, flying in curves and circles while with my hand and teeth I pulled back the belt which had become tangled in the elevator hinge joint, preventing it from working.

When I faced my opponent again, he was at a lower altitude than me. He dove. I immediately got behind him again. I stopped firing, hoping he would land peacefully. But then I saw the following: A man with a pale yellow leather jacket, puffed up by the wind, was sticking out of the pilot's cockpit. I couldn't explain it to myself, even though I suspected that something must have been going on over there. I felt some kind of jolt and bit the belt firmly in my teeth.

So we glided down a few meters, banking, until my opponent's plane belched white clouds of steam. He brought up his machine's nose sharply and began to fly forward at full power – his last attempt to escape. Immediately I closed my left eye again and took aim. The engine droned mechanically and I fired... on the yellow, round leather jacket.

After a while, the enemy lowered his nose and headed to the ground in long, slow spirals. I followed from curve to curve, seeing the shadow of the enemy aircraft drifting over fields and roads, getting closer and closer to the ground. My joy at seeing the "peacock butterfly"[61] below me was great.

Bright sun lay on the field between the stands of woods east of Caulincourt. The giant bird swooped down, threw up a thick cloud of dust, and the four large blue-white-red roundels lay lifeless on the ground.[62]

A soldier from a nearby convoy took courage and ran to the spot just ahead of fifty others as I flew back to my hangar nearby at Vaux. Cars full of men rolled to the crash site. I climbed aboard one too. Before we got to the place, we stopped. I got down and asked what the situation was. I was told that one of plane's crew was dead.

I let the others continue on and I went to the village where the prisoner was supposed to be. I had never seen a person killed in such a way, and I was always wary about seeing things that were in the least way sad that would stick with me for the rest of my life.

So I went and spoke to Stott, who now described the exact course of events to me. Laughing, he showed me his clothes and the yellow leather jacket. It was torn to pieces through and through.

"You are some shot?" he asked.

The French landlady with whom he was staying gave us lunch together. Like most English people, when they are alone, he was a good, open person who was not lacking in friendship. I have had this experience many times. If there were several of them, then of course things were otherwise. In front of each other, they did not find the honest courage to acknowledge a German.

When I later visited Stott in St. Quentin and told him that in the meantime I had shot down a second of his comrades, he just shook his head and made the suggestion, which was clearly in the British interest, that I should go on leave for four weeks.

Chapter 8

The Big Program

By Hans Buddecke

Early morning. When my orderly came into my room to wake me up, I had a rather heavy head. He opened the curtains. A wonderful thick blanket of cloud hung almost to the ground. Then he gathered up the pieces of uniform that were scattered around the room and went away again.

I rolled over on my other side to slumber for a moment. After five minutes my boy came back and said I had slept three more hours! So. The memory came slowly, comrades circled around me ... Mumm – Schülerfranz* ... I was supposed to fly for the Duke of Brunswick ... Right, the Duke and Prince August Wilhelm wanted to come. – Oh, my head was buzzing something awful.

The sun broke through. Flying weather... terrible! Berthold wanted to go to Abbeville with Duck and Gnome, the two observers. And Althaus? He was certainly still asleep.

I got up. I ran into Berthold in the wide corridor. In sweater and sports stockings *à la Vaux*. He always had big plans, which is why he never said anything. He was already thinking about the first gusts of wind, the first flak over the lines, the hours of flying that would bring him to the coast via Amiens. He visualized the camp at the mouth of the Somme and maneuvered his approach. He was agitated. It was always that way with him until everything had been completed successfully. In the meantime, he expressed his nervous tension with the most exquisite profanities, which he only too easily discharged

* First Lieutenant Schüler, who as an observer had received the epithet 'Franz.'

onto his two observers – even during the most difficult moments in the air.

Quietly I accompanied him out onto the field. That stuff about fliers approaching their missions with flippant remarks is made up for books; we ourselves know better. Of course, there's not always time before an action to think about its outcome and to consider how it should be carried out. Sometimes, however, your softly pounding heart whispers: "Remember that you might …" Then words get scarce, joking is difficult, and you prefer to keep to yourself until the moment when the rumbling motor with its power releases the tension and frees your bound spirit. Then suddenly everything becomes easy and free, and you wave a laughing goodbye.

The aircraft's two engines were running. Berthold's orderly Bart stood ready with his master's completely oily belongings to help him put on his sportswear. Off to one side Duck and Gnome, the two observers, took counsel with each other.

You look at every plane, you will always find something personal to the pilot – usually a very dirty little pouch that hangs from his neck with strange things in it, without which the pilot will refuse to fly.

Even the bravest person has his little superstitions. Most of the time, this manifests itself in clothing choices, but often also in behaviors, for example a comrade who forced his observer to stroke the propeller before each flight.

Whether it was superstition with Berthold or something else – in any case, a whole shop's worth of charitable donations always flew with him. First he put on his tunic, which really wasn't much of a tunic anymore, although it had been created as such in the spring of 1914 and had faithfully served its master in all manner of wild combats. His orderly, Bart, was a similar phenomenon. He had gone into the field with Berthold, and soon proved to be in no way appropriate; he was always dirty from top to bottom. But without Bart and that tunic, it just couldn't work. A fur coat went over the tunic, then a scarf, horn-rimmed glasses on the face, large aviator goggles over them, a thick woolen bashlyk[63] around the head. On top of that, the crown in the form of an oily brown, leather beach hat. Orderly Bart had washed this talisman – with water – so the hat of course shrank, transformed into a miniature of itself, so it was no longer useable as headgear. That didn't matter. The hat had to be there. It had to fly, along with the tunic.

The tail of the Great Aircraft lifted heavily, while back in the turret Gnome was grimacing. It rose from the ground and headed toward the enemy. The roar of the engines got quieter and quieter, the two lines with the three dots smaller[64] … then only an indistinct something in the white of the sky. Quite impersonal …

Gradually the watching mechanics bestir themselves, and their thoughts return to duty.

This Vaux was a beautiful piece of earth. Years before, Fallières[65] held large parades on the airfield. We didn't move here because of the little castle, but because of the field and the large barn on it.

Today we were supposed to receive a distinguished visitor.

Everything was neatly prepared. I went back to the castle to take my simple lunch, since I still had half an hour left. Althaus wasn't back from his conference; I was alone. That would give a great impression if I had to report: "Everything is falling apart."

We frequently had visitors at Roupy. When a guest arrived at the A.D.K., he was shown the aviation unit as the closest interesting thing. We were already set up for it. Usually we flew over Roupy, and might even take the guest up with us. To conclude, we would fire off some old flares and drink tea. We called this the "small program."

But for the guests who were to come today, we scheduled the "big program." First: "The Highnesses arrive in Vaux at two o'clock to inspect the airfield," said the order from the Grand Captain, our unit leader.

There I was standing alone in front of the hangar that housed the two Fokkers. I had put on my good tunic and was waiting for things.

1345 hours. The booming of cannon near Ham … The telephone rings three times … Enemy aircraft! … Now of all times!

Not a moment to lose. Machine out ... Jacket on ... Head protection ... Goggles ... Gloves.

"Clear?"

"Clear!"

One swing on the propeller and the engine throbs to life.

"Chocks away!"

The first mechanic gives me the sign.

"Go!"

In the direction of St. Quentin there are flak bursts. I get higher and higher above the ground. I follow the flak bursts as they move, which pulls me in a high arc around Quentin.

I don't see the enemy.

He must have been faster, and in any case, he had the inside shorter line.

The flak bursts were becoming more and more unreachable, so after fifteen minutes I gave up and flew back to Roupy to look for the signals from the ground that should tell me whether it was worth staying up there. Nothing was there. I was just about to turn off the engine[66] when I looked around me again, and just then flak explosions appeared again in the direction of Ham.

A moment later a silhouette peeled away from the torn trench lines below and rose closer. I flew along innocently, as if I were up to something completely different. The blue haze became more transparent. I was looking for the rudder – the tricolor!

The next moment my bird stood on its wing as I heeled over to match course with the enemy. Over the roar of the engine I could hear the first "tak-tak-tak" from his rear gunner over there. The surrounding villages were occupied by regiments of the division to which I had belonged in peacetime.

The Roupyers were ready for inspection. At the fork in the St. Quentin-Roupy-Vaux road I saw our Grand Captain, who with his hand raised stopped the automobiles of the high-ranking guests.

The performance began. At fifty meters I put my head against the padding, my eye firmly over the front and rear sights; then the black barrel in front of me began to hammer, until I believed that my propeller would chew into the enemy's elevator after another instant, so I executed a volte[67] and fell on him again.

This may have been repeated three or four times. The enemy was still firing and not evading. Again, I lined him up in my sights and hammered away until his fire finally fell silent. Then I noticed that he was slowly losing altitude, and I stopped firing. I flew slowly after him. I smelled it – had time to smell it. The B.E.-type[68] had a peculiar smell. The engine exhaust left a path behind her that, to a combat pilot, was sweeter than a perfumed lace handkerchief. After every long fight I had the smell in my nose for days.

The break gave me time to look around to see where we actually were. Exactly between Roupy and Vaux. Just what I wanted. Of course, I was not thinking of our guests downstairs, who must have arrived by now, but only had my opponent in mind, who drifted very suspiciously slowly downward, as if he was looking for any favorable moment to get away. That was certainly not my intention for him. Rather, I wanted him to go down quickly so I wouldn't have to shoot any more. So I stayed close behind him on his starboard side.

At a height of 200 meters we flew over a village, over a field. I clearly saw an infantry officer who cupped both hands around his mouth to shout to his men the command to hold fire. However, I could hear a few shots coming out of the village.

We were approaching the Roupy airfield.

100 meters.

At that moment another Fokker appeared from above in a wild dive, shot up the tail of the enemy bird, and zoomed over it. I knew immediately who I was looking at: Althaus.

So he had come after all and immediately brought his machine up too, to look for the enemy that had drawn all that flak. Cruising at

1,500 meters, he spotted us both far below, heeled his machine over and brought himself to my side in an outrageous dive. It would have been a terrific spectacle.

The enemy in front of us didn't last long. He descended in a curve and ran into the ground. I flew down close, over the crash, to see if anything stirred in the wreckage. Nothing.

A black swarm of people broke away from the edge of the Roupy airfield. Four cars rolled up on the road. So I flew to Vaux. Tenderly I put my good bird on mother earth. Once the propeller stopped, a "Hurrah!" roared out of hundreds of throats. It was a beautiful moment; I had to make an effort not to spoil it. The hands of my two mechanics stretched out towards me. I grabbed them and walked around my Fokker with the people to look at the holes. Then I stripped off my gloves and went to my room, where I took a rather heavy cigar from the box.

Meanwhile, a dead man and a dying man were pulled out of the wreckage.

Lawrence had brought his observer to Earth with the last power of his life.[69] The other had died up in the air.

I believe it's harder to die in the air than on the ground. Just as flying itself connotes a longing to return to Earth, from which one is far separated by space and circumstance, and during which one embraces from above, and loves in their greatness, the small details of which one can see disappear beneath one; so it seems to me that dying in the air is a fight against death with double energy, a fight against saying goodbye to the earth as well as to life.

The Grand Captain had the place where the enemy aircraft lay cordoned off immediately. In particular, the department's flying officers were not admitted. Then the wreck was cleaned up.

The Highnesses had followed everything and, after the two stretchers had been carried away, examined the broken machine. It looked bad with its 212 hits. The fuselage was later exhibited as an example of the effectiveness of our weapons.

A few puffs on the cigar were enough for me. A little soap on my face; then I went down to the hangar. I would have preferred to be alone with myself, but now I belonged downstairs, where the second part of the program was supposed to take place.

In the meantime, Berthold had come back in the large aircraft. A heavy rag hung from one wall of the observer's seat. At Abbeville, the observer had had a shell explode between his legs after the attack. It was a splendid achievement that these brave men had accomplished. They had worked their way 120 kilometers behind enemy lines.

He just had time to remove the protective clothing the lad was wearing. The Fokkers were quickly arranged in rank and file as the cars were rolling in.

Berthold reported, and he and I were introduced. The duke and the prince shook our hands silently and seriously. The mood was subdued, yet excited.

We forced our attention to the apparatus to be demonstrated; there was still room to admire new things. Meanwhile we stood arm in arm with our faces flushed from flying and from excitement and almost held on to each other.

Then came – because it's what the program called for – the Grand Captain's request to demonstrate a takeoff with the Fokker.

The two aircraft were rolled out by hand, and the propellers started. I gave the signal and we rolled across the field side by side. As we reached low altitude there was an incessant tossing of the little monoplane to the left and to the right, which must have been amusing for the spectators. Althaus flew at me so audaciously at every opportunity that I chose to back off. I didn't feel like bumping into a comrade at that speed. His arrogance, as it happened, literally came before the fall. He put his aircraft into a power dive and then pulled up. The engine stalled, however, and he couldn't restart it, so that he had to instead make a landing. He was too low to make it back to the landing field. The astonished spectators saw him roll towards a ditch along the road and a hillside at dangerous speed. In an instant the wheels crashed into the ditch, the tail flipped skyward, and the bird lay on its back, motionless, with its underside facing up.

The terrified onlookers rushed forward to bring help, but they were stopped by poor little Althaus waving them off as he climbed out, signaling that he was still alive. Thank God he hadn't hurt himself. Immediately after the crash I flew over the site to see if my reckless comrade were still alive. Then I landed too. It didn't look as if too much permanent damage had been done. Eventually our Highnesses seemed to conclude that the entertainments of our program were not too bad.

Althaus arrived, crestfallen, and it took considerable effort to console him. Despite his endearing recklessness, he could easily be seized by a deep *Weltschmerz*.

Now the procession moved to the parade ground in Roupy. From the light aircraft we moved to the heavy ones. Here, the exhaust pipes of two 160-hp machines shook the air with their garrulous whispers; then the whispers became the chest-thumping tones of the absolute power of these beings, as they slowly lifted themselves off the ground.

While one of the planes demonstrated the flight possibilities of these types at low altitude through a few curves and then landed again, the other spiraled itself up to combat altitude.

Roupy's parade ground was a wide hollow. On one side were the groups of guests, on the other – about 700 meters away, but appearing very close – a large white square was drawn on the ground: the target for the bomber, which had now reached his desired altitude. He flew skillfully toward the target, heading toward the audience. Very high, visible only as a dot, he came at us. Everyone knew he was carrying four heavy bombs.

The duke and the Grand Captain observed through binoculars. The bomber still hadn't dropped his bombs. Our excitement grew. We were already expecting that he would have to turn around and make another pass when the captain finally lowered his glasses and said: "Now."

Everyone waited calmly; no one dared to admit his fears to the others. It was an anxious moment for both laymen and professionals. Especially for the latter, who knew only too well how easily a bomb can go wrong.

Then came the hissing sound of the bomb falling, and a mighty head of cabbage made of earth and smoke burst from the innocuous field in the center of the target. A second later the roaring sound of the explosion smote our ears.

Our harmless friend repeated this maneuver, with all its excitement and fear, three more long times. An exhalation of relief blew through the crowd, when it was realized that he had nothing left to drop and the eight-mark rocket, which was a part of the great program, signaled him to land. In the meantime, our comrade the pilot had sat happily in his crate, perhaps contemplating God-knows-what natural beauties on the earth below.

The Grand Captain asked the Highnesses if they had any further orders. The duke thanked him kindly and said no. Without a doubt, no key on the keyboard of the human soul was left untouched. We were all dead tired.

So it came about that at the little round tables in the dining room at Roupy over tea and cakes between flowers and a hum of activity, that conversation was really quite subdued.

As the Highnesses got into their cars and shook hands warmly with all of us, the duke handed us three of his crosses with the beautiful blue and yellow ribbons.[70]

That was a conclusion we could easily live with.

Chapter 9

The Western Front, 1914–1915

On 4 August 1914, Germany invaded Belgium, opening up a front that stretched from Switzerland to the Dutch border. The German Army then drove through Belgium and into northern France. They reached the outskirts of Paris and advanced to the east of Paris before they were rolled back, starting on 6 September, by the French and British broad multi-army counterattack that became known as the (First) Battle of the Marne (6–12 September). The German and Allied forces then raced to the English Channel in attempts to outflank each other before winter set in. Both sides then began entrenching across the entire front. The Germans tried one last failed breakthrough attempt against the Allied forces with the (First) Battle of Ypres (19 October – 22 November 1914); then the front settled across 450 miles from Switzerland to the English Channel, with few major actions until the spring of 1915.[71]

Buddecke's First Assignments:

According to his account Hans Buddecke was at the front in September 1914. He was given minimal flight training. He was assigned to the *Flieger Ersatz Abteilung* (Aviation Replacement Section) in Darmstadt on 2 September, and transferred to *Flieger Ersatz Abteilung 3* (FEA 3; 3rd Aviation Replacement Section) near Reims, France on 27 September. He then moved to *Etappen Flugzeug Park 2* (EFP 2; 2nd Aircraft Staging Depot) near Bellenglise, France on 20 October.[72] While he states he was at the front in September 1914, he was still training in November 1914 with EFP 2, although it was located in occupied France. It was during this training that he became acquainted with Rudolf Berthold. He was then transferred to the *Feldflieger Abteilung 27* (FFA 27 or Field Aviation Section 27) on 12 January 1915.[73]

The dates of his assignments do not mesh well with his claim that:

> Because of the flight skills I had acquired in America, I naturally reported to the flying service. At the replacement unit near Frankfurt [this probably refers to the aviation replacement section at Darmstadt], the old pilot Faller from Baden took me up three times in his double-decker … But after just fourteen days I was transferred to the front. I had never been asked to take any exams, and I have to admit that I was only gradually able to really control the aircraft in the aviation unit after a number of flights.

It does appear that he was near Frankfurt for at least two weeks or more before he was transferred to a replacement section in France. This was still not front-line service, although it was near the front. It then appears that he went through almost three months of training before he was sent to an active combat section.

This unit, FFA 27, was commanded by Captain Alfred Keller. Buddecke was assigned to the second shift crew of a new two-seater armed with a rear-firing machine gun.[74] Buddecke criticized the airplane (see below) and he also claimed that he and his commander disagreed over the use of the Fokker. This last statement is puzzling, as he was transferred to FFA 23 in early June 1915. At that time, the Fokkers had yet to shoot down a single plane. They were only first deployed in May, and even then only one or two of them. So did he really have an argument with his commander in May 1915 over the Fokker that led to his transfer? This appears to be an overstatement, made after the fact, especially in light of how and why he ended up flying the Fokker at his next unit.

Buddecke says of his disagreement with the commander:

> Back then, everyone had his own idea of how to fight to the air. I was no exception; I saw the ideal in the small, fast-moving Fokker aircraft in which the pilot did everything on his own. My unit leader disagreed, so I requested a transfer. This does not mean, however, that I do not still very much admire this man today – not only because he wears the *Pour le Mérite.*

Captain Alfred Keller was awarded the Iron Cross 1st and 2nd class in 1914. He was awarded *Pour le Mérite* (the Blue Max) on 4 December 1917 due to bombing missions flown in September 1917 on Dunkirk.

Alfred Keller (1882–1974) continued in aviation after the war, working for the Weimar Republic and then for Luftwaffe under Nazi Germany. He ended up being promoted to Colonel General (equivalent to a U.S. four-star general) during World War II. He was awarded the Knight's Cross to the Iron Cross on 24 June 1940 as the commanding general of the IV Air Corps during the Battle of Britain. He was then promoted to command the First Air Fleet from 20 August 1940 to 12 June 1943, which mostly operated on the Eastern Front. He passed away in Berlin in 1974 at the age of 91.

According to photographic evidence, while Buddecke was at FFA 27 he was awarded the Iron Cross 2nd Class and the Bavarian Military Merit Order, 4th Class with Swords.[75]

The Aircraft Buddecke Flight Tested:

Buddecke describes the first German fighter aircraft he flew thus:

> Our first fighter aircraft arrived. It had a machine gun that fired to the rear, and was greeted with joy. Finally, we were finally able to do "tack-tack-tack" like those gentlemen flying Farmans on the other side ... I got the chance to be the second one to

> give it a test flight. I did, and lo and behold, the apparatus was so inferior in design … that it barely tolerated a steep curve and took minutes to make a half turn. When my unit leader asked me for my verdict, I did not hide my opinion from him.

It is not known which aircraft this was. Germany at this stage had a number of two-seater designs that were underpowered. Adding the weight of a machine gun, its mount and the ammunition to these designs probably made their performance even less impressive. Germany had a large number of airplane manufacturers even at these early stages of the war.[76]

At FFA 23, to which he transferred in June 1915,[77] they were reporting that they had new swivel-mounted Parabellum MG 14 machine guns for their planes. These were operated by the observers. FFA 23 had been re-equipped with Rumpler B.I and Albatros B.II biplanes, with Rudolf Berthold flying an armed Albatros.[78]

A Comparison to Immelmann's, Boelcke's and Berthold's Flight Training:

The fact that Hans Buddecke claims he was given very little flight training is unusual, as German standards tended to be fairly rigorous. As both Max Immelmann and Oswald Boelcke carefully documented their flight training regimes in dated letters and Rudolf Berthold left a diary, we can compare their training regimens to Buddecke's claims.

Boelcke underwent a ten-week flight course at Halberstadt and Darmstadt from 2 June to 15 August 1914, which was mostly during the period before the unexpected outbreak of the war, and before the urgency of getting pilots to the front. Immelmann began his flight instruction at Adlershof on 12 November 1914. Due to bad winter weather and a few landing mishaps during training, he did not earn his pilot's badge until the end of March 1915 – a period of four-and-a-half months.

Rudolf Berthold started at the same flight school as Boelcke in Halberstadt in June 1914. On 1 July, he was recalled to his regiment at Wittenberg, interrupting his training. He then drilled with the regiment for two weeks before returning to Halberstadt. On 17 July he was formally transferred from his regiment to the air troops and returned to Halberstadt on the 20th. By that time, Boelcke had finished his second examination, while Berthold had not yet taken his first two pilot's exams. At the end of the month he was sent to Großenhain airfield and assigned to FFA 23 as an observer, as his training as a pilot was not complete. That unit deployed to the front at Montjoie, Belgium, on 7 August, and conducted their first reconnaissance flight on 15 August with Berthold as the observer. On a flight two days later, his pilot got lost and made a forced landing that damaged the plane. They landed between the lines at a time when the opposing armies were maneuvering in the area, which risked getting them both captured. They were able to make their way back to their own lines on foot and eventually recover their aircraft, but this navigation error by the pilot reinforced Berthold's resolve to become a pilot himself and take charge of his own destiny. As a result of his excellent work while serving as an observer, he was awarded the Iron Cross 2nd Class on 13 September and the Iron Cross 1st Class on 4 October. Both medals were awarded to him by Colonel General Karl von Bülow, commander of the German 2nd Army. Sometime after 29 October 1914, Berthold convinced his commander to release him to EFP 2 so he could resume his pilot training.

It was at EFP 2 in November that Berthold met Buddecke and they became friends. He returned to his section in early January but was still not fully qualified, so while at FFA 23 he fulfilled his next test on 10 January at Château de Grand Priel and then returned to FFA 23. He finally completed all his requirements on 18 January 1915 and qualified for his Military Pilot's Badge. So, given a full month of training in June, some in July, and then a full month in November and

December, and some in January, it appears that Berthold was trained as a pilot in three full months and maybe another thirty days in July and January, although it was almost eight calendar months before he qualified as a pilot.

From Hans Buddecke's account it appears he re-joined the German Army in September and deployed to the front after fourteen days. This is probably not the case, and it appears that he had almost three months of training between 20 October 1914 and 12 January 1915; so his claim of only two weeks of training compared to two-and-a-half to four-and-a-half months for Boelcke, Berthold, and Immelmann is hard to believe. As we have seen, this would not be the first time in his memoir that he overstated his accomplishments.

Buddecke's Second Section:

In November, Berthold arranged to continue his pilot's training at a nearby facility, which is where he met and befriended Buddecke. Berthold finally qualified as a military pilot on 18 January 1915 and was awarded the Prussian military pilot badge. He returned to his squadron shortly thereafter. It appears that Buddecke was qualified as a military pilot in early January. He transferred to FFA 23 on 10 June 1915;[79] at that time the unit was commanded by Captain Karl Scher.

In June 1915, Berthold described the section:[80]

> I succeeded in having Buddecke transferred to my section. Now we have all splendid fellows, such as: Oblt Fritz Böhmer; Lieutenant of the Reserves Anton Hirsemann; Ltn.d.Res Erwin Tütschulte; Rittmeister [Cavalry Captain] Friedrich Schueler von Krieken and Ltn. Josef Grüner – all forceful officers of the good, old style, firm as iron in performing their duties and in service overall.
>
> In terms of distance flown and numbers of combat missions, each crew seeks to surpass the others. True flying spirit. All

for one and one for all! Moreover, we have the splendid … Hptm Karl Seber [commanding officer] and Hptm Eberhard Bohnstedt [executive officer] at the head of the section. Both constantly strive to keep us all out of trouble, the emphasis and attitude is always refreshing and the same spirit is raised among the non-flying mechanics and non-rated men. They do not have it easy, but they do the job.

Ltn Hans-Joachim von Seydlitz-Gestenberg – or, as I call him "Seidenspitz"[81] – is, to be sure, the most superb of them all. Although severely wounded in an air fight and not yet completely healed, he fled from the military hospital and tried desperately to be able to continue to fly; to do that, he had to be lifted into the aeroplane.

FFA 23:

The German word *Abteilung* can have a number of translations depending on context, but usually refers to an organized unit of some kind. The direct translation of the word into "detachment" often confuses people as to what the unit really is: it usually denotes a battalion-sized unit but can occasionally be used to refer to something else. In this case it refers to a section, or a unit smaller than a squadron. An *Abteilung* can be as small as a section (larger than a squad) or as large as an army (for example, *Armee Abteilung Kempf* in July 1943, which had three full corps attached to it).

In this usage, FFAs (*Feldflieger Abteilungen*) were units of six aircraft, which is smaller than what the British would call a squadron or the French would call an *escadrille*. At the start of the war, there were thirty-three or thirty-four of these units in the German Army.[82] One was assigned to each of the eight Army headquarters and one to each of the twenty-five regular Corps headquarters. So, by nature, they were reconnaissance assets that directly reported to senior headquarters. This is part of the reason that the Iron Crosses awarded to Oswald Boelcke, his older brother Wilhelm, and to Rudolf Berthold, were awarded directly to them by corps and army commanders. In many cases, the pilots themselves made their reports directly to the army or corps headquarters and were known by their commanding general officers.

By March 1915 the number of these flying sections had doubled. In late 1916 the FFAs were reformed into *Staffeln* (sing. *Staffel*; effectively squadrons) and *Geschwader* (effectively wings even though the name also translates as "squadron." Note that the plural is the same as the singular.)

FFA 23 was initially armed with two-seater Taube monoplanes, but by 1915 the mix of planes in the section had expanded.[83] It was commanded by First Lieutenant Otto Freiherr (Baron) Vogel von Falckenstein. He was a pre-war flyer. He was flying an Aviatik C when he was shot down and killed on 10 January 1915 by the famous French pilot Eugene Gilbert.[84] He was 32 at the time.

Though Berthold and Buddecke would become the most famous alumni of FFA 23, also with the unit was the future ace Ernst Freiherr von Althaus, whom Buddecke mentions frequently in his memoir.

FFA 23 was attached to the German 2nd Army. This army was part of the giant outflanking maneuver conducted in August 1914 that marched through Belgium, taking Liège and Namur before pushing across the Meuse River into France. By 7 August, when Berthold joined the unit, FFA 23 was encamped at Monschau, Germany, near the border with Belgium. They flew their first reconnaissance mission on 15 August, consisting of one aircraft with Berthold as observer. The airplane took bullet holes in the wings from anti-aircraft fire. Two days later, the same crew on another mission became lost and landed behind enemy lines. Luckily with the fluid situation of the front, the two men were able to regain the German lines and recover the airplane. That same day, FFA 23 lost another airplane over French territory and the crew was captured. Another plane went down on 26 August 1914.

Rudolf Berthold:

Rudolf Berthold became one of the top German aces of the war. He was born 24 March 1891 in the Kingdom of Bavaria within the German Empire. He joined the 3rd Brandenburg Infantry Regiment and after a year-and-a-half as an officer candidate, was commissioned as a lieutenant. Still, he had to go through the military flying schools, and underwent his flight training in the summer of 1914.[85] As noted above, he was a classmate of future top ace Oswald Boelcke, but while Berthold refers to Boelcke in his diary, the published letters of Boelcke make no mention of Berthold.

When Berthold was awarded the Iron Cross 2nd Class on 13 September 1914, he was only the second person in Second Army to be so decorated. On 4 October, General von Bülow awarded him the Iron Cross 1st Class. He was the first man in the 2nd Army after von Bülow himself to receive this award. It was very much due to the important role that aerial observation played in helping the 2nd Army protect its flank during the French counterattacks from the Marne and at the Aisne River.

In November Berthold requested to complete his pilot training and was assigned to EFP 2 at Château de Grand Priel just north of St. Quentin, France, fifteen miles from where FFA 23 was deployed. He qualified as a military pilot on 18 January 1915. He spent the latter part of 1915 flying missions in the large four-man AEG G.II biplane bomber.

Berthold's biography continues in Chapter 16.

"Mr. Vedrines"

In his first chapter on his actions during the Great War Buddecke mentions:

> Everything worked out nicely. I received a nice new aircraft, and flew extensive reconnaissance operations, during which

> I encountered Mr. Vedrines, who ignited my tracer ammunition with his machine gun while my observer was pulling out his carbine; and I finally got my Fokker, which hardly anyone else wanted to have.

Jules Charles Toussaint Védrines (1881–1919) was a colorful French aviation pioneer who in the early stages of the war flew a Blériot XXXVIbis monoplane he called *la Vache* (the Cow), emblazoned with that name in large letters on the fuselage and painted with a picture of a cow. Perhaps this is how Buddecke was able to identify him. Later in the war he was also known to fly a Morane-Saulnier Type L armed with a forward-firing Hotchkiss machine gun.[86]

It appears that in this passage, Buddecke is making an oblique reference to the first time he got shot down. This would have occurred after May 1915 and before September 1915. It is reported in the 27 August 1915 issue of the *The Indianapolis News* that Captain Hans Buddecke had received the Iron Cross 1st Class for a feat of daring in a recent battle with French flying machines. His airplane caught fire but he was able to extinguish the flames with his feet and returned in safety to the German lines with some especially valuable information. One wonders if this is the same incident as the reference in Buddecke's book to "Mr. Vedrines" igniting his tracer ammunition.

Ernst Freiherr von Althaus:

The Baron von Althaus was born in Coburg, Bavaria, in 1890. He was one of the original fifteen Fokker Eindecker pilots who started the "Fokker Scourge" of 1915. At the start of the war, he was a Lieutenant in the Hussars. He led a patrol of fifteen Hussars into an occupied French village and captured twenty-two enemy. In January, he was awarded Bavaria's highest decoration for valor, the Knight's Cross of the Military Order of St. Henry. In April 1915 he transferred to the air service, was promoted to senior lieutenant in August, and transferred to FFA 23 on 20 September. There he served with future aces Hans-Joachim Buddecke and Rudolf Berthold.

Flying for *Kampf Kommandos Vaux* (Battle Command Vaux) he obtained his first kill on 3 December 1915, a B.E.2c; and by 30 April 1916 he had become an ace with five victories. He was wounded at this time, and during his hospital stay he met his future wife, a nurse. On 22 July 1916 he scored his eighth victory and earned the *Pour le Mérite* (the Blue Max). He was wounded again on 4 March 1917 and scored only one other victory in the war, on 24 July 1917. Because of failing eyesight, he was shifted out of air commands and moved to the infantry. Althaus was captured by the Americans on 15 October 1918 and repatriated to Germany in September 1919.

After the war he became a lawyer, despite a total loss of vision by 1937. During World War II he served as the Director of the County Court of Berlin. After the war he worked briefly as an interpreter for the Allies. He died of illness in 1946.

Articles about Buddecke continued to appear in the Indianapolis newspapers, recounting his exploits in France. This was almost certainly at the instigation of his uncle, Albert Lieber. The first of these articles appeared in *The Indianapolis Star* on Sunday, 11 April 1915. It reads:

WRITES VIVIDLY FROM GERMANY: Rudolf Lieber, in Letter to Father from Duesseldorf, Deplores Use of American Shrapnel by French. HANS BUDDECKE WITH HIM: Lieutenant Who Spent Year in Indianapolis Has Had Many Exciting Experiences as Member of Aviation Corps.

Albert Lieber has just received a vividly interesting letter from his son, Rudolph, a student at Wabash College, who is visiting in Duesseldorf, Germany. Hans Buddecke, to whom young

Lieber frequently refers, was for more than a year a resident of Indianapolis and he left here at the beginning of the war to report for duty. Following is the letter:

"Dear Father:

"You will be glad to know that Lieut. Hans Buddecke is with us on a furlough.

"Immediately upon his arrival in Europe he entered the flying corps, and up to date has made between 275 and 300 flights. His main duty is to take photographs and to also direct the artillery, giving the position of the enemy. He has had many narrow escapes in the air, with French and English aeroplanes, but has always been successful up to now. He described to me that the difference between American shrapnel and the French is great.

American Shrapnel Deadly.

"The American shrapnel, when it explodes, is enveloped in a yellow cloud, and explodes very true. It is much superior to the French and more deadly.

"I am very sorry that America is furnishing such unheard-of quantities of war ammunition to murder the Germans, who have never injured America. The reports here are that Japan is very antagonistic to America and unfriendly. I hope we will not have a war with them.

"The Germans are permitted to drink all the beer and light wine that they wish, but whisky and brandy can only be had upon a doctor's certificate: and there is no hardship for the Germans. Can you send some chewing gum to me for Lieut. Buddecke? He can't get any here.

"The enthusiasm of Germany is as intense now as when the war first broke out. The universities will close somewhat earlier than usual, as about 75 per cent of the students entered the war.

Aviator's Experiences Exciting.

It will be of interest to you to learn that Lieut. Buddecke sailed for Europe upon a Greek vessel, and was immediately attached to the aeroplane department, which is under the direction of the Marine. Soon after he arrived, the Germans captured 100 French aeroplanes and he had charge of putting them in order and drilling new flyers. He has seen most of the great battles in France and says that it is quite different to fly a machine in war. When they get an order, no matter if there is a storm, they must execute the same, and although they may be attacked, they cannot return until their mission has been fulfilled. They usually fly at an altitude of about 3,000 feet.

"He says it is very exciting to see the maneuvering of friend and foe, and especially so when they are in battle with another machine. They always fly in pairs, one, to observe, and the other to guide the machine. It is astonishing but true, that even at 8,000 feet, the artillery can reach them with deadly effect. Immediately they get into this target practice, they zigzag and dive as quickly as possible.

"The position of Germany, both on the east front and the west, is excellent. Do not be alarmed about food, as we have everything in that line, and the prices are very little higher, and in many instances lower than during the times of peace. The Germans are very sanguine and grandfather says they will surely win."

This is the best description we have of Buddecke's activities before the days of the Fokker. The article confirms that he travelled to Europe on a Greek vessel, as described in his account. It also states that Buddecke was a resident of Indianapolis for "more than a year:" As Buddecke left in early August 1914, then this would indicate that he was there since July 1913, though there is no other evidence of him being in America before February 1914.

Boelcke and Immelmann had already brought down three enemies:

Hans Buddecke starts Chapter 7 with the statement: "So far, aerial combat had really been just a lawless shootout. Chance hits may have forced one of the combatants to go down – rarely to crash. But it seemed unbelievable to us that Boelcke and Immelmann had already brought down three enemies and were still intact."

It appears that parts of his memoir were written at the time of the events. Oswald Boelcke had shot down his third aircraft on 19 September 1915, while Max Immelmann downed his third on 21 September 1915. Buddecke also shot down his first aircraft on 19 September 1915.

Boelcke shot down his fourth aircraft (his third by a Fokker) on 26 September, and his fifth on 16 October 1915. Immelmann shot down his fourth aircraft on 10 October 1915. This strongly indicates that Buddecke's account was written between 21 September and 10 October 1915.

Max Immelmann:

Max Immelmann was one of a pair of German triple aces in 1915–16 who were a major part of the "Fokker Scourge."[87] He was born on 21 September 1890 in Dresden in Saxony and was an officer in the German Army from 1911–12. He then left the military to attend engineering school in Dresden. When the war broke out, he was called up by his previous unit, the 2nd Railway Regiment, but he had already applied in August to become an aviator based upon a poster he had seen. In November 1914 he happily transferred to aviation for training and deployed first to FFA 10 in France from February to April 1915 and then to FFA 62 in early May 1915. This newly created unit also included the veteran airman Oswald Boelcke, who had already been awarded the Iron Cross, 2nd and 1st classes, for his actions with FFA 13. The unit was equipped with LFV two-seaters.

On 3 June he was shot down by a French pilot but managed to land safely behind German lines. Immelmann was awarded the Iron Cross 2nd Class for preserving his aircraft.

The first Fokker Eindecker was delivered to FFA 62 in early July, with Boelcke taking over the M.5K/MG production prototype, now numbered E.3/15. In later July, a production Fokker E.1 arrived (model number E.15/15) armed with a synchronized Spandau IMG 08 machine gun. Taking possession of this Fokker Eindecker, Immelmann shot down his first plane on 1 August 1915. He was awarded the Iron Cross 1st Class for this achievement. By 21 September 1915 he had shot down three planes and had become an ace on 26 October 1915.

He was in competition with his friend and squadron mate Boelcke to see who could shoot down the most planes. This competition continued, with Immelmann leading the competition more often than not until 18 June 1916, when he was shot down near Lens, France. At the time of his death, he was credited with seventeen kills.[88]

Immelmann left his name on three subjects. First was the Immelmann turn, an aerial combat maneuver credited to him. Second is the "Immelmann Squadron" (AG-51) in the present German Air Force. Third was the "Blue Max," the nickname for the *Pour le Mérite*, which was Germany's highest award at the time. He and Boelcke were the first two pilots to be awarded the *Pour le Mérite*, receiving them from the Kaiser himself on 12 January 1916 after they had both made their eighth kills. It was then nicknamed the "Blue Max" on account of the blue medal and Immelmann's first name. It also served as the title for a fictional 1966 novel and subsequent movie on German Great War aviators.

Oswald Boelcke:

Oswald Boelcke was the other of a pair of German triple aces in 1915–16 who were a major part of the "Fokker Scourge." He was born 19 May 1891, also in Saxony, like Immelmann. He joined the army in 1912 and, inspired by an aviation display by Frenchman Adolphe Pegoud in Frankfurt in late 1913, he decided to become an aviator. In the meantime, he qualified for the German Olympic Modern Pentathlon team in 1914. The VI Olympics were scheduled to be held in Berlin, Germany in 1916, but were cancelled due to the outbreak of war.

Boelcke started his flight training in June 1914, and Rudolf Berthold was a classmate. Boelcke was assigned to FFA 13 on 31 August 1914 at his instigation so as to serve with his older brother. The two brothers made a hard-working observation team that flew more hours than anyone else in the unit, becoming leading aviators in the unit. They both ended up being awarded the Iron Cross, 2nd and 1st classes, for their efforts. Because of difficulties they were having with some of their fellow officers in the unit, his older brother was transferred out of the unit in April 1915 and Boelcke was transferred to FFA 62 in May 1915. There he befriended Max Immelmann and started flying the new Fokker Eindecker.

He shot down his first plane on 4 July 1915 using a two-seater LVG C.I with Lieutenant Heinz-Helmuth von Wühlisch as his observer and machine-gunner. This was his one victory in a two-seater plane. After that, he primarily flew Fokker Eindeckers and upped his count of kills to three planes by 19 September 1915, becoming an ace on 16 October 1915. At the time of Max Immelmann's death in June 1916, Boelcke had shot down eighteen planes compared to Immelmann's seventeen claimed kills. He then went on a killing spree in September and October, primarily flying an Albatros D.II, that raised his count of kills to forty, the highest total ever achieved by any pilot up until that time. On 28 October 1916, in the middle of a large air battle, he collided with one of his squadron mates, Erwin Boehme, and was killed in the crash. Boehme survived. Boehme was an ace with five claimed kills and would be credited with twenty-four victories before he was shot down in November 1917.

At the time of his death, Boelcke was the most renowned German airman, both as a fighter pilot, as a leader of men, and as a developer of aerial tactics and organization. The first fighter squadron he had formed, *Jagdstaffel 2* or *Jasta 2*, was renamed in his honor and his name continues to adorn the coat of arms of a modern German Air Force fighter-bomber wing (JaBoG 31).

A Short History of the Fokker Scourge:

The first plane shot down by a machine gun firing through a propeller was on 1 April 1915 by Roland Garros using a Hotchkiss machine gun fired from a Morane-Saulnier Type L. This was done by mounting steel wedges on the propeller to deflect any bullets that might strike the blades. Roland Garros shot down two more planes during the month of April using his new firing arrangement before an engine problem forced him to land behind German lines on 18 April 1915.[89] He was captured and his plane taken before he could completely destroy it. The Germans then realized that they could produce a similar arrangement so as to also have forward firing scout planes. On 19 May 1915 the German Army displayed the plane at Döberitz, the Imperial German Army proving ground established in 1894 outside Berlin. Various airplane manufacturers attended to examine this innovation, including Dutchman Anthony Fokker, who was an acrobatic pilot, airplane designer, and the head of the small *Fokker Aeroplanbau* airplane manufacturer primarily based in Schwerin. He and his German engineer Heinrich Lübbe examined the French arrangement. Fokker was then able to convince the senior officers present to support his efforts to develop a synchronization, or interrupter, gear (the terms are used interchangeably) that would allow a machine gun to fire through the propeller. This was an idea he had first started working on in December of 1914 and was already near completing a working prototype.[90] It was based in part on an arrangement patented by August Euler (1868–1957) back in 1912. With the French having developed the crude but working deflector system, Fokker was able to convince the German military to support his more sophisticated arrangement. He then quickly finalized his design, installed a machine gun and his synchronization gear on a single-wing Fokker, and ran it through a battery of successful tests.

In late May Fokker installed a Parabellum MG 14 machine gun and the synchronization system on one of his pre-war Fokker A.IIIs (a Fokker M.5 in the company terminology) flown by German Army pilot Lieutenant Otto Parschau. The plane had been nicknamed the "green machine" because of the unique "jaeger regiment" green paint job given to this privately owned airplane that was now in service to the German Army. The first demonstration of the system for the German Army was conducted on 13 June 1915 at Stenay, a French town occupied by the German 5th Army. The German Army was suitably impressed with the demonstration and authorized armed aircraft to be developed using the machine gun and synchronization gear. This series of planes was based upon the Fokker M.5 that Anthony Fokker had designed and built in 1913. It was a single-seater light-reconnaissance plane, very closely based on the 1913 French Morane-Saulnier H. This was similar to the airplane that Roland Garros was using, except his model L used a parasol wing[91] and instead of a wooden structure for the fuselage, Fokker used a welded steel tube frame. The power plant was initially an Oberursel U.0. 7-cylinder rotary engine, which was a licensed version of the French seven-cylinder Gnome Lambda radial engine. It produced 80 hp, as did the same type of engines used on the Morane-Saulnier H and L versions. Fokker had used the M.5 for acrobatic demonstrations, including looping the plane. Roll control of these planes was accomplished by "wing warping," similar to what was done with the Wright Flyers and Morane-Saulniers.

The German Army in early 1915 had ordered ten M.5Ks (K for short wing) that were designated as the A.III, but before delivery five were modified to add the 7.92 Parabellum MG 14 machine gun and synchronization gear. These were the five new prototype Fokker E.Is. Subsequent production E-types had their wings lowered slightly to improve pilot visibility. An additional ten production E-types were completed by the end of July, giving the Germans 15 E-types. One of the first five planes (Fokker E.3/15) was given to Oswald Boelcke of FFA 62, who shared his plane with squadron mate Max Immelmann until he could get his own plane (E.13/15). Others were provided to Kurt Wintgens (E.5/15) of FFA 48 and Hans Buddecke of FFA 23. Otto Parschau started with the "green machine" which was the prototype Fokker A.16/15 armed with the Parabellum machine gun. He was then provided with Fokker E.1/15 while the "green machine" was shipped back to the factory.[92] In late 1915 he picked up another production plane Fokker.[93] These five pilots started in the second half of 1915 what would later become referred to as the "Fokker Scourge."

Since the start of the war, pilots had been carrying rifles, carbines, and pistols with them in flight and this had resulted in multiple combats and even a few planes shot down over the course of the first nine months of this war. The French then armed their rear-engine Farmans with machine guns, and several other French and British two-seater planes were given rear-facing machine guns. These planes were able to take down more opposing enemy planes. The most successful pilot at this was Adolphe Pegoud who had shot down, or forced to land, five German planes, three on 5 February and two on 3 April 1915.[94] Pegoud's five "kills" were scored with a Maurice Farman while Eugene Gilbert made three kills flying a two-seater Morane-Saulnier. The actual shooting was done by the observer, which for at least three of Pegoud's kills was Private Leon Lerendu, his old mechanic at *Blériot Aeronautique*. The British pilot Louis Strange also achieved one kill with his own machine-gun armed Maurice Farman. The situation had become a little lop-sided with some of the French and at least one British plane type armed with a machine gun, and no German planes similarly armed. It was the Germans who were at the losing end of this early air war. Then Roland Garros shot down three planes in April 1915 and was captured.

Part of the reason the French and British reconnaissance aircraft were armed with machine guns early in the war and the Germans were not, was that the French had the lightweight gas-actuated and air-cooled Hotchkiss light machine gun (27 lb) while the British had the lightweight drum-fed Lewis gun (28 lb).[95] In 1914, the Germans did not have a lightweight machine gun. These were first deployed in 1915 with the belt-fed Parabellum MG 14 (21 or 22 lb), the Bergman MG 15na (28 lb), and then the Spandau IMG 08 (which weighed around 26 or 27 lb in its final version).[96] These lighter guns finally allowed the Germans to arm their reconnaissance planes. They also gave their new 'C-series' of planes considerably more engine power with the 160-hp Mercedes D.III 6-cylinder water-cooled in-line piston engine. The 'C series' – the Albatros C.I, the LVG C.I and C.II, and Aviatik C.I – first appeared around April 1915.[97] The Albatros and LVG two-seat reconnaissance planes were fitted with a rotatable ring for the observer's machine gun, a superior arrangement to most of the Allied mounting arrangements. This was designed by Franz Schneider of Switzerland. This German-based engineer and aircraft designer, who had previously worked for Nieuport, had also patented a synchronized firing system in July 1913, and published it in September 1914, but was unable to develop it because his request for a lightweight machine gun was rejected.[98] Instead, the credit for creating the first working synchronized machine gun went to Anthony Fokker.

The Germans were finally able to turn the tables on the Allies starting in July 1915 when Wintgens claimed he shot down two French planes on 1 and 4 July with his Fokker E.I. These claims were not confirmed but are probably correct. This was followed on 4 July 1915 with a confirmed kill by Boelcke, but he was flying a two-seater LVG, not a Fokker. The first confirmed Fokker kill was made by Kurt Wintgens on 15 July 1915 flying for FFA 48. By the end of July, Wintgens had two confirmed kills and two unconfirmed victories. At that time, around fifteen Eindeckers were operational, including the original five. Immelmann had had his own production plane armed with a Spandau IMG 08 lightened machine gun.

The killing continued in August with Wintgens upping his account to three confirmed kills, while Boelcke downed a second plane and Immelmann scored his first. In September, Boelcke increased his confirmed kills to four while Immelmann had three. This is mentioned in Buddecke's account. Boelcke and Immelmann were serving together at FFA 62. Hans Buddecke got his first kill on 19 September 1915, his second on 23 October and his third on 11 November. By the end of November Boelcke had six claimed kills, as did Immelmann. Wintgens had his three claimed kills and two unconfirmed kills, and Otto Parschau and his "green machine" had one claimed kill.

By December, there were around forty Fokkers in service, including the very similar Pfalz E-type fighters.[99] According to another source, by the end of October the Germans had around seventy-five Fokker Eindeckers in "frontline inventory."[100]

On 12 January 1916, Kaiser Wilhelm personally awarded the *Pour le Mérite*, the highest German award for bravery and service, to Oswald Boelcke and Max Immelmann for having shot down eight planes each. They were the first two airmen so awarded.

The "Fokker Scourge" continued until around April or May of 1916, when new armed Allied planes like the French Nieuport 11, the rear-engine British DH-2, and the two-seater rear-engine F.E.2B became common and control of the airspace was once again contested.

The phrase "Fokker Scourge" was first used in mid-1916 by the British press and politicians. One member of parliament also referred to the British airmen as "Fokker fodder." At this point, dozens of Allied aircraft had been shot down by the marauding Fokkers, but the "Fokker Scourge" had already ended. Still, Oswald Boelcke had claimed nineteen airplanes by the end of June 1916 while Max Immelmann had claimed seventeen. Max Immelmann went down on 18 June 1916, probably as a result of a malfunction of the synchronization system.[101] By the end of June, Wintgens was credited with eight kills while Parschau had five, Ernst von Althaus (FFA 23) was credited with six, and Buddecke's friend Rudolf Berthold (also

FFA 23) had five confirmed kills. Buddecke was credited with seven confirmed kills later over the Dardenelles.

While the kill claims of Boelcke and Immelmann were impressive, they were being seriously chased by the French and British aces, with Frenchman Jean Navarre credited with twelve kills, Charles Nungesser with ten kills, Georges Guynemer with nine, and the late Adolphe Pegoud credited with six. The British pilot Lanoe Hawker was credited with seven kills and his actual score may have been higher.

Farman aircraft:

Three French-born brothers of British parents, Richard, Henri, and Maurice Farman, established the Farman Aviation Works (*Avions Farman* in French) in 1908 near Paris. They built a number of plane models before the war that ended up being major components of both the French and British air forces. Of the first four squadrons the British deployed to France, there were fifteen Henry Farmans among them.[102] The French also made extensive use of the Farman aircraft.

The British started the war with the Farman MF.7 Longhorns and Farman MF.11 Shorthorns. As of 1915, the Farmans in service with the British and French air forces were mostly Farman HF.20s (a refinement of the MF.11). They were two-seater biplanes, rear engine with the 80-hp Gnome Lambda engine. With the observer in the front seat and the engine in the rear, this allowed the aircraft to carry a flexibly mounted Hotchkiss or Lewis machine gun in the front. It could also carry a small bomb load. This gave the Allies the ability to shoot down German airplanes and this was part of the somewhat one-sided exchange up until the beginning of the "Fokker Scourge" in July 1915.

B.E.2c:

The Royal Aircraft Factory B.E.2c was the most common British reconnaissance plane in 1915. It was a two-seater tractor biplane (meaning engine in the front) that had the observer seated in the front and the pilot in the rear, which was not a common arrangement on a tractor plane. It was powered with the RAF 1a V-8 air-cooled piston engine with 90 hp. It was a pre-war design that first flew on 30 May 1914 and went into squadrons shortly after that, along with earlier models of the B.E.2s. In 1915 it usually did not carry a machine gun, as the weight of gun and ammunition would seriously degrade range and performance. These vulnerable aircraft were Hans Buddecke's first three kills.

Fokker Eindecker:

The Fokker Eindecker was a single-seater monoplane with a single belt-fed Parabellum machine gun mounted on the cowling, with a synchronization gear that allowed it to fire through the propeller. Both the plane and the synchronization gear were designed by Anthony Fokker. His Fokker E.I, E.II, and E.III versions were the primary planes of the "Fokker Scourge." He also produced a version with two or three machine guns, the Fokker E.IV.[103] This final version of the Eindecker fighter aircraft had more horsepower and more firepower.[104]

The Fokker Eindecker was fundamentally a copy of the French Morane-Saulnier H design, except it used welded steel tubes for its frame. The engine was a German-manufactured version of the French 80-hp Gnome Lambda radial engine. As such it was not a superior plane to what the French and British were flying. Its main advantage was the belt-fed Parabellum MG 14 that could fire through the forward propeller. As it was belt-fed with a hundred rounds, and the machine guns on the French and British planes were drum-fed (the Lewis drum carried forty-seven rounds), this gave it a slight firepower advantage.

The pilots of FFA 23 received their Fokker Eindeckers in July according to Berthold's account. The unit had also received the large AEG G.II twin-engine bomber. This bomber had a wingspan of 52 ft 6 in a length of 29 ft 10 in and a loaded weight of 5,434 lb. As Berthold noted in his diary for August:

> For months we have flown the *Grosskampflugzeug* [large battle plane], which we call the 'Big Barge.' It has two engines that together produce 300 hp. It has places for two or three observers, two machine guns and can carry a bomb-load of 200 kilograms. I have flown it in combat and it is well suited.

Enamored with this new bomber, Berthold passed on the opportunity to fly the Fokker Eindecker. As he stated, "In July, I was supposed to receive a Fokker Eindecker. I gave it up in favour of Buddecke, who asked me to do so. He was familiar with the type from his time in America."[105]

As the synchronized machine-gun armed Fokker was unique, the German command wanted to make sure they were not captured, as had happened with Roland Garros' airplane. The pilots were therefore restricted to only flying on their side of the lines and had orders not to cross over the front lines in any circumstances.[106] As Berthold described his thinking at the time:

> I do not want a Fokker yet, as one may not fly over the frontlines … and I do not want to be a rear-area flyer. The little bird is indeed good in attacking, but it is flown too little at the Front; it would be ideal if I had both [my AEG and the Fokker] and could fly each as needed. It is unfortunate that one cannot attack with the G-type, but it is too unwieldy for that purpose. Controlling the long wings, which are like arcs, takes a great effort in terms of flying.[107]

As Buddecke notes in his account, "I finally got my Fokker, which hardly anyone else wanted to have." This is partly confirmed by Berthold's diary, but it's not clear how much it was because "hardly anyone else wanted to have" it and how much was due to Buddecke asking for it.

The Fokker Eindecker (E.1) had a wingspan of 29 ft 0 in a length of 23 ft 8 in and a gross weight of 1,241 lb. The first planes used the

80-hp seven-cylinder Oberursel U.O rotary engine. Later versions of the Fokkers (E.II and E.III) used the 100-hp nine-cylinder Oberursel U.1 engine.[108] The Oberursel engines were license-built copies of the French Gnome rotary engines. The Nieuport monoplane (the Nieuport IV M) had a wingspan of 39 ft 8 in a length of 26 ft 11 in and a tare weight of 1,065 lb. The Nieuport IV originally had a 50-hp Gnome rotary – the engine Buddecke had installed in his American-built Nieuport copy – but was later upgraded to the 100-hp Gnome. The Nieuport IV and Morane-Saulnier N both looked very similar to a Fokker E.III.

Referring back to the Friday, 27 August 1915 issue of *The Indianapolis News*, the article mentioned above continues:

> **RECEIVES IRON CROSS**
>
> **-----**
>
> **Captain Buddecke, Formerly of This City, Honored in European War.**
>
> Albert Lieber has received a letter from his son, Rudolph Lieber, who is now a student at the Handels Hoch Schule [*sic*: *Handelshochschule* or trade school; what we would call today a graduate school of management] in Cologne, Germany, containing the news that Captain Hans Buddecke, nephew of Albert Lieber, has received the Iron Cross, first class … It will be remembered that Captain Buddecke was in Indianapolis for some time and that one week after he left here the aerodrome at the Speedway burned destroying his aeroplane as well as some flyers of Captain Bumbaugh. Immediately on the declaration of war by Germany, Captain Buddecke took the first ship available, going by way of Greece [*sic*]. Had it not been for the war he would have remained in Indianapolis and continued flying over the state throwing advertising matter down on the cities.

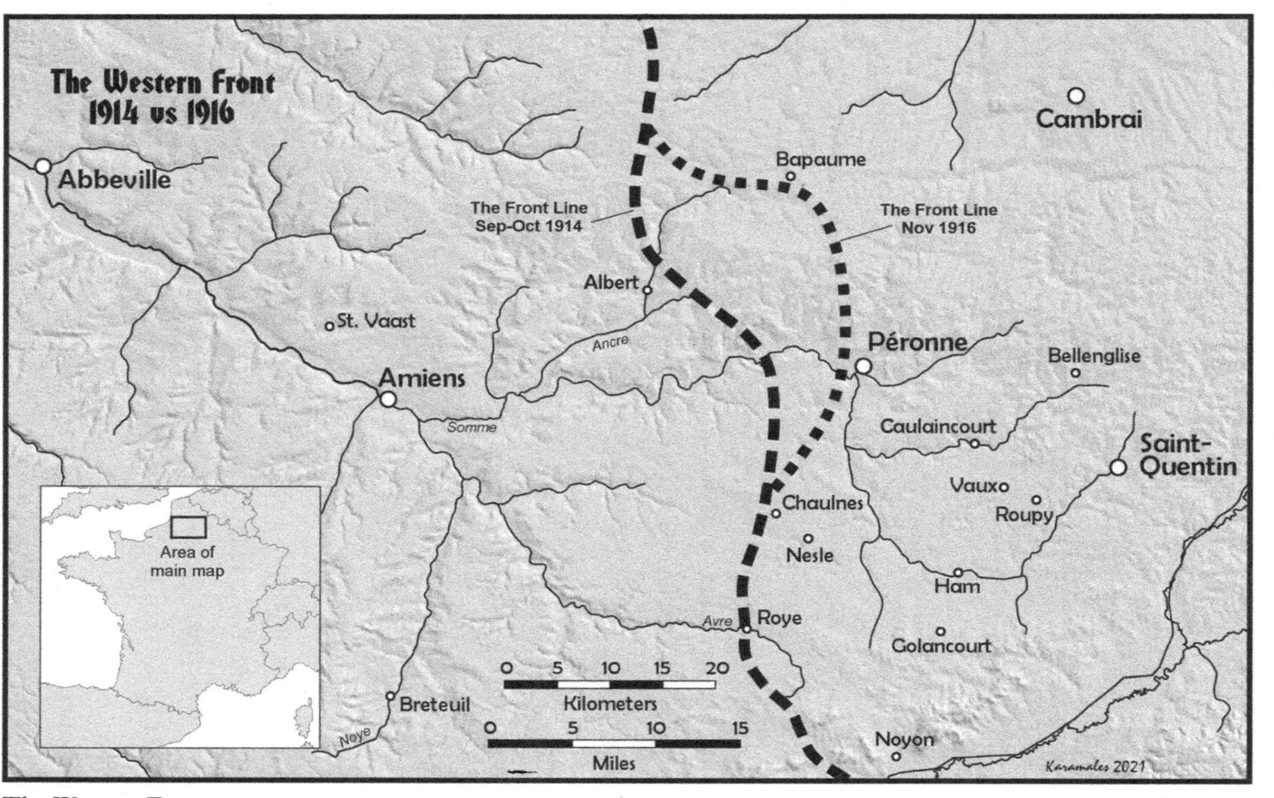

The Western Front

Buddecke's Kill List in the West:

The list of Buddeckes's confirmed kills are as follows:[109]

Date	Unit	Aircraft	Opponent	Location
19 Sep 1915	FFA 23	Fokker E. III	B.E.2c (2008)	Near St. Quentin
23 Oct 1915	FFA 23	Fokker E. III	B.E.2c (2017)	St. Quentin
11 Nov 1915	FFA 23	Fokker E. III	B.E.2c (1725)	Near St. Quentin

In contrast, at this time Max Immelmann was credited with six kills, Oswald Boelcke also credited with six kills, Kurt Wintgens with three confirmed kills (and two uncredited) and Rudolf Berthold had none. This makes Buddecke in November 1915 one of the four top fighter pilots in Germany.

In comparison, at this time among the French pilots, Adolphe Pegoud was credited with six kills, Eugene Gilbert with five, Jean Navarre with three, Roland Garros also with three, and Charles Nungesser and Georges Guynemer each had one victory. Among the British, Lanoe Hawker was credited with seven kills, making him the top ace on either side as of the end of November 1915.

What is interesting is the number of rounds used to shoot down these planes. Buddecke claims that his first victim "received 108 hits." It is claimed that the second plane reportedly had 212 bullet holes in it.[110]

The occupants of the first two planes he shot down were identified in Buddecke's account. The third plane he shot down was manned by Lieutenant W.A. Harvey of No. 8 Squadron, who was making a raid on a German airfield at Bellenglise. His plane flew without an observer because of the weight of the bombs he was carrying. He was wounded and forced to land behind his own lines near St. Quentin. In a later operation, he ended up interned in Switzerland and died there of tuberculosis on 7 November 1917.[111]

Two of the planes Buddecke shot down (on 19 September and 11 November) were from the No. 8 Squadron.

Lawrence of Arabia:

In Chapter 8, Buddecke makes the reference: "Meanwhile, a dead man and a dying man were pulled out of the wreckage. Lawrence had brought his observer to Earth with the last power of his life. The other had died up in the air."

This reference to Lawrence was almost certainly Second Lieutenant William George Lawrence (1889–1915), the younger brother of Thomas Edward Lawrence. He died in action on 23 October near St. Quentin flying a B.E.2c (serial number 2017). He served with the No. 13 Squadron of the Royal Flying Corps and had been serving in France for less than a week. He is recorded in many sources as an observer, whereas Buddecke states he was the pilot.[112] The pilot of the plane was Captain Cecil Hoffnung Marks.

Lawrence's older brother, Thomas E. Lawrence (1888–1935), is better known as "Lawrence of Arabia," who in 1915 was a lieutenant in the British Army and based in Egypt. (The co-author of this book is not related to these men.) He was then assigned as one of the British liaison officers to Hussein bin Ali, the Sharif of Mecca. T.E. Lawrence became famous for his role in the Arab Revolt which began in June of 1916. He ended up playing a major role in coordinating the forces which wreaked havoc on the Ottoman lines and resulted in the Arabs taking Aqaba and later Damascus.

The other man in the plane was the 27-year-old Captain Cecil Hoffnung Marks, (1887–1915). He was Jewish and was a graduate of Eton. He was one of the first English officers to be qualified as a flyer.[113]

There is some question about their deaths. The two men were initially buried in the German Soldiers' Cemetery, where they remained until being reburied at St. Souplet British Cemetery after the war. In 1919, a deposition of officials from St. Quentin implied that the two airmen had been murdered. It was alleged that the town clerk, M. Vatin, had illicitly examined their bodies, identified multiple gunshot wounds, and noted that they were covered in mud, which he suggested was indicative of some form of struggle.[114]

Hans Buddecke's autobiography does not hint at anything unusual, other than he went back to his room and had a cigar before coming back out to greet the visiting dignitaries. He does note that there was "A black swarm of people [that] broke away from the edge of the Roupy airfield … Meanwhile, a dead man and a dying man were pulled out of the wreckage." He does not recount going over to the plane. It is possible that he was aware that they had been killed by the crowd and was distraught over that. Perhaps this is why he discusses going to smoke a cigar, before washing his face to go out and meet the dignitaries.

Chapter 10

On the Road to Gallipoli

By Hans Buddecke

We all got to know a lot about saying goodbye during the war, if we hadn't known it before.

One evening, Schülerfranz came up to me in the officers' mess.

"Have you heard? You are being sent to serve in the Turkish service."

"And you?"

He shook his head.

We had volunteered for Turkey together and did not want to part. I already knew then that I would never again belong to such a dear circle of comrades, where everyone was so congenial, under the leadership of our Grand Captain, who held us wildlings at bay with admirable wisdom. He didn't even have to give an order; we tried to read his wishes in his eyes.

I said goodbye to Althaus in Vaux. He widened his eyes and lit a cigarette.

A fortnight later I boarded a train with a new comrade, Schütz, and my mechanic. We travelled from Berlin to Vienna, from there to Budapest and via Bulgaria to Turkey.

We only stayed in Constantinople for a few days (which I will return to later), then we got into an automobile that took us to Uzunköprü in an hour-long drive. With true contempt for death we fought our way through the meter-deep mud to get to the flight station, which was located on top of the mountain. "Flight station." In reality, of course, there was a wooden house and a hangar was being built. That was all.

We visited our mechanics, who had been camping here in a tent since the end of December, and examined their meager accommodations.

While Schütz was busy elsewhere, I went to the little house to warm myself up. I had a cold with a first-class fever, and hot tea was good for that. It perked me up. I gained interest in my surroundings and now saw one of the German builders carving up a large carp. The mere sight of it gave me a certain pleasure, since we had been feeding on bread and canned food for a week.

So, I went over to talk about the fish, and it turned out that it was Christmas that evening. My first thought was: hopefully Schütz won't find out what festival is coming up today, otherwise there will be a big Christmas party in the dirty hole down in the village where we lived with our interpreter and our last bottle of red wine will be on. It would be terrible. So, I did everything to keep Schütz away from the carp, and I thought I had succeeded when he quietly admitted to me that he knew something special: it was Christmas, and we had to celebrate that.

Over the ancient river bridge, which is a kilometer long and narrow as an alley, we pushed our way through camels and buffalo carts to reach our home. Then a dignified feast was prepared and cognac was bought from the shopkeeper. For the special celebration of the day, however, we wanted to eat for the first time in the Turkish officers' mess.

With great difficulty we made our way through the night and rain to a back yard, where a large tent was pitched. There were two long, white-covered tables with garden chairs. Except for two officers, nobody was there. One squatted in front of the stove, into which he was tossing coal; the other sat quietly in his place.

We came to attention, then began discussing the art of managing a fire. Gradually the tent filled up. The conversation grew louder until the colonel and commander of the installation arrived. Everyone fell silent and bowed. We were introduced, got a friendly handshake, and then sat down. We remained silent until the first courses were served.

On small tin plates there were about four different dishes: a bowl of soup, a piece of meat, a mountain of rice, and an unidentifiable dessert. Everything tidy and well prepared with oil. There was also a fist-thick piece of bread.

Only the rattling of eating utensils could be heard. The colonel spoke but a few words. After the meal he rose quickly, with the others, and left the room. An officer came up to us to ask us to see him. The house he lived in, like ours, was quite simple. Property of a wealthy Turkish farmer: bare wood and whitewashed walls. He was extremely friendly and spoke French to us.

Schütz spoke significantly more than I did and was often drawn into conversation by all Turks. He seemed to them to be more German than I was because of his blond hair, as opposed to me being a black sheep.

Once we had finished sipping our coffee from small cups, we were dismissed.

We were hardly outside when Schütz remembered, to our horror, that it was Christmas. So to celebrate the day in our hut, where because of the beds, suitcases, table, and storage equipment there was barely even room to turn around, we lit three candles instead of one, heated some red wine and ate biscuits. After we had finished the red wine, it was the cognac's turn.

Schütz had shot down an enemy aircraft in France, which is why we understandably spoke of nothing more than flying and dogfights until we fell into bed. This conversation seems to have had an effect, because in the middle of the night I woke up to a roar from Schütz, who repeatedly proclaimed in a booming voice: "The dog has to go down!" That was Christmas.

By the way, I slept quite well. Small, flat, mahogany-red insects served as sleep aids. They tormented one until, exhausted from hunting for them, one sank into nothingness.

Thus, the days passed until the day Major Serno, the head of Ottoman aviation,[115] arrived in his automobile on his way to Gallipoli to see the Commander-in-Chief of the Dardanelles Army, Marshal Liman von Sanders. The only major road at that time led from here via Keschan–Bulaiar,[116] the narrowest part of the peninsula, to the front.

The need for planes was great at Gallipoli. Enemy squadrons dropped their bombs wherever they liked. The observation biplanes were not capable of mounting an adequate defense, but their sacrificial attempts to do so didn't garner them much sympathy from the troops being bombed. The maneuver of approaching a bomber and turning around to open fire, made necessary by the way their armament faced, made it look like they were running away. But now there was hope for redemption. Three well-crewed Fokkers could be announced. They comprised a unit that consisted of three airmen, six mechanics, and an interpreter. But that was all that was handed to me as the commander of this unit. I would have to find the rest of my strength and resources on the spot.

In order to learn what I needed to know, I started the 120-kilometer journey early in the morning with Major Serno in the little 16-hp, ancient car of unknown design. I quickly realized that, like everything here, driving a car has its own peculiarities. At first the road was just barely passable, but then there were gradients, and we had to get out to push the damn thing up the steep clay road. How we managed this so often is still a mystery to me today. Some strange situations also arose as a result of our very new means of transport. I saw a very good old man and his donkey disappear sideways into the bushes and roll down a slope to avoid being run over by us as we sped by. Despite our pity for the unfortunate old rube, we had to laugh at the sight.

At first the area remained desolate, stretches of dry grass or bare limestone soil. Now and then we caught the shining glow of the Maritza[117] over to the west as it made its way through mountains and ridges to the Aegean.

By noon we had pushed our way to Keschan, a large Turkish village that was not very lively despite its size. A Greek church and the minarets and domes of small mosques towered over the clay roofs.

Caravans of camels, donkeys and wagons clogged the road, which was busily being repaired. The phlegmatic pedestrians were hardly disturbed by our passage. Soldiers would occasionally salute us, but they too were sluggish and sleepy-looking. If they were in uniform, however, at least they looked pretty clean despite the many patches. In this the Mohammedan religion, with its five daily ablutions, has a lot to recommend it.

It is peculiar how the Turk can pray. People can be cooking, singing, talking, smoking; and close by, perhaps even in the middle of all this, someone kneels in the direction in which he thinks Mecca is, and prays. His complete focusing of his mind enables him to be utterly indifferent to all that is going on around him.

Our driver didn't seem to take too much pleasure in his craft. He also had to stop every ten minutes to clean the oily spark plugs on his engine. He drove fast or slow, not according to the road conditions, but apart from any outside influence. For a long time I therefore considered driving a motor vehicle to be almost impossible for Orientals, but I also noticed exceptions. And just as with the automobile it was also with sailing.

Much later, I got into severe storms twice in the Gulf of Smyrna. The first time was at one o'clock in the afternoon, when we were out at sea, and high waves blocked our course. The tiny launch we were in seemed to be about to disappear into the troughs between the waves. She was bound to capsize at any moment. The Turkish guide sat on his knees with a map and seemed to be at his wits' end. I intervened at the time and, albeit with great difficulty, we managed to bring the boat home. The second time, however, a little Turkish sailor impressed me immensely. I sailed across the Gulf with him with a small group of people. He had been wearing his nose bandaged for months, which is why he acquired the name "Nose King" from us. We were about in the middle of the gulf when a great storm came up in the mountains one night. The little sailboat could hardly make any headway. The assistant in front had already loosened the bow sail and cried incessantly for "Allah!," but our Nose King at the wheel only said: "Ben javus kapitano" ("I am a mighty captain"), laughed, and won our trust. Indeed, even though we were completely soaked, he got us safely out of those waves, when hundreds of others have perished under similar circumstance.

With our driver, however, it was the opposite. The further we got, the clearer it became to me: the man would never learn. We fought our way up some switchbacks. It was arduous work, but it was rewarded on the crest of a high ridge, where a magnificent view opened up. In front of us the Gulf of Saros with those two little sugar cones, the Saros Islands, the eyes of the English. In the middle distance, the Gallipoli peninsula. Over its mountains we looked into the Dardanelles and the towering mountains of Asia Minor. The gulf widened, and the rugged rock massif of the island of Samothrace rose out of the blue; to the right of it the flatter island of Imbros, the main base of the English. The blue waterways must have been beautiful from above, as is common when there is fighting in such wonderful surroundings.

Endless road still lay between us and our destination, so we rolled on down through the mountain switchbacks. The weather, which had been prone to rain, got better with every kilometer that brought us closer to the Aegean Sea. We had passed the weather divide. At first we drove right along the peninsula. I would have liked to beat the simple-minded engineer who built this road.

In order for the water to be able to run off, the local nobleman had dug a deep ditch across the road every hundred meters for this purpose, a circumstance that surely caused deep grief for many motorists after me.

At the narrowest point, where at Bulayr the Turks had defended the peninsula against assaults from the mainland side in the Balkan War and thus kept the isthmus and Marmara secured,[118] we drove across to the Dardanelles. What a desolate, bleak country if the viewer didn't have the memories of the history of all the ages forced upon him. Soon we had reached the city of Gallipoli on the inner side of the peninsula. It already showed traces of British attacks. Major Serno knew a place nearby. He was on the *Barbarossa*[119] when it was torpedoed by an English submarine not far from the shore. The ship is lying on the bottom; from a plane you can see it clearly. Since then, we had gained some consolation: numerous large enemy battleships that had attempted to enter the Dardanelles had been compelled to withdraw before the cannon of the Dardanelles forts and Hersing's torpedo tubes.[120]

Twice more we had to push our car uphill; then the valley of Egos Potamoi[121] spread before us, offshore of which the triremes of the Spartans had crushed the Athenian fleet into the ground in the misty past. The airfield was there.

We arrived at the camp around six o'clock in the evening. The reception was brief, and we soon saw the reason. Anything that had legs for miles around took off running, cross-country. The noble officers assembled in the Heroes' Bomb Shelter. A low whirring and hum approached from above. We got the picture right away. It was just the afternoon visit by the English from Imbros. We quietly waited until the three Farmans had dropped their ten bombs,[122] which they scattered randomly on the airfield, and were gone. I took a good long look at them. These lads had been coming over every day since the start of the action; we had to put a stop to this, and soon.

The facilities of the airfield and the quarters differed significantly from those in France. Every newly arrived officer had built for him a little house in the draughty side valley; or rather, a shack, made of clay, stone, bricks, and a little wood. The material for this was laboriously hauled in by buffalo carts, whose wheels are so musical that you can hear them for miles. I moved into the palace of a true artist of disorder, who had just vacated, and undressed in the evening, dancing from one leg to the other on the wet floor. Then I wrapped myself up on the cot with a leather jacket and coat and put some waterproofing on them, so that the water penetrating through the roof could run off. That's how we all lived there.

The next morning Major Serno decided to ride along the banks of the Dardanelles on horseback. We were to proceed to the high command.

Chapter 11

At Gallipoli

By Hans Buddecke

The headquarters of armies usually look different. Here we climbed down a flight of steps into the bottom of a low, pine-covered ravine, on the bottom of which house after house was huddled. Thick leafy trees towered over them so that nothing could be seen from above or outside.

One end of the gorge was the German quarter, the other the Turkish one. The officers from the highest to the lowest lived in little huts. A slightly larger house had space for a longer officers' mess table, around which about twelve people could sit. Behind it was the so-called smoking room, which was also used as a guest room. There was a fir tree there. Everything still smelled of Christmas, and that gave the little damp barracks a sense of home.

The Turkish quarter looked similar to the German one. There, too, pages from *Jugend*[123] or maps served as wallpaper for the damp, whitewashed walls. We arrived shortly before dinner and were to be introduced to His Excellency Liman afterwards.

Not all strangers could be treated as guests, otherwise there would have been too many guests. But there were other things on my mind here. I noticed that because of my claim that I was an aviator, I was the subject of many over-the-shoulder stares. The explanation soon became clear. People didn't think much of us pilots. Here pilots were always in the minority in the air, four against forty, but the picture the people on the ground saw was always the same: the aircraft zoomed up, turned, fired, and flew away – that same characteristic of aerial combat that was a result of the design of our machine.

So it was inevitable that a young officer asked me: "Have you ever shot one down?" And when I modestly replied: "Three," he said, amazed: "What, and you haven't been mentioned in Army dispatches yet?"

The food was quite simple and modest; it barely satisfied my hunger after the long drive. But a large cup of coffee made up for everything that was lacking.

Serno introduced me to the Marshal's adjutant, Major Prigge, and with him we went higher up the ravine and waited in front of a fence that surrounded the commander-in-chief's house. Soon he stepped out and I was standing in front of an army commander who had just inflicted one of the greatest defeats of this war on the English, which was immeasurable. Now this fighter had been brought to the heart of Turkey. His success would mean five fewer combat fronts for our opponents. Who knows whether the Russian war would ever have ended like it has if the British and French had been able to come to the aid of the Russian Empire through the Bosporus and the Dardanelles.

I spent the afternoon in the mess hall poring over a map. Then I ran from place to place to get soldiers, wagons, a tent, and some bread. Just before evening we got on horseback and rode the trail back over the mountains. Around ten o'clock we got lost on the last mountain. Eventually we left the reins to the little animals and they found their way home without stumbling over walls and ditches, boulders, and paddocks.

The next morning we rode in the small car and battled our way on the poor road back to Uzunköprü.

Everything was in order; we could get started.

Chapter 12

Surprise Attack Across the Dardanelles

By Hans Buddecke

But it was really only a coincidence that we caught the train that brought us back to Constantinople. There I boarded my plane the next afternoon, my light baggage, blankets, and my ever-present crooked walking stick stowed behind me. I headed south under low clouds. Orientation was no problem, as there was only one road to the south. The terrain, though barren, offered a great variety of colors and shapes. Soon the ridge before the Gulf of Saros came into view. It too was still below the cloud layer, so I could get by it with no difficulty. I had the ridge just below me, my speed boosted by a strong north wind, when I saw a few eagles in front of me. They didn't seem to want to be bothered by me, but when I came near them they turned on me from behind, just as enemy fighter pilots tend to do. But I was faster and left my big, beautiful companions behind me. Then I steered across the Gulf of Saros over the Dardanelles.

You could fly hundreds of kilometers here without worrying about your orientation, once you had looked at the globe. Around me lay the row of islands of which ancient Greek legends tell. Samothrace was particularly eye-catching. It looked like a large fruit ice cream bombe on blue glass. Chocolate below, then purple, red, and white on the top. It occurred to me that hunting aerial targets would be a pleasure here. After fifty minutes I was over my airfield. There was a landing indicator. Since I noticed that the wind was blowing at an angle to it, I landed on my own against the indicator on the spacious field. My aircraft had already touched down on the earth and was rolling. Instead of stopping, however, it slowly lifted its tail into the sky and stood there. I got out of the plane, equally angry at the wrong landing indicator and amazed at my peculiar position, and saw that the wheels were stuck up to the axle in the mud and that the propeller had smashed about a meter deep into the mud. Everything was completely wrecked. Ashamed and annoyed about this peculiar introduction to the new comrades, I soon retired to my little house with its exemplary disorder and set about cleaning this stable.

In the morning I went on horseback in the pouring rain to look for a new airfield. As fighter pilots we were too far to the rear of the front lines. I only saw crumbling villages and deserted vineyards, and gray and brown land. I stayed the night in the office of a hospitable Turkish officer and rode on the whole next day. I found nothing that could have served as an airfield without some real preparation. But since quick action was required, I decided to stay in the old place. I visited the higher headquarters again, where in the meantime the German Major S. and Major Serno had arrived for the briefing on the overseas route. I joined them. Late in the evening we boarded a gunboat at the airfield. Schütz had also arrived, but the mechanics were still a long time coming. Nevertheless, we got our machines ready by the next morning.

By 7 o'clock in the morning I was out on the landing field, and was busy taking my cartridge belt out of the machine gun to replenish the remaining 150 cartridges to several hundred when there was a distant hum, and the battle cry rang out: "Tajare gelior!" ("Aircraft approaching!"). In no time, all the soldiers working on the field were in motion, scattering into the distance. The situation was annoying. Neither of us was really ready. Moreover, I had no intention of attacking the incoming English at this moment. With my 150 rounds I could perhaps shoot down one at best, but then they would know that Fokkers were now stationed at the field, and would never again venture so far into Turkish territory. Schütz felt as I did. He had discovered a problem with his machine and had to wait for the mechanics to arrive.

I had my battle plan clearly laid out. I wanted to finish preparing our machines in peace; give our youngest, who was due to arrive in the afternoon, a good briefing on how to bring down a bird; and then we could deliver a Turkish coup. It had already been discovered that by conducting a bombing raid with our big planes, we could gently goad the enemy into sending over ten or more Farmans in retaliation. Maybe we could shoot down all ten of them.

[When the next raid began,] an aircraft approached from over the sea at an altitude of 1,800 meters, and planted his four cabbage heads in the middle of the airfield. It was typically expected of bombs at that time that they would never hit anything; that was true in this case. But a second aircraft was already approaching. The tingling in my fingers that I felt watching the first one intensified, especially when I detected numbers three, four, and five on their way in. Then, relief! Major Serno's order came from the shelter, and I immediately started off.

While bomb after bomb was crashing all around, I got the bird out of the hangar with the help of Schütz and a few courageous Turks, and got into the cockpit in no time. But the engine repeatedly failed to start. Schütz threw the propeller again and again, while one new Farman after another flew towards us.

Finally! As I gave the engine full power and rolled across the field, there were two bomb explosions behind me. The crews hit the ground and let the dirt spatter down on them like rain, then they brought out Schütz's Fokker.

I immediately fixated on the Farman above me and let myself rise from below against him. Above him I saw his comrades, who must have realized what was coming, but did not think of helping. After 16 kilometers I reached his altitude and fired until my machine gun jammed. By this time we had flown down the Dardanelles. At the Narrows of Chanak,[124] where Xerxes once oversaw the crossing of his armies from a golden throne, my opponent spun into the ground. But by now the situation was: I had no more ammunition! I looked sadly after the cheeky gentlemen high above me and flew home.

There Schütz met me with bloody hands. He had already known in advance that he would not be able to do anything with his machine.

He had indeed attacked one of the Farmans, but after two shots his gun jammed. The blood on his hands came from his frantic attempts to clear it. I bemoaned both our fates. I was not satisfied with my shooting. It should have been much better. It took so long to bring down my quarry, and it was so far away when it finally fell, that it was impossible to recover anything, even the smallest piece of the enemy aircraft. It was now impossible to have a souvenir of that great time when the clean-up of the air over the blue strait of the Dardanelles was begun.

Incidentally, I met a base commander who was the only one to complain about a certain fact. It was so original that I bring it up here. The man lacked any means of punishing his subordinates. Arrest would have been considered by them as leisure time. Corporal punishment was permitted, but he didn't want to schedule it every day. So he came up with another diabolical means. At the bay of the port of Akbasch, which was bombed almost every day by the enemy, he set up three white soldiers' tents – clearly visible from above. An excellent target, and now for punishment he imposed arrest as needed. Sentence was to be served in these tents. And it was as simple as that.

My comrades in the camp congratulated me warmly; they were openly and honestly happy about this first success, although I took away a lot of honor and success from them, who had been wrestling with this opponent for months.

The evening came, and with it another enemy squadron. I was standing by my bird, which I had lovingly repaired myself, when I saw them coming. It was already getting dark. After taking off, it was only with difficulty that I kept the last one in sight. I cut off his way back and attacked him at short range. I was about twenty yards from him when the huge bird suddenly soared straight up in front of me. Immediately I threw my machine to the left, then to the right, so as not to let it fall on me but so that I could still see it. The mighty machine lay half on its back and fell. Near me, something – I shuddered to think what it was – fell like a stone into the void, as a cloud of white smoke shot out of the enemy plane ... immediately afterwards it burst into flames, and the burning machine shot downwards like a comet. After a few hundred meters it righted itself, suddenly flying normally again. The fire went out, the wings collapsed upward, and, spinning like a shuttlecock it got smaller and smaller, vanishing from my sight ... six kilometers from the airfield. I landed. As my bird rolled to a stop, there was a loud bang and my machine lurched. The fleeing soldiers had left the chocks, which I needed for takeoff, lying on the field to flip my aircraft arse over teakettle. One of those blocks had torn through one of my main wing cables. I realized immediately that I would be out of action for a few days. Anger added to the dejection I brought with me from the horrific spectacle from the air, and I could provide only a sympathetic smile for the people who rushed to kiss my hands, shoes, and the sleeves of my jacket.

"God is great!" they cried, "and so are the Germans!"

I don't know whether my two comrades at the time, Boelcke and Immelmann, would have felt the same way. Every downing of an enemy plane left me with emotional impressions. At that time every fight was a duel of individuals in a large volume of space, which of course could leave a very lasting impression. My opponents were people to whom life, which spread in all splendor before them, just as for us, had a double helping of promise and *joie de vivre*, and yet they were unable to fire a single shot out of the barrels of their guns in defense of that life.

What is it like today? Are we not disappointed if the opponent does not immediately burn, if we do not immediately get the thick plumes of smoke in our faces? Doesn't it try your patience when you might have to accompany him "downstairs," instead of being allowed to look above for a new target?

It rained congratulations that evening, but my mood wasn't too rosy. Because of the broken cable, I had to wait until the mechanics, who happened to have a replacement cable with them, arrived via the long way from Constantinople. There was nothing like that here.

The following days came to my aid. It rained. The English used the low visibility to withdraw their troops from the peninsula. We got the news and knew that one of the greatest campaigns of the war had been won here.

That same day a Turkish farmer who had watched the dogfight the previous evening brought me a large pot of yoghurt as a present. The food was excellent.

A few days later, as the sun shone down on the empty English trenches, where Turkish soldiers were having a go at the mountains of abandoned provisions, two Fokkers hung over the yellow land. Schütz flew a hundred meters behind me.

Below me I spotted a colorful gentleman. In no time I was on his tail. We went around in three spirals, and my aim was good … he flipped … plunged … fell into the sea. English torpedo boats came to pick him up.

In the evening I was ordered to report to Enver Pasha, who had come to visit the captured positions, in his camp the next day. Faller, whom I had met again here, flew Schütz and myself ahead to look for an airfield near my destination. We landed on the Alçitepe, a mountain that dominates the lower peninsula,[125] whose possession had been a key objective of the English. They had never achieved it. It was wonderful here. In a wide circle one could see islands, ships, the battlefield, the Strait of the Dardanelles, and in the distance the scenery of Asia Minor. The sun was shining, and we rejoiced in our lives.

No sooner had we pulled our caps off our ears than we heard the melodic hum of a foreign engine above us, nearby. Schütz took off first – Faller had brought his mechanic with him. At first I thought: I want to let Schütz take this enemy, since so far he has only had bad luck. But then other considerations prevailed. Better is always better, and two are better than one. That's how I came to take off too. With my quite empty fuel tank I climbed quickly and soon had the enemy in my sights above me. When I saw that Schütz was still looking, I was already above him. By waving I showed Schütz the direction in which the gentleman was circling who was about to try with his bombs to blow up buried ammunition together with a large number of Musselmen.[126] Soon I noticed from his movements that he had spotted me. However, he believed he was safe at his altitude and circled calmly on.

I was getting closer to him. When he turned back homeward, he noticed that I was already in front of him. Skillful and determined, he took his advantage and attacked me from above. With an evasive movement I could have avoided his fire, but I knew that a thousand heads were waiting below for me to run him over the houses.

So I flew sideways to his course, let him come close in order to fire, then I slewed my muzzle around to point at him, jerked the machine up as high as it could go, and fired until he was over me. We lay flat on our backs for twenty meters, pointing straight up.

The Fokker only barely held up in the subsequent U-turn since it had lost all its momentum in the climbing maneuver. But then I saw that my opponent had already had enough. In spirals, with a few warning shots, I accompanied him downstairs, where the pilot landed his machine in the tangle of trenches and broke his neck in the rollover.

A few minutes later, Enver Pasha and his staff arrived to inspect the plane, whose death struggle they had been observing. Back on the Alçitepe I noticed that my opponent had inflicted on me a shot in the center of the propeller. The bullet had ricocheted off and hit the engine, damaging it a little.

After a rain of good wishes – which Heaven would have had a hard time fulfilling – had descended on me, a sinner, I was told I had to hurry to report to Enver Pasha.

An officer on his horse had stopped nearby, and behind him an orderly on a beautiful old white horse. As best I could, I asked him if he knew where Enver's camp was. He said yes. Although he strongly urged me to take his own horse, I mounted his orderly's and off we went.

He showed me the way. A 14-year-old German boy, a little ne'er-do-well, who was already at home in all sorts of saddles, escaped from his parents and, who knows how, came down here, had told me that the place was no more than ten minutes away. We rode. Ten minutes, fifteen minutes.

Twenty minutes had passed and there was still no sign of the Vice-Generalissimo[127] at all, but the terrain was growing bleaker step by step. My guide began to look anxiously to the right and left. Again I asked, with many hand movements, where the camp was. He reassured me in that way people have when you don't know the language of the country and that makes them think you are not a rational adult: they treat you like a little child who, for God knows what foolish reason, begins to cry.

And again we rode for ten minutes, when another bey came along. My sheikh[128] then asked him where Enver was, and the newcomer replied that he knew exactly. Who wouldn't know that? At least that's what he seemed to have hinted at via the hand movements that were the same as my guide had used with me. I was handed over to this man with great courtesy, and now rode off with him in a different direction. We rode fifteen minutes farther away, then things got too stupid for me. So after a polite farewell I let my bey ride around the area on his own, while I gave my animal the spurs with dreadful forcefulness, whereupon it turned into a Russian swing[129] and took me back to my airfield in another twenty minutes.

Now the young German boy, who had come back after inspecting the dead Englishman, explained the way to me. I had been gone five minutes – again on the wrong path, of course – when the fellow rode after me on a good horse.

He had taken it away from a Turkish officer, who grabbed him by the ears. He triumphantly told me that Enver was aboard my plane. When I arrived at my Fokker, Enver was already gone. He had had everything explained to him by the mechanic, had seen the scar of the strange shot, and then returned to his camp.

Several Austrian officers drove past in automobiles on the nearby road. I rode after them. The way was easy. After hugging the neck of my decrepit old mare to get under some low branches, I soon arrived in a small ravine.

A group of officers had gathered on a small rise there. With a gallant swing I dismounted myself from my Rocinante[130] and slowly climbed up to them. I realized immediately that this time I was in the right place. The Austrians had also arrived to give a report. I walked calmly towards the group and greeted them properly. Several photographic cameras flashed towards me, but I did not see an Enver Pasha.

A colonel came up to me and asked quietly: "Have you already been introduced to His Excellency, the Minister of War? Please come."

The group parted and I saw an officer dressed in field fatigues, without any special medals or braids, neither tall nor short, with a kind, well-groomed face. The two deep-set, beautiful eyes under the straight brows were directed at me.

Enver.

He spoke flawless German, praising and thanking me for the battle of which he had been an eyewitness. His brief words indicated an extraordinary kind of deep thinking. They were like his appearance: beautiful by unpretentiousness and attractive and friendly.

Then he took the little gold medal of merit from the hand of one of his adjutants and pinned it on me.

"It's not really a reward, just a little souvenir," he emphasized.

When I stepped aside and the officers of his staff shook hands with me, I was afraid of losing my little medal. The Austrian gentlemen also stepped forward. Then the vice-generalissimo retired to a tent where breakfast was served. With a happy heart I mounted my animal and rode back to my bird to show him what he had earned.

The sun had been shining, but now dense storm clouds were gathering from all sides over the peninsula. I took off for the flight home.

Above the valley where I had met Enver, and where Marshal Liman von Sanders had arrived with his adjutants in the meantime, I placed my yellow bird with the black menacing eyes on its wing tips in the bright sunlight in front of the blue wall of clouds, banking once to the right, once to the left. I knew that those below would enjoy the sight. So I also enjoyed my life and plunged into the darkness of the atmosphere: that was the coup d'état over the Dardanelles.

For months there were no more enemy planes over the peninsula. The task that had been set was solved in no time. Our ships were able to sail unconcerned; troops who travelled to take part in expeditions on the coasts of Asia Minor and Thrace were able to march along the roads, singing. Only the cannon fire of a monitor shook the air over the castle of the ancient caliphs at the exit of the Hellespont. But they never dared to block the road again through aerial observation.

Many weeks had passed when squadrons of new types of bombers – covered by fighter planes – carefully felt their way towards the peninsula at enormous altitudes. Then, after seven weeks of unsuccessful fighting with these now quite superior machines, I succeeded in getting an eighth kill from such a squadron after firing twenty-five rounds, which was all that my weapon would fire since the mechanism was worn out by the changing weather. It was quite a fun battle.

I spotted the bombers below me and threw myself on the foremost, coming in at a slight sideways angle. After about twenty-five shots at close range, it spiraled downwards. But it was still a long way to earth. My gun stopped firing.

I sat so close to the tail of my opponent, a Farman type, that I couldn't take my hands off the controls long enough to fix my gun's jam, and had to turn the engine off and on in order to fly slowly enough to maintain position.

I could already see behind me the crowd of other enemy planes approaching. However, they couldn't shoot because I was between them and their comrade.

So I watched as the enemy observer right in front of me aimed his machine gun at my wing and showered me with a wonderful spray jet of smoke-trace ammunition. When he started to fire for the second time, I let myself fall into the void.

At that moment a rattle of gunfire broke out behind me that made my heart laugh despite the anger at my machine gun.

400 meters above the sea, the last Nieuport fell away.

As I flew home to rebuke my mechanics, the merry comrades from the Navy in Chanak, where I had moved my camp, had already come out to greet me.

The Farman was still falling.

We drank a bowl of punch and, accompanied by the plucking of a violin, sang the beautiful song:

'Nur immer ran ans Leder, Leder,
Hier heißt es enten oder weder,
Hurra Soldatenlust!'[131]

And then a soldier brought a yellow telegram. The translator had not mastered the German language. There was nothing I could read, only three French words prominent at the end: *Pour le Mérite.*

There it was, the Blue Max.

Chapter 13

The Air War over Gallipoli, 1915

A Short History of Gallipoli Air Campaign:

Gallipoli is the peninsula that caps off the northern side of the entrance to the Dardanelles. It is also the name of a town at the base of this peninsula that was originally the ancient Greek city of Kallipolis. There were still 32,000 Greeks living on the Gallipoli peninsula in 1915.[132] Two straits, the Dardanelles and the Bosporus, connect the Mediterranean Sea to the Black Sea. Control of the Dardanelles opens up the waterway that leads to the Sea of Marmara, to Constantinople (now Istanbul), to the Bosporus, then to the Black Sea and Russia. Control of these straits either helps isolate Russia or can create a naval supply route to Russia. At the start of the war, the Ottoman Empire had control of the Dardanelles and Bosporus, and control of the land on both sides of these straits. Germany and Austro-Hungary were at war with Russia (and Britain and France, called the Entente or, more commonly if slightly less correct, the Allies). The Ottoman Empire, centered around the modern nation of Turkey, was neutral at the start of the war.[133]

At the start of the war, two warships made up the Germans' Mediterranean squadron. They were the modern battlecruiser *Goeben* and the light cruiser *Breslau* led by Konteradmiral Wilhelm Souchon. Their mission was to intercept French transports moving troops from North Africa to France. The two ships set sail from Pola, in the Austro-Hungarian Empire (now part of Croatia), around 1 August 1914. The British squadrons in the Mediterranean attempted to track them before the war began, and moved to intercept them once war was declared by the United Kingdom. Instead, the two German warships dashed off to the east to the Dardanelles. These two German ships were then assigned to the Ottoman Navy, allowing them to "legally" pass into neutral Turkey's waters. They were flagged and renamed as Ottoman ships but the German crews remained on board and the German admiral was appointed commander-in-chief of the Ottoman Navy. Relationships between the United Kingdom and Ottoman Empire had already been undermined by the British requisition without compensation of two almost completed battleships being built in British shipyards for the Ottoman Empire. These were to have been the first two modern battleships in the Ottoman fleet – their first dreadnought-type battleships. The arrival of the German ships further reduced British support in Turkey and emboldened those Turks that favored joining Germany in the war. Still, the Ottoman government was split on whether to enter the war.

To bring Turkey into the war, plans were developed by the Ottoman War Minister Enver Pasha, German Admiral Souchon, and the German foreign ministry. Enver Pasha was one of the triumvirate of "three Pashas" that were the *de facto* rulers of the Ottoman Empire at this time. On 29 October 1914, Admiral Souchon led the two German-manned warships and seven smaller Ottoman ships in raids on the Russian Black Sea ports of Novorossiysk, Feodosiya, Odessa, and Sevastopol. On 2 November, Russia declared war on the Ottoman Empire, followed by Britain and France three days later. The Ottoman Empire reciprocated on the 11th. These provocative actions dragged Turkey into a war that many Ottoman senior leaders, including the Sultan, were hesitant to join. The Sultan nevertheless declared a *Jihad* (holy war) against the Entente on 14 November 1914, although this had little practical meaning or effect.

On 17 February 1915, the British Navy conducted a reconnaissance of the Dardanelles using a UK-produced Wight (not Wright) pusher-prop floatplane from the British seaplane carrier HMS *Ark Royal*. Two days later, a strong Anglo-French task force began bombarding Turkish coastal artillery batteries in an effort to force the Dardanelles.

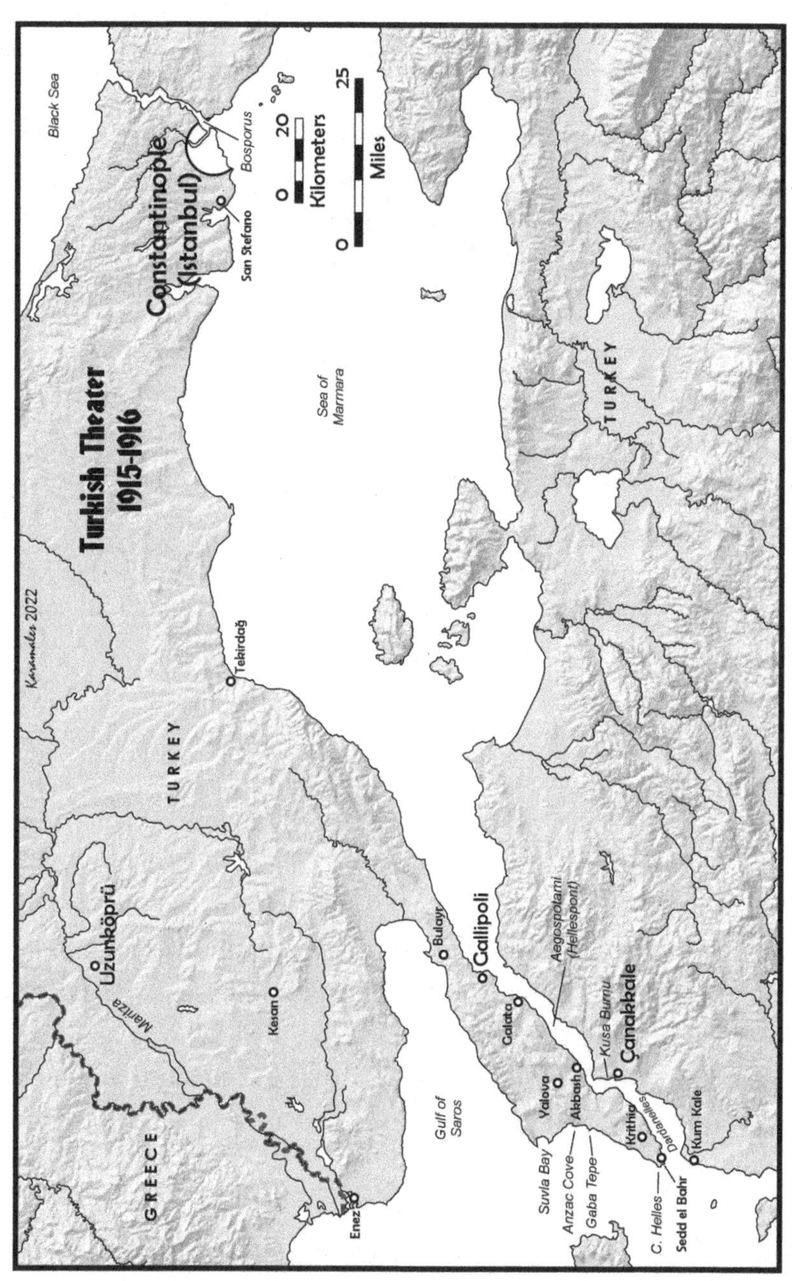
Turkish Theater
1915-1916
Karamolas 2022
Black Sea
Constantinople
(Istanbul)
Bosporus
San Stefano
0 20
Kilometers
0 25
Miles
Sea of
Marmara
TURKEY
TURKEY
Tekirdağ
Uzunköprü
Meritza
Kesan
GREECE
Enez
Gulf of
Saros
Bulayır
Gallipoli
Galata
Aegospotami
(Hellespont)
Kusa Burnu
Çanakkale
Yaloua
Akbash
Suvla Bay
Anzac Cove
Gaba Tepe
Krithia
Dardanelles
C. Helles
Sedd el Bahr
Kum Kale

This effort was halted by weather, recommenced on the 25th, then halted by weather again.[134] At this time, the Ottoman 1st Squadron had up to three aircraft operational at the town of Gallipoli, manned by German and Ottoman pilots under command of German Lieutenant Ludwig Preussner, and starting on 17 March, a seaplane at Canakkale.[135] The *Ark Royal* had up to eight aircraft operational, but lost a Sopwith Type 807 on 5 March 1915 due to a mechanical issue. This was the only Allied air support for these naval operations. This effort to force the Dardanelles was initiated again on 18 March with a major attack by eighteen British and French battleships that resulted in three pre-dreadnought battleships being sunk and three battleships seriously damaged.[136] The Anglo-French fleet then withdrew.

As forcing the straits by naval action had proved unsuccessful, the Allies then decided to conduct an amphibious operation. On 25 April Anglo-French forces, consisting of a large number of Australian and New Zealand troops, conducted a sizable amphibious landing in two areas of beaches on the Aegean shore on the lower part of the Gallipoli peninsula. The two major landing forces included primarily the British 29th Division and the Royal Naval Division at Cape Helles with an initial force of around 21,000. The other landing further up the coast was at the beaches that became named Anzac Cove (named for Australian and New Zealand forces), just north of the headland Gaba Tepe, and was conducted by the 1st Australian Division and the New Zealand and Australian Division, a force of around 25,000.[137] A French brigade made a diversionary landing on the Asian shore of the Dardanelles before withdrawing and joining the British 29th Division. This was the first modern amphibious operation, with naval gunfire support and air support. It was poorly coordinated.

The landing at Anzac Cove moved slowly inland and did not seize the high ground in the area. Because of its slim foothold on the beach, that evening the commanders began discussing withdrawal and re-embarkation. Instead, they decided to dig in. The landing at Cape Helles was also slow to advance, losing an opportunity to move inland. The Turkish defenders were quickly reinforced. This resulted in a stagnated position with two separate beach areas ringed in by Turkish defenders situated on higher, more defensible terrain. The reinforcing Turks then conducted a series of determined and bloody counterattacks that also stalled.[138] This was followed by continued Allied attacks which made no progress. After 8 May, everyone consolidated their positions and the battle settled down for a while in what was clearly a stalemate.

To support this operation the Royal Naval Air Service (RNAS) provided eleven seaplanes and a kite balloon from HMS *Ark Royal*[139] and at least eighteen aircraft from the No. 3 (Naval) Squadron, RNAS, commanded by Commander Charles Rumney Samson.[140] They operated from the island of Tenedos, a fifteen square mile island over fifteen miles (almost twenty-five kilometers) due south of Cape Helles. Tenedos, referenced in both the *Iliad* and the *Aeneid*, is now referred to in Turkish as Bozcaada. The No. 3 (Naval) Squadron became active on 27 March.[141] Also providing observation support was HMS *Manica*, a kite balloon ship with one kite balloon of German design and French manufacture. It became active on 19 April.[142] A small French seaplane section also deployed at Tenedos on 1 April consisting of two Nieuport X floatplanes.[143]

These air forces were almost unopposed by the small Ottoman air force. The Ottoman contingent is reported in February 1915 to be four German land planes and five seaplanes.[144] In March, the Ottoman Empire had only eleven aircraft available for operations in Gallipoli: five Albatros B.Is, an Etrich Taube and five seaplanes based at Canakkale.[145] The count of operational aircraft was considerably less.[146]

The first Central Powers air attack occurred on 28 March when a German Taube flown by the German pilot Lieutenant Erich Serno ("Major Serno" if using his Turkish rank) tried to bomb HMS *Ark Royal*.[147] Serno was part of the German military mission and was the primary German officer operating with the Ottoman air force. At this stage, the whole Ottoman air force in the Dardanelles area consisted of two sections of up to four planes each. The German aviators and crew that made up a significant part of the section at Galata wore Turkish uniforms. The Ottoman air forces also had a land, seaplane, and training base at San Stefano (renamed Yeşilköy in 1926, and currently the site of Istanbul Atatürk International Airport), just outside of Istanbul. It was less than 155 miles from Gaba Tepe and Helles. They developed an aerodrome at Galata and a seaplane base at Canakkale, on the Asian side of the Dardanelles. They would later add an airfield for land-based planes just outside of Canakkale.[148]

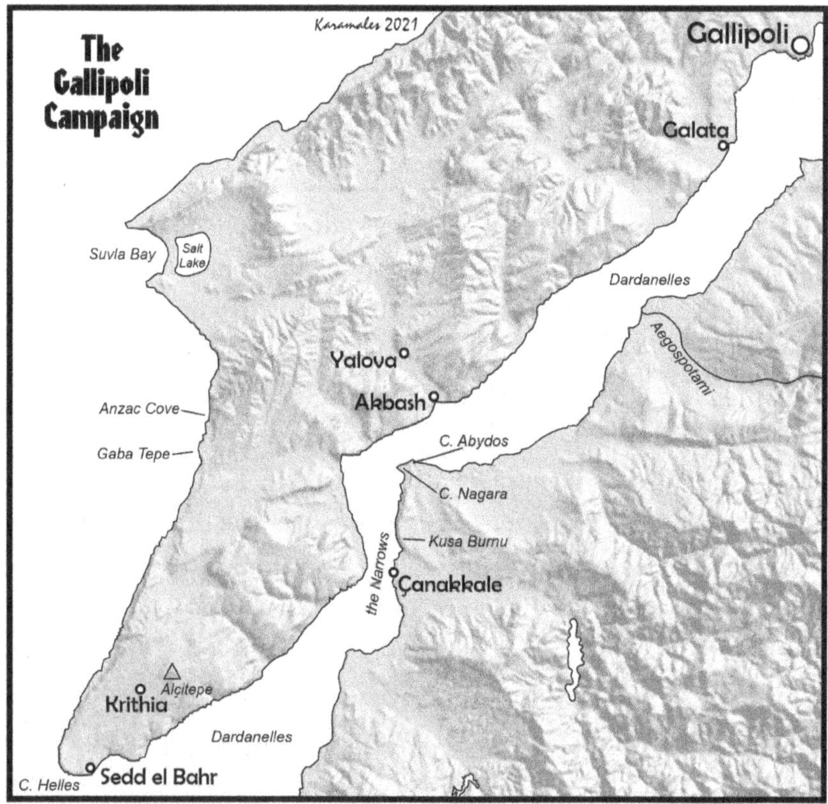

Gallipoli

On 16 April the British airbase at Tenedos was attacked by a German-built Taube, which dropped two bombs to no real effect. They were bombed again, perhaps by the same aircraft, on 18 April with three bombs – again, with no real effect. The British conducted a retaliatory bombing mission with three airplanes on the Ottoman airfield at Canakkale with significant hits claimed.[149] The one land-based plane there appeared to have been neutralized. The Ottoman air base was inactive for several weeks after this attack.[150]

The UK airbase at Tenedos was supplemented by French squadron MF-98T under Captain Antoine Césari. They arrived on 29 April, several days after the landings of 25 April. Their first aircraft was operational on either 4 or 11 May.[151] They initially deployed eight pilots, in addition to Captain Césari, and eight aircraft, Maurice Farman MF XIs.[152] They also had the quality photographic equipment that the English were lacking (but which they shared). By 18 May 1915 they were reduced to seven aircraft, having lost one at sea in an accident.[153] On 23 June 1915, they were reinforced with seven more pilots, four Farman 80-hp planes, and three Morane Parasols, which may have been machine-gun armed.[154] On 5 July they were able to field fourteen aircraft.[155] As the squadron name "MF-98T" indicates, it was armed primarily with Maurice Farmans (the MF) and was based on Tenedos (the T). The two-airplane French seaplane section was withdrawn on 25 May and returned to Port Said, Egypt, to be reunited with its squadron.

HMS *Ark Royal* and the kite balloon ship HMS *Manica* were assigned to support the forces ashore at Anzac Cove while the No. 3 (Naval) Squadron supported the Cape Helles force. By virtue of their larger numbers, better reliability, and more experience, the No. 3 (Naval) Squadron did a much better job providing air support than did *Ark Royal*, which had terrible reliability rates. For example, during March, *Ark Royal* only completed twenty-five of the seventy-five missions they attempted.[156] As a result, most of the artillery observation and aerial reconnaissance work for Anzac Cove was done by the ship-mounted kite balloon, which was effective. The balloon was often winched up at a height of 1,500 ft and could stay aloft for hours. The observer had an oblique aerial view of the battlefield and a telephone line entwined in the tether cable which allowed him to communicate with the ship. The ship's radioman would then relay the messages to other ships. Eventually the No. 3 (Naval) Squadron also provided support for Anzac Cove in addition to Cape Helles.

Ottoman air activity in April was very limited. Although the Ottoman air force had deployed two squadrons in the area, their operational air strength through most of the month remained one plane in Galata and two or three planes at Canakkale.[157] In late April the Ottoman air force received a couple of Albatros aircraft and other general supplies from the Germans.[158] The Ottoman air force was now rejuvenated and these Albatros airplanes conducted daily reconnaissance flights of the Allied positions.

Ottoman ground forces conducted a large counterattack on 1 May to try to push the Anzac forces off the beach, but with the Anzacs well supported by naval gunfire, this attack stalled. The Ottomans also launched a night attack on 1–2 May against the beach at Cape Helles, but this also failed. The Anzacs counterattacked the next day, but similarly made no progress. At this point, both sides were entrenched and unable to easily move forward, analogous to what had happened on the Western Front the previous year.

On 1 May, the British were able to conduct another large group bombing mission using all their spare aircraft (about a half-dozen) to go after a large Ottoman supply convoy. On 2 May, the commander of the No. 3 (Naval) Squadron reported that as of that day they had flown 18,851 miles total with the average number of planes operating each day being six. On the first day of the landings (25 April) they flew 2,400 combined miles.[159] In the same correspondence Commander Samson expressed his preference for the Maurice Farmans. He stated:

> I am still of the opinion that the only war machines are fast *Pushers* with good climb. The M Farman with 100 Renaults

> and 1241 are absolutely splendid. Other types of machines cannot compete at all. Avros etc., are just so much waste of money. These M Farman's can do 75mph, carry wireless and 2 100lb bombs, therefore they can spot, reconnoiter or attack, whichever is wanted. They can also fight. Their only drawback is that they turn slowly and wallow about in the wind ... one of the B.E.2Cs chased the German [aircraft] today but we could not catch him.[160]

They also conducted another large group bombing mission that day against attacking Ottoman forces (probably using another half-dozen aircraft). Also of significance, they intercepted and forced down an Ottoman seaplane, but it landed near Ottoman positions.[161] On 3 May. the Ottoman air force twice attempted to bomb the *Manica*, but all the bombs missed. The British conducted additional ground offensives from 6 to 8 May, for which the No. 3 (Naval) Squadron put up twenty-two sorties in support: ten spotting and twelve reconnaissance missions.[162] This was still a fairly low level of support, but sufficient to be noticed.

Both sides also dropped propaganda leaflets during the month of May. In the lull in the fighting after 8 May, the British dropped leaflets encouraging the Ottoman soldiers to desert. On 27 May, the Ottoman air force dropped pamphlets over the enemy lines appealing to Muslim Indians and French colonial troops not to fight their fellow Muslims. The British responded four days later with their own pamphlet drop. British propaganda efforts were probably of limited value as most Ottoman troops and even officers were illiterate.[163]

Operations on the ground quietened down after 8 May but not so in the air or at sea. On the night of 12–13 May, the British pre-dreadnought battleship HMS *Goliath* was sunk by torpedoes from an Ottoman destroyer commanded by a German officer. It went down quickly with a loss of 570 of her 750 crew. On 16 May, the French squadron lost one aircraft at sea, reducing their active complement to seven. They also lost one pilot that month due to an accident while making bombs. By 19 May, the No. 3 (Naval) Squadron was reporting that it had covered 30,000 miles. As they reported they had covered 18,851 miles on 2 May, it appears that they managed over 11,000 miles of flying over the course of seventeen days, from 3 to 19 May. A back-of-the-envelope estimation indicates that if an average of six planes were flying each day, and there were no weather issues, then each plane covered 109 miles each day. With Tenedos being fifteen miles from Cape Helles, then this was potentially seventy-nine miles over the front line area or over an hour of loitering time over the battlefield. On 18 May, the No. 3 (Naval) Squadron also started flying missions to cover the Anzac beach. This beachhead was twelve miles further away from Tenedos Island.

On 17 May the Airship Expeditionary Force No. 1, RNAS, was landed at Imbros Island, which was located over ten miles (over sixteen kilometers) due west of the Gallipoli peninsula. It consisted of two Sea Scout airships (No. 3 and No. 19) and the unit had six officers, twelve non-commissioned officers, and fifty ratings. The Sea Scout (or Submarine Scout) airships were non-rigid blimps developed to counter German U-boats. Developed in two weeks in March 1915, these airships consisted of a B.E.2c fuselage and engine slung beneath a blimp of 60,000 cu ft. Each carried a crew of two and could fly around 50 mph. Their endurance at full speed was seven to eight hours. On 19 May, the two airships took to the sky, but the unit spent most of the next month training, as it had only been formed after 14 April and had had no time to train before deployment.

Meanwhile, in the middle of May, three German Gotha WD.1. seaplanes arrived by train, were assembled, and underwent training at San Stefano. They were then transferred to Canakkale under command of German Captain Ernst Liebman. Ludwig Preussner's land-based 1st Ottoman Squadron was also established at Canakkale, consisting of three recently arrived Rumpler B.Is.[164]

On the night of 18–19 May, and for the next six days, the Ottoman forces conducted a major offensive against the Anzac Cove beach area, with around 42,000 Ottoman troops trying to push 17,000 Australians and New Zealanders back into the sea. It was supposed to be a surprise attack but the Breguet of No. 3. Squadron had spotted the preparations the day before and the Australian and New Zealand forces were placed on alert. With a shortage of artillery and ammunition, this Ottoman offensive (the third one on Anzac Cove) stalled out with heavy attacker casualties and a lop-sided casualty exchange rate.[165] While the Ottoman ground actions were not doing well, a German U-boat in the area, *U-21*, managed to sink two pre-dreadnought battleships, HMS *Triumph* and then HMS *Majestic,* on 25 and 27 May respectively. The continued loss of warships effectively "clipped the wings" of HMS *Ark Royal*, as it and many of the other Allied ships were now mostly confined to harbor in Mudros on the island of Lemnos for their own safety, except when actually shelling Gallipoli.

During the month of May, the No. 3 (Naval) Squadron flew 303 missions while HMS *Ark Royal* recorded only thirty-seven seaplane take-offs in a twenty-day period in May,[166] total flight time for the latter being just sixty-three hours and fifty-four minutes.[167] The carrier still fielded around six seaplanes and two landplanes, but its effectiveness was going to be even less in the future, as operating from the port at Mudros put it further away from Gallipoli.

Meanwhile, late in May, the No. 3 (Naval) Squadron received six new Voisins with 140-hp engines.[168] Using one of the Voisins, the British damaged the Turkish battleship *Barbarossa.* The French Escadrille MF-98T lost a pilot and plane when his unused bomb exploded as he landed.[169]

June saw the arrival of the improbably named HMS *Ben-my-Chree* (translated from Manx Gaelic as "Woman of my Heart"). This smaller seaplane carrier could carry a half-dozen seaplanes, but only had four planes, including one Sopwith Schneider and two Short Type 184 torpedo bombers.[170] It joined the Eastern Mediterranean fleet on 12 June, but did not immediately operate in the area of the Dardanelles. The torpedo bombers had some success, which was the first use of torpedo bombers in war (the first actual aerial torpedo attack occurred in August; see below). The British had also built a temporary airstrip at Cape Helles. The squadron was renamed on 21 June as the No. 3 Wing, although it had no additional aircraft.

Also arriving the night of 14/15 June at Imbros was a second kite balloon ship, HMS *Hector.* It did not immediately deploy, but instead trained for the next three weeks, eventually becoming operational on 3 July. Finally, there was the Sea Scout section with two Sea Scout airships, the Airship Expeditionary Force No. 1 which had arrived a month earlier. Their operations were limited by their lack of training and having only one hangar erected, and the crews had spent much of June and July training. They conducted their first patrols on 19 May. The Allies now had around thirty operational aircraft (including balloons) deployed in the area, and about forty aircraft total.[171] The Ottoman deployment was considerably less.

From the beginning of June the number of Allied air operations increased, with bombing raids by both sides becoming more frequent. Ottoman anti-aircraft fire had also gotten more effective, forcing many of the reconnaissance flights to operate thousands of feet higher.[172] The No. 3 (Naval) Squadron had also taken over operations in the Anzac Cove area, as HMS *Ark Royal* planes had proven to be unreliable.[173] The nature of the missions had also changed, with fewer reconnaissance flights and more bombing missions being conducted now. In the middle of June they closed down the temporary airfield they had established at Cape Helles near the British headquarters there. While it was conveniently located, operations from that airfield had claimed at least one British airplane and two French airplanes and their pilots.[174]

On 22 June a British Voisin forced down with rifle fire an Etrich Rumpler Taube, which landed on the Ottoman side of the lines. The pilot was Captain Charles H. Collet and the observer with the rifle was Major R.E.T. Hogg.[175] This was clearly an airplane disabled and forced to land due to opposing fire, and was therefore the first confirmed kill by either side due to enemy air combat in the Gallipoli Campaign. Later that day, the French were able to find the empty plane and destroy it with artillery fire. It appears that the crew survived.

On 23 June the MF-98T Escadrille was reinforced with seven new planes and seven pilots. The aircraft included four more Farmans and three Morane Parasol "fighters." These "fighters" were two-seaters with rear-firing St. Étienne machine guns.

The British actually attempted to bomb Istanbul itself using their large Breguet airplane, the only plane with the range to get there, bomb, and return. They launched a flight to the Ottoman capital on 22 June, but had to call it off due to engine troubles. They never attempted to bomb Istanbul again.[176]

The British at Cape Helles conducted another offensive on 4 June that went nowhere (the Third Battle of Krithia), even though they committed the 29th Division, Royal Naval Division, the 42nd Division, and two French divisions. They were then reinforced by the 52nd (Lowland) Division and another attack was conducted on 28 June that achieved only local success. On 21 June the French also launched a bloody attack that made little progress, but was well supported by their MF-98T Escadrille. The Ottoman forces counterattacked several times between 28 June and 5 July, also with no success. On 12 July, the British staged another bloody attack that gained only a little ground. It was supported by a dozen missions from the No. 3 (Naval) Wing.

In early July, the No. 3 (Naval) Wing was down to nine pilots (three newly arrived) and eight to ten operational aircraft.[177] There was continued Ottoman air activity at this time, including an attempt in early July to shoot down the kite balloon attached to HMS *Manica.* In response to this increased Central Power activity, on 5 July the British and French squadron commanders coordinated the biggest air raid of the Dardanelles Campaign, consisting of eight British planes and fourteen French planes, to bomb the Ottoman air field at Canakkale. This force represented almost all operational Allied airplanes in the theater. The British claimed that most of the buildings at the base were destroyed, along with "all three" airplanes.[178] This effectively removed the Ottoman air force for the moment, but they were receiving reinforcements. A small naval aviation section of Gotha seaplanes arrived that same day from Germany, and on 13 July four new Albatros C.I aircraft, armed with rear-firing machine guns, arrived from Germany to reinforce Preussner's First Ottoman Squadron. This unit now set up at a new aerodrome at Galata, just south of Gallipoli. Two days later the British tried a night bombing mission against this airfield but to no effect. As of 18 July, due to the strain of continued operations on aircraft maintenance, the No. 3 (Naval) Wing was down to three operational aircraft. On 23 July HMS *Ben-My-Chree* was finally operational, and none too soon, for HMS *Ark Royal* accidentally sank one of its few seaplanes, a Schneider, on 28 July. The British part of the Allied air effort was now in sore need of reinforcement. During July, the No. 3 (Naval) Squadron had flown 188 missions, while HMS *Ark Royal* only managed seventeen.[179] As mentioned, the No. 3 (Naval) Wing moved from Tenedos Island to Imbros Island in late July, a move that was not completed until the end of August.

The French took over the British airfield at Tenedos. They were then attacked by two Rumpler B.Is. and two Gotha seaplanes at 04:45 on 31 July, in a morning attack that dropped five bombs and 500 metal darts.[180] This led to what amounted to the first aerial fight of the campaign using machine guns. Flight Lieutenant Marix of No. 3 (Naval) Squadron intercepted one of the Gotha seaplanes with his Lewis gun-armed Nieuport and fired at the enemy at close range. The damaged Gotha force-landed on a beach near the stream called Soghan Deré on the Gallipoli peninsula. Seven planes from MF-98T then bombed where it landed. That evening, Captain Césari, flying solo in his Farman, intercepted a Rumpler, fired three rifle shots at him, and pursued him back to his airfield. Both of these engagements were supported by Corporal Baynay in a Morane Parasol, who was on call at the airfield.

In August, the operations continued with multiple Allied ground offensives and Turkish counterattacks. At this point, the Allies' original five divisions had been increased to fifteen while the original six Ottoman divisions had increased to sixteen. The bloody fighting in August opened with two diversionary attacks out of Cape Helles and Anzac Cove on 6 August that both stalled, while a nighttime amphibious landing on the 6th by two British divisions was conducted at Suvla Bay, just north of Anzac Cove. This force failed to advance inland early enough and was quickly bottled up. By that evening some 20,000 British troops had been landed at Suvla Bay.[181]

The Allies now held three isolated beach areas, all bottled up by the Ottoman forces. The diversionary attack out of Anzac Cove was thrown back by a Turkish counterattack on 10 August. The Suvla landing was reinforced by three more Allied divisions and they tried to break out on 12 August, but this attack also stalled. The Allies again began considering the evacuation of both Suvla and Anzac Cove.

Meanwhile, naval war also picked back up. One of Turkey's two pre-dreadnought battleships, the *Barbarossa* (*Barbaros Heyreddin* in Turkish), was moving down from Constantinople to the Dardanelles to support Ottoman defenses when it was intercepted in the Sea of Marmara by British submarine HMS *E11*, which hit it with a single torpedo. The ship capsized after seven minutes, then remained floating for a few minutes more before slipping beneath the waves. It sank with the loss of 21 officers and 237 men out of an authorized crew of 38 officers and 530 men. The remaining crew were picked up by her escort and another torpedo boat patrolling the area. Major Serno, the head of German aviation in Turkey, was on that ship but survived (see Chapter 10). The ship had seen extensive service in both the German and Ottoman navies, having survived two naval battles in 1912 and 1913 with the Greek navy.

British air support for all the action in August was greatly improved by the arrival on the first of the month of six Henry Farmans with 100-hp engines (earlier ones had only 80 hp and had been rejected) and some Nieuports.[182] On 8 and 9 August they also received two new Farman HF.24s[183] and two Nieuports, and around the same time two new pilots. The Nieuports were converted to fighter aircraft with a Lewis machine gun mounted on the top wing. This was a significant improvement, as the No. 3 (Naval) Wing was reporting only three planes ready for action on 18 July and had still managed to fly more than ten times the number of air missions as HMS *Ark Royal*. Now the No. 3 (Naval) Wing had a total of eleven pilots, although only seven or so were available most days due to rotations and leaves. At this point, they had more planes than available pilots.[184]

HMS *Ben-My-Chree* also received a new Short seaplane on 1 August, which was assembled, tested, and became operational on the 10th. Their balance sheet remained at four aircraft, as they lost one when one of their two Schneider seaplanes was wrecked on the 3rd. Finally, as of 6 August, the two Sea Scout airships were finally also available for operations. Operations on the 6th also included a French and British combined strike at the Turkish/German airfield at Galata, where five aircraft had been spotted. The strength of this combined strike was not recorded, unlike the unprecedented twenty-two-plane strike against Canakkale airfield the previous month. A report prepared on 6 August stated that among all their air assets, the British had eleven floatplanes of five different types, and thirteen land planes of five different types with six different engines.[185]

Between 9 May and 6 August 1915 the Royal Navy Air Service (RNAS) carried out the following missions:

Spotting flights for naval and army artillery	203
Photographic reconnaissance flights by airplanes	71
Bombing and/or reconnaissance flights	291
Bombs dropped: large (100 lb)	120
Bombs dropped: small (20 lb)	190
Anti-submarine patrols by SS (Sea Scout) airship	40
Fighter defense patrol	10

Although not specifically stated, it is assumed that this collection of missions encompasses the operations of the No. 3 (Naval) Wing, HMS *Ark Royal*, HMS *Ben-My-Chree*, and the two Sea Scouts (which is stated above).[186] It is not certain if it includes the missions by the two kite balloon ships. It does not include the missions of the French MF-98T squadron, which had fourteen or more planes active. This is 615 missions over a ninety-day period or an average of almost seven missions a day.

Escadrille MF-98T lost an aircraft on 6 August when Farman No. 459, flown by Sergeant Dumas with Captain Aubert, was hit in the engine by shell fire at 1,800 meters and glided back toward Tenedos, landing in the sea. Three days later a Morane was downed by friendly ground fire, although the aircraft was recovered and the crew uninjured. On 25 August a Farman crashed at sea, killing 2nd Lieutenant Saint André and Sergeant Dumas.[187] The squadron was now down to twelve aircraft. In late August they received additional aircraft, including the 130-hp Farman (MF XI bis). With these new aircraft, Captain Césari considered bombing Constantinople, but instead had Warrant Officer Lecompte bomb Enos (Enez) in Thrace.[188] This is similar to later British efforts (see below).

On 10 August, there was another aerial engagement in which the pilot of a British 120-hp Henry Farman opened fired with a rifle on a German Etrich Taube.[189] The Taube dove (no pun intended) away and escaped. On 12 August, an aircraft from HMS *Ben-My-Chree* torpedoed a ship, the first such attack in naval history. The ship was a 5,000-ton transport that had already been beached from damage received four days earlier because of a torpedo hit, and shelling by the British submarine HMS *E14*. It was hit again by a 14-inch torpedo from a Short 184. Two successful torpedo attacks on 17 August sank a Turkish steamship and a tugboat. On 19 August No. 3 (Naval) Wing lost two planes and one pilot from two separate mechanical problems. The pilot was the first the wing had lost since deploying to Gallipoli.[190]

The British air effort was now being reinforced with No. 2 (Naval) Wing (squadron), which sailed for the Dardanelles on 15 August. At the time of embarkation, this squadron consisted of sixteen officers, three warrant officers, 200 ground staff, and twenty-four aircraft: six Morane Parasols, six Caudrons, six B.E.2cs, four Bristol Scouts, and two Voisins.[191] They were a mix of designs, with the Morane Parasol being a two-seater monoplane with an 80-hp Rhone rotary engine, the Caudrons being two-seater biplanes with 80-hp Gnome rotary engines, the B.E.2c a two-seater biplane with a 75-hp Renault engine, the Bristol Scouts were single-seaters with 80-hp Gnome rotary engines, and the Voisins were two-seater pusher-prop biplanes with 140-hp Canton radial engines. The engines on all twenty-four aircraft were French engines or English-manufactured engines based on French designs. The two Voisins were being transported for transfer to the No. 3 Wing.

This new wing arrived on 25 August and was operational at Imbros on 31 August. Since the Caudrons were underpowered, being adversely affected by the warm August weather of the Aegean, they were of limited utility. Effectively, the wing had sixteen or fewer planes.[192] Also, on 17 August the No. 3 SS Airship Squadron arrived with one Sea Scout airship. The air strength of the British forces was at that point effectively doubled.

At the end of the month, the No. 3 (Naval) Wing was back down to only six planes operational, largely due to maintenance issues. Still, the wing had conducted 217 flights in August totaling over 400 hours aloft. *Ark Royal* had only managed eighteen combat flights during August, along with a number of test flights.[193]

The British tried one last offensive on 21 August to unite the Suvla Bay and Anzac Cove beachheads, but this effort failed like the ones before it. The Gallipoli front was now stalemated, with almost 200,000 British, French, Australian, and New Zealand troops trapped in and around the three beachheads, and around 200,000 Ottoman troops defending these three isolated lodgments.

By the end of summer 1915, Allied air power in the theater consisted of the very experienced No. 3 (Naval) Wing RNAS, originally with Voisins and now with Farmans and Nieuport Xs; and the French Escadrille MF-98T with Farmans. The No. 2 (Naval) Wing had now been deployed with around sixteen aircraft operational. They were primarily operating from the island of Imbros, which was also the site of many hospitals, support facilities, and the senior Allied headquarters in the area. Also deployed were the two kite balloon ships, two sea scouts (not operational), and two aircraft (seaplane) carriers. HMS *Ark Royal* had received new planes, now deploying a half-dozen Short Type 166 or Short Type C seaplanes with 200-hp Canton Unne engines. These turned out to be much more reliable than the older aircraft that had so bedeviled the world's first aircraft carrier. The Allies had around fifty operational aircraft and almost seventy aircraft in all, though some units had a shortage of pilots – for example, No. 3 (Naval) Wing had, as of 8 September, only eight pilots, which imposed an upper limit to how many operational aircraft they could have.

The Ottoman air force had around twenty aircraft, mostly of German manufacture. Eight were stationed at Canakkale, which is on the Asian side of the Dardanelles at the narrowest point along the straight (only 1.2 kilometers or 0.75 miles wide at this point). This included a seaplane base at Naga with five Gotha WD.1s and WD.2s.[194] At least five or six aircraft were operating out of the airfield at Galata.[195] These included Taubes moved from Canakkale, and newly arriving Rumpler B.Is, LVG B.Is, and armed Albatros C.Is.[196] The Ottoman air force only received their first machine gun armed aircraft (operated by the observer from the rear cockpit) in July 1915.[197] Until then, the Allies had undisputed air superiority.

Both sides dug in and stayed on the defensive after 23 August. Bulgaria entered the war on the side of the Axis on 6 September, declared general mobilization on 22 September, and declared war on Serbia on 14 October. This allowed the Central Powers to directly provide reinforcements to Turkey via rail, including German and Austro-Hungarian heavy artillery; while in September the Allies transferred two divisions from Gallipoli to Salonika, Greece, for the sake of reinforcing the Serbian front.

In early September the Ottomans began receiving more aircraft: one Albatros C.I flown across "neutral" Bulgaria, two new Gotha WD.1s delivered to Naga, and more pilots and observers.[198]

The British and French still continued operations, losing an airplane (but no crew) due to mechanical problems which forced it to land, whereupon it was shelled by Turkish artillery, on 5 or 6 September. They also armed their two Nieuports with machine guns on 11 and 12 September. These machine guns were in a fixed forward-firing position and angled at 45 degrees upward to avoid shooting through the propeller.[199] On 27 September, there was an aerial engagement between these machine-gun armed German and British aircraft. The Germans claimed a victory by an Albatros C.I piloted by Lieutenant Preussner, with Lieutenant Karl Kettembeil as his observer and machine gunner. This appears to be an incorrect claim as the British record no aircraft being shot down that day.[200]

Starting on 16 September, each side began to regularly attack the other's airfields. On 28 September an Ottoman bombing raid on No. 3. Wing at Imbros, one of several such raids that had been carried out that month, killed the commander's batman and wounded another man. In response, a combined French and British air attack of ten planes was made the following day on the Galata and Canakkale airfields. Thanks to intelligence from a prisoner, they were also able to send a six-plane strike against the headquarters of the German commander, Liman von Sanders, on the peninsula. Earlier in the month Samson, commander of No. 3 Wing, had strafed a staff car that was later claimed to have contained the Ottoman general Mustafa Kemal (later known as Atatürk, president of Turkey), although this claim has never been verified.[201] Despite the fact that air operations had been going on continuously since March, there still had not been any aircraft shot down, ignoring the claim by Preussner on 27 September. One Ottoman plane had been forced down on 22 June by the British and later destroyed by French artillery. A Gotha seaplane had been forced down by the British on 31 July but its final disposition is not known.

On the night of 6–7 October, a storm collapsed the Ottomans' main hangar at Galata, damaging five aircraft and leaving the airbase with only one operational armed Albatros C.I. That plane also broke down after a couple of days. This significantly reduced Ottoman air activity for the rest of the month.[202]

With the Gallipoli Campaign clearly stalemated, on 11 October the British once again started discussing evacuation, but nothing was done at that time. The front remained static until early December. Events happening elsewhere in the area were complicating the situation in Gallipoli. To support the Serbians, the British and French moved three more divisions to Salonika in early October. Meanwhile the Germans, Austro-Hungarians, and Bulgarians collapsed the Serbian defense. Their offensive opened up the rail line from Berlin and Vienna to Istanbul. The Central Powers were now able to move Austrian and German artillery down to Gallipoli. At the end of October, HMS *Ark Royal* left for Salonika, removing it from Gallipoli air operations.

The Ottoman air forces were reinforced in November with another three armed Albatros C-types. Allied operations in November continued with a significant number of bombing raids against troops, facilities, airfields, and supply lines. On 19 November the British lost an aircraft to ground fire while conducting a five-plane attack on Ferrijik Junction in Bulgaria, deep behind enemy lines. The pilot was rescued from behind the lines by the new squadron commander, Richard Bell Davies, who was awarded the Victoria Cross for the rescue. This may have been the first aerial "combat search and rescue" mission in history.

Arriving sometime in November, a third kite balloon ship was added to the Allied inventory, HMS *Canning*. As the weather worsened there was less flying, but no less drama. On 26 November an airplane from No. 3 Wing flipped on landing, killing both occupants. In late November the "first" air combat loss occurred over the Gallipoli battlefield when an Ottoman crew flying a German Albatros C.I shot down a French aircraft over Gaba Tepe. As discussed later, this was arguably not a valid claim.

At this time the French squadron had around ten planes operational. They had racked up 639 flying hours in November, or over twenty-one hours per day on average. This is particularly good considering that the poor weather this month restricted a lot of the flying.

On 1 December, there was an aerial engagement as two planes from No. 2 Wing were bombing the Ottoman Kusa Burnu seaplane base. This was initiated by a German plane engaging them with its rear machine gun. The targeted British plane then maneuvered to the German's tail and returned fire with its Lewis gun. After twenty rounds the gun jammed, ending the duel. The following day there was another engagement when a British No. 3 Wing aircraft dived upon an armed Taube. They chased the aircraft away, but took some damage from ground fire. The British were able to dominate the air during this time, and provided aerial observation, artillery spotting, and other air support to the troops. This resulted in the Germans sending down Hans Buddecke with three claimed kills, the experienced Lieutenant Schütz with one claimed kill, one other young pilot, and three Fokker Eindeckers to break the British air supremacy over the battlefield in January. The section consisted of the three airmen, six mechanics, and an interpreter.

As Buddecke noted in Chapter 10 of his account:

> The need for planes was great at Gallipoli. Enemy squadrons dropped their bombs wherever they liked. The observation biplanes were not capable of mounting an adequate defense, but their sacrificial attempts to do so didn't garner them much sympathy from the troops being bombed. The maneuver of

> approaching a bomber and turning around to open fire, made necessary by the way their armament faced, made it look like they were running away.

As he also noted in his account (see Chapter 11), "Here pilots were always in the minority in the air, four against forty." This is a reasonable estimate of Allied air strength. He continues with: "but the picture the people on the ground saw was always the same: the aircraft zoomed up, turned, fired, and flew away – that same characteristic of aerial combat that was a result of the design of our machine [the two-seater observation aircraft with rear-firing gun]."

Buddecke arrived in December and celebrated Christmas in Turkey. It does not appear he was deployed for action until 6 January 1916. Some sources claim that on 6 December 1915 he shot down a Henry Farman over Nara.[203] Not only is this claim unconfirmed, but clearly, from Buddecke's account, could not have occurred because his first flight in the Dardanelles was on 6 January 1916. The two British air wings were active at this time, although operations were limited by the weather. They lost two planes (but not the crews) between 8–14 December, attacked and chased away one Ottoman aircraft and one British plane and pilot never returned from his mission.[204]

On 7 December, the British government, after weeks of debate, finally decided to evacuate Gallipoli. A discreet withdrawal was conducted at Suvla Bay and Anzac Cove at night over ten days from 10 to 20 December. The British had pulled completely out of both landing areas by the early morning of 20 December. This ended what was a nightmarish combat experience for the Australian and New Zealand troops. The British and French still maintained their forces at Cape Helles.

No. 3 Wing started disbanding at the end of December, with its personnel either sent home, or some men and equipment being transferred to No. 2 Wing. Still, No. 2 Wing was reinforced at the end of December with six new Bristol Scouts each armed with a machine gun that could fire through the propeller arc.[205] This was a significant air superiority asset, but it's not clear when they became active.[206] Meanwhile, the Germans continued to build up their air assets, with another two Albatros C.Is, and three Gotha WD.12s sent down in addition to Buddecke and his three Fokkers. The German seaplane unit based at Canakkale now had six available planes.[207]

On 19 December, as the Allied evacuation was being completed, it is reported that every British plane that could fly did fly at least one sortie. This included eight patrols by No. 2 Wing and seven patrols by No. 3 Wing. The two RNAS wings were in the air for a total of twenty-seven hours and thirty-five minutes that day. The French squadron was in the air for about eight hours. Two machines (but no crew) had been lost the week of 8–14 December: No. 3 Wing had lost an aircraft (but no crew) to anti-aircraft fire on 16 December and another aircraft was lost due to an accidental bomb explosion (no crew lost); then another aircraft was lost due to accident on 20 December that resulted in one crewman killed and one captured.[208] On 25 December, as Buddecke and Schütz celebrated Christmas, the long-standing No. 3 (Naval) Wing, which had first deployed to Belgium on 27 August 1914 and which had been in continuous operation since then, was finally ordered home. Their last aerial engagement in the Dardanelles was an inconclusive one with an Ottoman Taube. In all, between February and December 1915, only two planes were forced down by the British in aerial combat, of which one was destroyed by French artillery. There was one British plane claimed on 27 September (but was probably not shot down) and one French plane claimed on 30 November (also probably not shot down).[209]

No. 3 Wing, from March through December 1915, had flown over 2,600 hours and nearly 156,000 miles during the Gallipoli Campaign.[210] Having arrived and become operational around 28 March,[211] and having been ordered home on 25 December, the squadron was active for an estimated 273 days in and around the Dardanelles. This averages out to 9.5 hours of flight per day for the wing and around

571 miles per day, equivalent to around five sorties a day. The mileage divided by hours indicates that the average operational speeds were around 60 mph. No. 2 Wing would remain at Imbros until the end of May 1916.[212]

The French Escadrille MF-98T was withdrawn from Tenedos on 13 January 1916. They lost one aircraft to combat on 6 January 1916.[213] Their total losses for the campaign were given as one airman killed in combat, two by accident, and eleven aircraft lost, including eight following their forced landings due to mechanical problems.[214] On 5 July 1915 they had fourteen aircraft, all operational. Their strength after that time varied and is not well documented.

Hans Buddecke and Lieutenant Schütz arrived in the Gallipoli area around 25 December. Their three Fokkers arrived on 3 January 1916 and became operational around 6 January.[215] On 6 January, Buddecke claimed a Farman east of Cape Narors and another Farman east of Jalova. The first plane was confirmed, giving Buddecke his fourth confirmed kill. The second kill was not confirmed, but was probably a British plane.[216] These two claims are discussed by Buddecke in Chapter 12, starting with the fourth paragraph. This was the first day his and Schütz's Fokkers were operational in the Dardanelles. Their third pilot ("our youngest") had not yet arrived, and is not mentioned again in Buddecke's account.

It is clear that the arrival of Buddecke and his flight mates had ratcheted up the intensity of the air war. Before his arrival the British and French had not lost any airplanes to aerial combat (and the British had two claimed kills of their own, one assisted by French artillery). Now they had lost two planes to Hans Buddecke and his Fokker. It appears that as late as 12 January, still only the two Fokkers were operational.[217]

Anticipating the British withdrawal, the Ottoman Army attacked the British positions at Cape Helles in a bloody offensive on 7 January 1916. The British then withdrew from Helles, the last units leaving on

9 January. This ended the Gallipoli Campaign on the ground and at sea, although the air forces remained and continued to engage.

On 9 January Buddecke is credited in some accounts with another Farman off Cape Helles.[218] This was not confirmed and not mentioned in his book. It seems unlikely that he would neglect to mention the incident if it had resulted in even an unconfirmed victory.

On 11 January Buddecke claimed another Farman at Jalvari, Cape Helles (see Chapter 12). It is clear from his description of the engagement that the enemy plane went down, fell into the sea, and the pilot was rescued by English torpedo boats. Most likely, the unconfirmed claims on 6 and 11 January did indeed occur (see discussions below).[219]

His next confirmed kill was on the 12th when he shot down a Farman at Galata. His account notes that the pilot landed in a "tangle of trenches" and broke his neck in the rollover. He then notes that a few minutes later Enver Pasha and his staff arrived to inspect the plane. Later that day a young German boy inspected the dead Englishman and reported back to Buddecke. This appears to have been his last kill in the first half of January.[220]

This confirmed kill gave him his fifth victory, making him an ace – although this term was not in use yet in the German air force. The German air force would later decide that ten victories would constitute an ace.

At this point, Buddecke was the third-highest scoring German pilot after Boelcke and Immelmann, each of whom scored their eighth kills on 12 January.

The Gallipoli Campaign had lasted eight-and-a-half months, from 25 April 1915 to 9 January 1916. Allied casualties in the campaign are given as 56,707 killed, 123,598 wounded, and 7,654 missing or captured for a total of 187,959. Ottoman casualties are given as 56,643 killed, 97,007 wounded, and 11,178 missing or captured for a total of 164,828.[221] Other sources give higher losses for the Turks. For example, a New Zealand government website gives Allied losses at

44,150 killed, 97,397 wounded and total casualties of 141,547, which is probably too low. Ottoman losses are given as 86,692 killed and 164,616 wounded for total casualties of 251,309.[222]

While there were no Allied ground forces on Gallipoli after 9 January 1916, air operations continued since Allied air forces remained based on islands in the vicinity of the peninsula. Continuing to patrol the area, Buddecke claimed three more kills on 25–27 January, all Farmans: two near Dardanelles (one unconfirmed) and one at Seddülbahir (often spelled Sedd-ul-Bahr or Sedd el Bahr), which is at Cape Helles. These are not addressed in his account. After his last claimed victory on 11 or 12 January, he wrote that "For months there were no more enemy planes over the peninsula." It's odd that he didn't discuss these additional victories in his memoir, but as his account may have been a very rough first draft and was published after he died, perhaps he simply forgot or had not gotten around to mentioning them at the time. The source of the claims for 25–27 January is unclear.[223]

Buddecke remained in the Gallipoli area for several months afterwards, claiming two more unconfirmed kills: on 30 March 1916 a Farman again at Seddülbahir and on 4 April 1916 another Farman east of Felahie, Gallipoli. He oddly described these claims as: "Then, after seven weeks of unsuccessful fighting with these now quite superior machines, I succeeded in getting an eighth kill from such a squadron after firing twenty-five rounds." This was probably the unconfirmed kill on 30 March. The engagement is described in depth. At this point he had five confirmed kills as of 12 January, and is credited with the two kills on 25 and 27 January which he does not discuss in his account, so he is clearly counting this unconfirmed kill as a kill. His count of eight kills reinforces the notion that he did shoot down two planes on 25 and 27 January but forgot to mention them in his account. Shortly after the 30 March kill he got word that he had been awarded the *Pour le Mérite* (the Blue Max), which he was awarded on 14 April 1916.

He was the third German airman to be so awarded, after Boelke and Immelmann, who both had eight kills at the time of their award. At the time, he had seven confirmed kills and five unconfirmed kills. Perhaps one of these unconfirmed kills was also officially credited to him, possibly the one on 30 March. Most likely, the powers that be felt he had done enough to deserve the award, even though his last two kills had dropped into the sea and therefore remained "unconfirmed."

Buddecke is sometimes listed with another unconfirmed kill on 4 April 1916, but this is also not mentioned in his memoirs. Those were the final successes of his Gallipoli operation. In the end he had six unconfirmed kills, of which the two on 6 January and 11 January appear likely. The claimed victory of 30 March is doubtful. As of 4 April, both Boelcke and Immelmann were credited with thirteen confirmed kills, and they had no unconfirmed claims.

Enver Pasha:

Enver Pasha (1881–1922) was born in Constantinople (called Istanbul as of 1930) under the name Ismail Enver. His parents were Albanian Muslims. He graduated from the Army War College in 1903 and was posted to the Ottoman Third Army in Macedonia.[224] Politically active, he was a member of the Committee of Union and Progress (CUP) that initiated the Young Turk Revolution of 1908. He was promoted to major after the revolution of June 1908. He was sent to Berlin in 1909 as a military attaché but was brought back the same year to help crush a mutiny. In 1911 he married an Ottoman princess, then was part of the unsuccessful defense of Libya, which was taken by Italy. He led the *coup d'etat* of 1913 that brought the CUP to power. He had only recently been promoted to colonel and was 31 years old. He then led Ottoman forces against Bulgaria in the Balkan Wars, during which he retook Adrianople and eastern Thrace, considerably adding to his reputation. He became the Minister of War in January 1914, was promoted to general, and was part of the ruling triumvirate, the "three Pashas." They were the *de facto* rulers of the Ottoman Empire from 1913 until the end of the Great War.

His "military experience" was still fairly limited. He had served as the attaché to Germany in 1909 for a few months (he spoke German), commanded in Tripolitania in 1911 during the Italo-Turkish War, and held a senior command in 1913 during the Balkan Wars. He was still only 32 years old.

He played a principal role in bringing Turkey into the Great War. In early December 1914 he took command of the Ottoman Third Army in the Caucasus theatre. He was disastrously defeated in January 1915 at the Battle of Sarikamish. He then took command of the forces around Constantinople, but had the good sense to turn over command of the forces at Gallipoli to the professional German soldier General Otto Liman von Sanders, who considered Enver Pasha to be an incompetent buffoon.[225]

Enver was also one of the principal perpetrators of the later Ottoman genocides against the Armenians, Assyrians, and Greeks. He was dismissed from his post as War Minister on 4 October 1918 while the rest of the "three Pashas" government resigned ten days later. After the Ottoman Empire capitulated to the Allies at the end of the month, Enver fled into exile in Germany. In late 1921 he went to Uzbekistan in the former Russian Empire to organize Muslim forces against the Bolsheviks. This was an ambitious attempt to create a pan-Turkic Muslim confederation encompassing Turkey, Central Asia, and parts of China. He led the forces of the Basmachi revolt against the Bukharan People's Soviet Republic, having built up an army of over 10,000 men. He was killed in a cavalry charge in Tajikistan on 4 August 1922; he was 40 years old at the time. The Basmachi revolt was effectively suppressed by the Soviet Union's Red Army in 1923–4.

Marshal Otto Liman von Sanders:

Otto Viktor Karl Liman von Sanders (1855–1929) was a German general who served as an advisor to the Ottoman Empire throughout the Great War. He was considered a "marshal" in the Ottoman Army and is referred to as such in Buddecke's memoirs.

Otto Liman was born in Stolp (now Slupsk, Poland) in the Kingdom of Prussia. His father was Jewish although he was baptized a Christian. He joined the German Army in 1874, initially serving with the 115th Lifeguard Infantry Regiment, the same unit in which Buddecke served some thirty-seven years later. He worked his way up the ranks and through various more senior commands, and was promoted to Lieutenant General in 1911. Otto Liman was ennobled in 1913, adding the "von Sanders" to his name, that being the maiden name of his late wife Amelie von Sanders (1858–1906). In November 1913, he was appointed the head of the German military mission to the Ottoman Empire. He arrived in Constantinople on 14 December 1913 with about forty-one officers on his staff.[226] While von Sanders had already had a long successful military career, including service on the German General Staff, he had little actual combat experience, as was the case with many German generals at this time.

His role became critical when the Ottoman Empire entered the war on 2 November 1914. With Enver Pasha in the Caucasus, Liman von Sanders commanded the Ottoman forces in the Gallipoli Campaign from the start.[227] He promoted the able Ottoman commander Mustafa Kemal to command the 19th Division opposite Anzac Cove, which started the rise to fame of this Ottoman general who later became the ruler of Turkey under the name of Atatürk.

In 1918, Liman von Sanders took over command of the Ottoman Army fighting in Palestine. He replaced the famous General Erich von Falkenhayn (1861–1922), the general who served as the Chief of the German General Staff and commanded the Verdun offensive in 1916. But von Falkenhayn had failed to prevent British General

Allenby from taking Jerusalem, although he did thwart the Ottoman governor's plans for a forced removal of the Jewish population. Liman von Sanders was also defeated by Allenby in the Battle of Megiddo (19–25 September 1918) and taken prisoner.

Still held captive at the end of the war, Liman von Sanders was arrested for war crimes in 1919 by the British over his sanctioning massacres of Greeks and Armenians. They released him in 1920 and he returned to Germany and retired from the army. He published a book in 1927 about his experiences. Hans Buddecke is not specifically mentioned in the book, although there is at least one picture of him and Oswald Boelcke in Turkey standing with Liman von Sanders (see photo section). He died in Munich in 1929 at the age of 74.

Major Erich Prigge:

Major Erich R. Prigge (1878–1955) was the adjutant to General Liman von Sanders and is mentioned in Buddecke's account once (see Chapter 11).

Prigge was born on 19 March 1878 at Harsefeld in the Prussian Province of Hanover. He was commissioned in the German Army in 1897. In 1914, he retired from the Army as a captain and transferred to the German Military Mission to the Ottoman Empire. He was made a major in the Ottoman Army and placed in charge of an Ottoman Cavalry NCO school. When the war in Europe started in August 1914, he was appointed as adjutant to General Liman von Sanders, a post he retained for most of the war. In May 1915 he was awarded the Iron Cross 1st Class. In September 1915 he was instructed to write an account of the fighting at Gallipoli, which was published during the war in early 1916.

After a ten-month assignment to the Eastern Front in 1917, Prigge returned to Turkey and resumed his role as von Sanders' adjutant, being promoted to major in April 1918 (and to lieutenant colonel in the Ottoman Army). Captured along with Liman von Sanders at Megiddo in September in 1918, Prigge returned to Germany in 1919 and retired from the army.

Living in postwar Berlin, Prigge had a successful business career and in 1922, published a book on the war in Turkey. During World War II he was a reserve officer handling administrative assignments in Baden. He continued as the managing director of the Red Cross in Baden after the war. He passed away in Locarno, Switzerland on 1 February 1955.

Major Erich Serno:

Major Erich Serno (1886–1963) was a lieutenant in the German Army in 1915, and a major in the Ottoman Army. He had begun his pilot training in Germany in 1911 and flew on the Western Front in the early days of the war. He was assigned to the German military mission to the Ottoman Empire in October 1914 and was the prime German officer liaison to the Ottoman air force. He arrived in Turkey in January 1915, accompanied by a staff of twelve. He started work at the San Stefano (Yeşilköy) Flight School in February 1915, where he was involved in training Turkish pilots and aircrew. He also was involved in such issues as Ottoman air force uniforms and organizations. Over the course of the war he helped organize seventeen land-based and four seaplane squadrons for the Ottoman Empire.[228]

As recounted in Buddecke's memoir, Serno was aboard the Turkish pre-dreadnought battleship *Barbaros Heyreddin* when it was torpedoed on 8 August 1915 by the British submarine HMS *E11.* Over half the officers on the ship perished. He was extremely fortunate to survive.

Serno left two accounts of his experiences in the Ottoman air service. He returned to Germany and took a management role in the German Arado airplane company after 1936.

The Ottoman Air Force:

The Ottoman Empire did not effectively start setting up their air force until the second half of 1911, initially sending two officers to train at the Blériot school near Paris, followed by eight other students in 1912.[229] It was also at this time that they set up an air base just west of Constantinople in the town of San Stefano. By the end of 1912, the Ottoman Army had fifteen airplanes, all various French designs: Blériot, Deperdussin, and REP (Robert Esnault-Pelterie).[230]

These planes were not used in the Italo-Turkish War of 1911–1912 that was fought over Libya. The Italians did make use of their aircraft and dirigibles in the war. In October 1911, the Italian air force became the first to conduct airplane reconnaissance and bombing missions. They also suffered the first wartime aircraft fatality in August 1912 and first aircraft to be captured in September 1912.

The Ottoman air force was used in the Balkan wars of 1912–1913, with seventeen aircraft supposedly used for reconnaissance.[231] They did lose some pilots and crew. Still a small force at the start of the Great War in August 1914, the Ottoman air force had eight airplanes assigned to operations and four to the flying school in San Stefano.[232] In early 1915 it included two four-plane squadrons, one in Gallipoli and the other in the Caucasus. (Compare to British squadrons of the time, which consisted of between twelve and twenty-four planes, or French *escadrilles* and German *Staffeln* of 6–10 planes each). By the end of 1915 the Ottoman air force had expanded to seven squadrons,[233] one of which was composed completely of Germans, although they wore Ottoman uniforms. The Ottoman personnel in these detachments consisted of a total of thirteen pilots and eleven observers. Three of these squadrons – the 1st, 6th, and 9th – were involved in operations around Gallipoli, as were two seaplane squadrons. By the second half of 1915, the Ottoman air force was deployed to Gallipoli, Constantinople, western Thrace, the Caucasus, and Mesopotamia. By the end of 1916 the Ottoman air force had eighty-one pilots and observers and about ninety airplanes.

1st Squadron: Formed in February 1915 at Canakkale with three aircraft and a seaplane. Moved in March 1915 to Galata. Moved in July 1915 to Tekirdağ with three Albatros B.Is and one Rumpler B.I.[234] Shown in September 1915 at Galata with 3 Albatros B.Is.

The 1st Squadron was involved in operations during the defense of Gallipoli. It was tied to the Fifth Turkish Army, commanded by General Otto Liman von Sanders. The squadron was commanded by German Captain (Turkish rank) Ludwig Preussner in 1915. It received Albatros C.Is (which were usually armed with one rear-facing machine gun) on 13 July 1915,[235] and Preussner claimed to have shot down the first Allied aircraft on 27 September 1915, although his claim is improbable.

A single seaplane, a Nieuport Hydravion (Nieuport VI H), was purchased by the Ottoman government around July 1914. It was attached to 1st Squadron in March 1915. It was later moved to the 1st Seaplane Squadron.

6th Squadron: Formed at Galata on 5 January 1916 with three Fokker Eindeckers.[236] This included Han Buddecke and his three Fokkers. The squadron was in operation around Gallipoli.

The three new Fokkers were sent down with Buddecke and Lieutenant Schütz and their mechanics. They arrived at the Dardanelles on 3 January 1916 and the 6th Squadron became operational on 5 January 1916.[237] Their first action was on 6 January 1916 when Buddecke claimed to have shot down two planes (and probably did).

Schütz came to Turkey with Buddecke and is discussed in his account. Erich Muhra (1896–1972) was probably the "other young pilot" that Buddecke refers to. He is not otherwise discussed in Buddecke's account. He was assigned to the 6th Squadron in December 1915.[238] It is claimed that he obtained one kill in December 1915, was wounded in action on January 1916, the plane was damaged in the fight, and crashed near Canakkale. It is also claimed that he shot down another plane in July 1918, but was again wounded in action.

After the war he obtained a law degree from the University of Breslau in 1923 and was an officer in the Luftwaffe during World War II.

The 6th Squadron was later commanded by the German officer Lieutenant Theodor Jakob Croneiss (1894–1942) in 1916, who is also not mentioned in Buddecke's account.

Emil Meinecke (1892–1975) was assigned to the 1st Squadron in the autumn of 1915 after initially working as a flight instructor. He was transferred to the 6th Squadron in April 1916, later becoming the squadron leader, and scored his first kill on 27 January 1917 using an Albatros C.III with Prince Hugo Friedrich Hohenlohe-Öhringen as his observer/gunner.[239]

9th Squadron: Formed in 1916 for the defense of Istanbul. Armed with four Fokker Es and one Albatros D.III at San Stefano in December 1916. Involved in operations around Gallipoli. Commanded by Captain Fazil Bey.

Germany's involvement in the Ottoman war effort was significant. During the course of the war Germany would transfer 460 airplanes to the Ottoman Empire, of which around 260 went to Ottoman units and the other 200 were used by German units. There were around 400 German aviation personnel that served with the Ottoman forces. The Ottoman air force ended the war with around 200 aircraft.

Lieutenant Hans Schüz:

"Lieutenant Schütz" was most likely Hans Schüz. He was the other pilot transferred to Turkey with Buddecke. Buddecke spells his name with a "t" and never mentions his first name. Other accounts refer to him as Hans Schüz. He was an experienced pilot when he arrived in Turkey. According to Buddecke: "Schütz had shot down an enemy aircraft in France." According to other listings, Hans Schüz had yet to have any claimed kills as of the end of 1915 (Buddecke had three).[240]

Schüz was born on 3 September 1893 at Langen in Hessen, making him almost three years younger than Buddecke.[241] Schüz joined the Prussian Army in 1911, becoming a lieutenant in 1912. He was assigned to flight school in January 1914 and transferred to duty in Freiburg in July 1914, then to FEA 3 in Darmstadt. At the end of August 1914 he was assigned to FFA 34, which had been established on 22 August by FEA 3.[242]

Some accounts claim his first victory was on 11 January 1916 in Turkey.[243] This is not noted in Buddecke's memoir and this claim is questionable (see discussion below). Most likely this was the kill sometimes recorded as shared between Buddecke and Schüz that we credit to Buddecke.

Hans Schüz remained in the Ottoman Empire for most of the war, transferring to the 2nd Squadron by April 1916 with which he deployed to Iraq and participated in the Siege of Kut (7 December 1915 – 29 April 1916). By the end of 1916 he was credited with six kills, and he collected three more in 1917. In 1918 he deployed to Palestine where he claimed his tenth kill; then he was transferred to the 13th Squadron and obtained an unconfirmed kill. His total by the end of the war was ten confirmed kills (including the shared one on 11 January 1916) and one unconfirmed kill.

Schüz rejoined the German air force in 1934. In 1941 he was promoted to major general (equivalent to a U.S. brigadier general). He was responsible for airfield operations in Africa. He was lost over the Mediterranean on 31 August 1941 while flying a Heinkel He-111 from Derna, Libya to Rome.[244]

Lieutenant Theodor Jakob Croneiss:

Theodor Jakob Croneiss (1894–1942) took command of the 6th Ottoman Squadron in 1916. He started the war with the 1st Bavarian Chevauleger Regiment,[245] a cavalry unit, then trained as an aircraft observer. He took training as a fighter pilot at the Fokker School at Schwerin and in 1915 he was sent to the Dardanelles.

He is not mentioned in Buddecke's account, probably because Croneiss was still operating with the 1st Ottoman Squadron, completely independent of Buddecke.[246]

Croneiss is credited with three kills between 7 January and 4 February 1916. One of those kills is likely and two appear to not be likely (see below). It is assumed he was using the Fokker that was reportedly shipped to Turkey in September. His older brother, Carl Croneiss (b. 1891), also served with the Ottoman air force starting in the autumn of 1915.

Croneiss was peripherally involved in Hitler's putsch in 1923 and remained a friend and ally of Hitler afterwards, maintaining communications with both Hitler and Göring. He worked as a test pilot for the Messerschmitt company and had extensive contacts in the German aviation industry.

He did not join the Nazi Party until 1933. He served in the SA and later rose to the rank of SS-*Brigadeführer* before World War II. His brother Carl joined the SA around 1930 and sat in the Reichstag from 1938–1945.[247]

Theodor Croneiss died of natural causes in Munich on 7 November 1942. At the time, his son was serving in Stalingrad and took the nine-day train trip home from there as a result. This saved him from being encircled by the Soviet Army later that month, and he survived the war.[248]

Preussner and Kettembeil:

Lieutenant Ludwig "Louis" Preussner, pilot, and Senior Lieutenant Karl Kettembeil, observer, were the first Central Power airmen to claim to shoot down an enemy aircraft in the Dardanelles, on 27 September 1915. German Lieutenant Preussner, a Captain in

Turkish service, was flying an Albatros C.I.[249] Other planes had been lost due to operations on both sides, but none due to aerial combat.

Their claim is dismissed in some works, and probably correctly so.[250] This was not the first engagement between aircraft over Gallipoli. Both sides had fired rifles and even machine guns at each other. This was the first aerial engagement in the theater in which both aircraft were armed with machine guns. It was an indication that operations in the air were getting more serious.

Preussner was born in 1888 in Bavaria and became a pilot before the war at his own expense. He commanded the 1st Turkish Squadron for much of 1915 before transferring to training in 1916. He was seriously injured in a training accident flying a Rumpler B.I. with a Turkish pilot at San Stefano airfield on 16 May 1916. He died on 29 May 1916 as a result of his injuries.[251]

Senior Lieutenant Kettembeil started service with the Ottoman air force on 16 August 1915 and remained with Ottoman forces for most of the war. He then joined the Luftwaffe in 1935 and served in World War II commanding reconnaissance units. Promoted to Lieutenant General on 1 June 1943, he was sent back to Turkey. He passed away in Munich on 12 April 1976 at the age of 85.[252]

Aerial victories besides Buddecke's claimed kills (1915–1916):

Probably Not a Valid Claim: 27 September 1915: Lieutenant Preussner and Senior Lieutenant Kettembeil are claimed in many sources to have shot down a British aircraft with an Albatros C.I. Their opponent was most likely Charles Rumney Samson, flying Nieuport No. 24 or Richard Bell Davies in Nieuport No. 26, both from the No. 3 Wing. Both men and planes returned to their base this day.[253]

Probably Not a Valid Claim: 30 November 1915: Lieutenant Ali Riza with his observer 2nd Lieutenant Ibrahim Orhan, flying an Albatros

C.I, shot down a French plane over Gaba Tepe, the headland just south of Anzac Beach. Plane crashed on fire between Itepe and Cape Helles.[254] The British did not lose any aircraft this day and while the French records are sparse, one secondary source notes that all the French aircraft returned this day to their base.[255]

Probably Not a Valid Claim: 4 January 1916: It is claimed that Wilhelm or George Schubert (German) shot down a French Maurice Farman from Escadrille MF-98T.[256] The best detailed description of Escadrille MF-98T actions does not mention this.[257]

Probably Not a Valid Claim: 7 January 1916: Theodor Croneiss shot down a British Farman at Seddülbahir.[258]

8 January 1916: Theodor Croneiss shot down a Voisin III LAS (#8502) near Cape Helles[259] flown by F.D.H. Bremner (also known as "Bunnie"), and his observer Midshipman H.E. Burnaby.[260] Bremner always reckoned that he had been shot down by Buddecke, but this is certainly not correct.[261] Considering the date of the event, this appears to be confirmation of Theodor Croneiss's kill.[262]

The *Kriegs-Chronik der Leipziger Neuesten Nachrichten* [War Chronicle of the Leipzig Latest News] appears to mention this engagement about a week later, albeit with some minor errors: "12 January 1916. Our aircraft, piloted by Lieutenants Buddecke and Chonos [*sic*], shot down a fourth enemy airman on 9 January. He crashed into the open sea at SeddülBahr [*sic*]."[263]

Most people assume that "Chonos" is Croneiss as he was the only Fokker pilot with a name even close to that. It could be an unrelated report, as F.D.H. Bremner glided his aircraft into the Helles airfield, which was near Seddülbahir. One is left to conclude that this report either confirms Croneiss' victory for 8 January; is the basis for the claim that Buddecke obtained a kill on 9 January (which we dismiss); or is a report of an engagement that did not result in a downing. It appears to provide evidence that Croneiss was in the area and engaged in combat at this time.

The reference to a "fourth enemy" plane would seem to imply the two planes Buddecke shot down on the 6th and perhaps the plane shot down by Croneiss on the 8th.

Probably Not a Valid Claim: 11 January: Possible claim made for Hans Schüz. This is probably not the case and Buddecke's account strongly indicates that "Schütz" had yet to get a kill as of 12 January.[264]

There is a detailed account of the shooting down of a Henry Farman on 11 January. It was flown by Australian officer Flight Lieutenant Cecil H. Brinsmead and the observer was Lieutenant Noel Henry Boles. It reads:[265]

> Tuesday 11 January dawned bright over the Dardanelles. Perfect weather for flying. In the early afternoon, Cecil Brinsmead suited up and clambered aboard a Henry Farman. His observer was Lieutenant Noel Henry Boles of the Dorsetshire Regiment.
>
> Now, on that fateful afternoon in January, Brinsmead and Boles met Buddecke and Schüz in the cold, clear air over Cape Helles …
>
> The Fokkers appear to have taken the British airmen by surprise.
>
> Wing Commander Eugene Gerrard, in a letter to Boles' father, say the pair were attacked from behind simultaneously by two hostile aeroplanes.
>
> "A destroyer officer who witnessed it says that the machine was shot down before it had any time to reply."
>
> For the time of day, we can look to the log book of HMS *Ribble*.
>
> "2.47pm: Allied aeroplane brought down by two hostile machines, close at full speed. HMS *Laforey* picked up two bodies and proceeded to K."

> The bodies of Brinsmead and Boles, recovered from the Aegean, were taken aboard HMS *Hibernia*, anchored in Kephalo Bay [Imbros].
>
> Our medical officer went aboard and interviewed the PMO [Principal Medical Officer] of the ship who had made the examination. I learned from him that the only wounds sustained by Noel were a bullet through the left wrist – it passed through his wrist-watch – and some scratches. The pilot had only scratches. It seems as through some part of the control was carried away. Death was caused in both cases by fracture of the skull and must have been instantaneous. He particularly told me that.

This action is described by Buddecke this way:

> A few days later, as the sun shone down on the empty English trenches, where Turkish soldiers were having a go at the mountains of abandoned provisions, two Fokkers hung over the yellow land. Schütz flew a hundred meters behind me.
>
> Below me I spotted a colorful gentleman. In no time I was on his tail. We went around in three spirals, and my aim was good … he flipped … plunged … fell into the sea. English torpedo boats came to pick him up.

According to Buddecke's account, he alone shot down this plane on the 11th and Schüz did not participate. So the claim for Hans Schüz does not appear valid.

Probably Not a Valid Claim: Before 13 January 1916 (but after 15 November 1915): Sergeant Charles Denti and Corporal René Weisshaupt of MF-98T in a Morane Parasol drove a Turkish aircraft away in a dive. Victory recognized on 4 September 1916. Fight occurred near Tenedos and the French aircraft received twelve bullets.[266] This claim probably has little validity and was not claimed by the pilot at the time. Note that the Morane-Saulnier Parasol was operated as a two-seater with a St. Étienne machine gun mounted facing the rear.

Probably Not a Valid Claim: 4 February 1916: Theodor Croneiss shot down a two-seater (a Farman or a B.E.2) at Baba Tepe, off Imbros.[267] See discussion below on actions from 25 January – 4 February 1916 for further details.

Buddecke's Five Kills 6–12 January:

Kill/Claim	Date	Aircraft Type	Location	Notes
4	06 Jan 1916	Farman	E of Cape Narors	See Chapter 12. Probably was Maurice Farman MF.11 number 942 of Escadrille MF-98T piloted by *Ltt* Jules Charles Lecompte.
Unconfirmed	06 Jan 1916	Farman	E of Jalova	See Chapter 12. Probably was Flight Commander Hans Acworth Busk, who was killed.
Unconfirmed	09 Jan 1916	Farman	Off C. Helles	Not discussed.
Unconfirmed	11 Jan 1916	Farman	Jalvari, C. Helles	See Chapter 12. Australian Flight Lieutenant Cecil H. Brinsmead and British Lieutenant Noel Henry Boles killed.
5	12 Jan 1916	Farman	Galata	See Chapter 12. Flight Junior Lieutenant James Sydney Bolas killed; Observer Midshipman Douglas Montagu Branson wounded and captured.

Book cover. (Photo courtesy of Tobias Weber)

The Nine Photos in Buddecke's Book

(Captions are translations of those in his book.)

Cover photo.

Buddecke's first aircraft.

Above left: On his own two feet in America.

Above right: First Lieutenant Buddecke in service to the Turks.

Above left: Boelcke and Buddecke on a boat ride off Smyrna.

Above right: View of Smyrna through the dilapidated gate of the old city wall.

Bird's-eye View of Constantinople.

Scene of the Dardanelles Successes.

Buddecke's airbase on the coast of Asia Minor.

Photos from *The Indianapolis Star* and other newspapers

RING OF FENCING FOILS SOON MAY RESOUND IN HOMES OF INDIANAPOLIS SOCIETY FOLKS

En garde!

Soon you may hear the sharp warning followed by the ringing clash of blade on blade. Indianapolis seekers after something different in the line of pastimes are to be given an opportunity to take up fencing.

Hans Ioachim Buddecke, a nephew of Albert Lieber and formerly fencing instructor of the Royal Cadets Corporations in Prussia and an aviator in Emperor William's army, will make an effort to popularize fencing in the city.

Buddecke holds the championship of the Cadets Corporations in the "cut" and "thrust" movements in fencing and a part of his enlistment in the German Army was spent as fencing instructor to officers.

"I came to America," said Buddecke, "to get acquainted with your country's customs. Indianapolis people, I think, will eagerly take up fencing. It is one of the most entertaining sports and a recognized medium of development of the body and mind to accuracy and control.

"To become proficient in fencing means that the mind must have absolute control over the body. Muscles try to act involuntarily when a person faces a rapier,

FENCING POSES BY HANS BUDDECKE

be sure of a graceful movement in the dance, because the motor muscles are thoroughly developed."

Buddecke also will be an assistant to Capt. G. L. Bumbaugh in his flying machine and airship enterprises and will be engineer for the dirigible which Capt.

Right: Fencing Poses by Hans Buddecke (from *Indianapolis Star*, 22 February 1914).

Below: Hans Johann [*sic*] Buddecke (from *Indianapolis Star*, 22 July 1914).

terize public men."

ated to nearby barns

dition is critical

Amateurs in Weak Machines Principal Toll of Aviation, Declares German Flying Here

eroplaning Really Is Safe, Says Hans Buddecke, After Making Trial Flight at Speedway.

According to Hans Johann Buddecke, young German aviator who has just ome to Indianapolis and who intends aking some spectacular flights over the ty within the next week or two, the eason for the alarming frequency of acdents among aviators is easy to explain

'Most of the men who are hurt or illed in aeroplane accidents," said Mr uddecke, "are amateur flyers—they are zy fellows who don't want to work and ho think they see a chance for 'easy oney' in aviation They buy a cheap eroplane after getting backing from ome company, and decide to make the oney on taking a few risks They get is cheap aeroplane with a bad motor, nd give 'exhibition flights' at state fairs nd places of that sort, and, not thoroughly understanding aviation they mash the 'planes and themselves, too

ONTINUED ON PAGE 13, COLUMN 6.

HANS JOHANN BUDDECKE.

GERMAN SOLDIERS IN MEETING HERE.

FRONT ROW, LEFT TO RIGHT—WILHELM SAMUELLS, KURT C. VOLKHART, CHRISTOPHER BERTRON, ALBERT LIEBER, HANS BUDDECKE AND LEONARD SCHWARTZ. SECOND ROW--JOSEPH VEIT, JOHANNES GRUNNER, LEOPOLD RASSOW, FRITZ LINK AND FRANZ FISHER. REAR ROW—FRITZ SCHAEFER, ERNST PAEP-PER, FRITZ SEIFFART AND FRITZ HUBERT.

HERO OF GERMAN AERIAL CORPS WELL KNOWN IN INDIANAPOLIS

LIEUT. HANS BUDDECKE.

Above: German Soldiers in Meeting Here (from *Indianapolis Star*, 4 August 1914).
Front Row, left to right -- Wilhelm Samuells, Kurt. C. Volkhart, Christopher Bertron, Albert Lieber, Hans Buddecke and Leonard Schwartz. Second Row—Joseph Veit, Johannes Grunner, Leopold Rassow, Fritz Link and Franz Fisher. Rear row – Fritz Schaefer, Ernst Paepper, Fritz Seiffart and Fritz Hubert.

Left: Lieutenant Hans Buddecke (from *The Richmond Palladium and Sun-Telegram*, Tuesday, 18 January 1916).

Other Relevant Photos

Katherine Stinson, the 19-year-old girl aviator. Picture may be from around 1910. She was described by Hans Buddecke as "a nice, not exactly pretty, girl and happy owner of a Wright crate." (Source: Library of Congress)

Right: Katherine Stinson circa 1914–1915. (Source: www.flickr.com/photos)

Below: Buddecke is standing next to his Nieuport at either Cicero Field or Indianapolis Motor Raceway (probably the latter). (Photo courtesy of Tobias Weber)

Western Front 1915

Above: Spring 1915 with the FFA 27, standing in front of Golancourt house. From left to right: Lieutenant Volck (O), Lieutenant Viehweger (P), Lieutenant Hans Jochim Buddecke (P), First Lieutenant von Brederlow (P), von Mudra (O), Lieutenant Demmel (P) with dog Kiwi, Captain Alfred Keller (P & CO), Captain Wilhelm Baur-Betz (O), First Lieutenant Kurt Drobnig (O), First Lieutenant Schikali (P), Captain von Sillich, Lieutenant Hans Reitter (O), First Lieutenant Müller (O) with dog Joffre, Dr. Fantel.
Key: O = Observer, P = Pilot, CO = Commanding Officer. Photo and identification courtesy of Tobias Weber. Of these fourteen airmen, only Buddecke became an ace. Captain Keller became Colonel General in the Luftwaffe. Joffre was also the name of the commander of the French Army.

Below: (Photo courtesy of Tobias Weber. Source of caption is not known)

The first plane Buddecke shot down. (Photo courtesy of Tobias Weber)

Cecil Hoffnung Marks (1887–1915), pilot of the second plane Buddecke shot down. (Source: www.jewsfww.uk/)

The Lawrence brothers in 1910: from left to right: Thomas Edward (Ned), Frank, Arnold, Bob and Will. William Lawrence would be the observer in the second plane shot down by Hans Buddecke. (Source: Wikipedia)

William George Lawrence. (Source: T.E. Lawrence society website at: 23 October 1915 | T. E. Lawrence Society (telsociety.org.uk))

Gallipoli

Above left: Major Serno. (Picture provided by Paschalis Palavouzis)

Above right: *Ltt* Jules Charles Lecompte. This was one of Hans Buddecke's victims on 6 January 1916. (Picture provided by Paschalis Palavouzis)

Right: Flight Commander Hans Acworth Busk. This was one of Hans Buddecke's victims on 6 January 1916. (Picture provided by Paschalis Palavouzis)

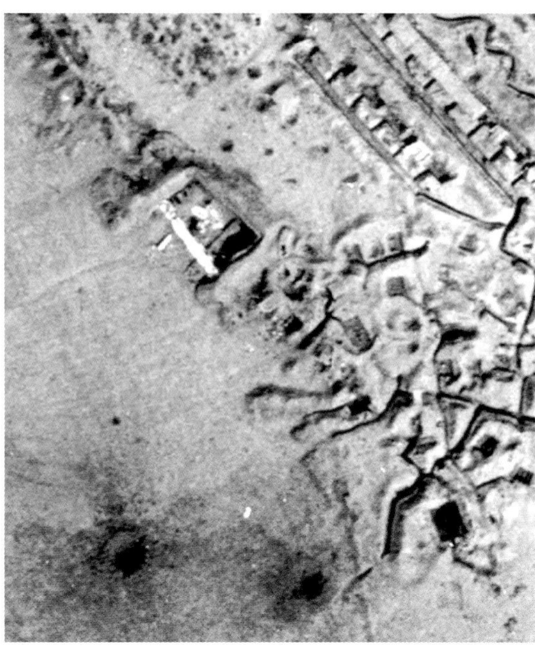

Above left: Theodor Croneiss. (Picture provided by Paschalis Palavouzis)

Above right: Picture of F.D.H. Bremner's Voisin 8502 on the emergency strip at Helles at 8 January 1916. He was shot down by Theodor Croneiss. He destroyed the plane later that day. In the bottom of the picture, one can see the presumed shell holes from the Turkish 6-inch shells that were reportedly fired at this airfield. (With permission from David Brenner, December 2021. bristolscout.wordpress.com/)

The Graphic, 20 January 1916. This was Hans Buddecke's victim on 11 January 1916. (Courtesy of Bernard de Broglio)

Noel Henry Boles (1893–1916), observer.

Left: A 1918 "Sanke" series postcard. Buddecke is shown wearing his Turkish officer's uniform with the lamb's wool kalpak headgear of the Turkish aviation service with the badge of the Turkish aviation service on his hat. He is wearing his *Pour le Mérite* (Blue Max) at his collar and down his uniform are his Ottoman Golden Liakat Medal (*Liyakat Madalyasi*), Iron Cross 1st Class, and Ottoman pilot's badge. The collar of the uniform is red and he retains the shoulder boards from his German uniform. This picture was most likely taken in 1916. (With permission from the Levantine Heritage Foundation. levantineheritage.com/)

Below: Buddecke in tropical pith helmet with Fokker E. III 96/.15, Ottoman serial F4. (Courtesy of Bernard de Broglio)

Ein Luftkampf über den Dardanellen: Der in türkischen Diensten stehende deutsche Kampfflieger Hauptmann Buddecke schießt einen französischen Doppeldecker ab.
Der hervorragende Flieger ist bereits durch den Orden pour le mérite ausgezeichnet worden. — Nach einer Zeichnung des nach der Türkei entsandten Sonderzeichners der Leipziger „Illustrirten Zeitung" Fritz Grotemeyer.

Above: Buddecke from a German magazine illustration. (Courtesy of Bernard de Broglio)

Below: Lieutenant Hans Schüz, Buddecke's section mate. Picture was from later in the war. (Picture provided by Paschalis Palavouzis)

Left: James Sydney Bolas (1892–1916), pilot. (Source: www.findagrave.com/)

Below: Picture was published in *Harb Mecmuasi* showing a French Farman brought down by Buddecke being visited by Turkish officers. The Turkish caption notes that after this event Buddecke received the title of Lieutenant and the Golden Liakat Medal. They also note that he had managed to crash four enemy planes so far. (Photo courtesy of Tobias Weber. Translation of Ottoman Turkish caption by Dr. Cigdem Oguz.)

Above: Senior Lieutenant Hans Joachim Buddecke, General Liman von Sanders, and Captain Oswald Boelcke in Turkey 1916. (Source: Bundesarchiv-Bild-183-S60853). Buddecke is now seen wearing an Ottoman Golden Imtiaz Medal.[1]

Below: Anthony Fokker (left), Captain Albert Mühlig-Hofmann (center), and Buddecke stand in front of what was probably a Fokker D.I. prototype, 140/16, at Schwerin. This would have occurred during Buddecke's leave in May 1916. A portion of this picture was later used in advertisements by propeller manufacturer Garuda. (Photo courtesy of Tobias Weber and caption borrowed from Bronnenkant, p. 19.)

1. Medal reference is from Bronnenkant, p. 20. He gives the date of this photo as 20 July 1916 and says that the medal was awarded to Buddecke sometime in June or early July by the Sultan, Mohammed V.

Buddecke and Senior Lieutenant Friedrich Schüler van Krieken pose in front of an observation plane from FFA 23 in May 1916. Krieken joined Buddecke in Turkey in June 1917 and subsequently became the Ottomans' Fifth Army aviation staff officer. (Photo courtesy of Tobias Weber and caption borrowed from Bronnenkant, p. 18.)

Western Front 1916

Attendees at *Jasta 4's* party honoring Berthold's award of the *Pour le Mérite*, held in the stately Chateau Vaux, included four other recipients of Prussia's highest bravery decoration. Sitting second from left was Ltn Walter Höhndorf and beginning with fifth from left: Olblt Rudolf Berthold (with the ribbon of the newly presented award visible around his neck, Oblt.d.Res Hans Joachim Buddecke, Ltn.d.Res Wilhelm Frankl and Oblt.d.Res Earnst Freiherr von Althaus. Third from right in the third row was Oblt Fritz Otto Bernert, who received the award in October 1917. Often mischievous, the flyers posed a white uniformed dummy behind and between Berthold and Buddecke. (Photo courtesy of Tobias Weber and caption from Kilduff, p. 73.)

This F.E.2b was Buddecke's ninth confirmed victory on 22 September 1916. (Photo courtesy of Tobias Weber)

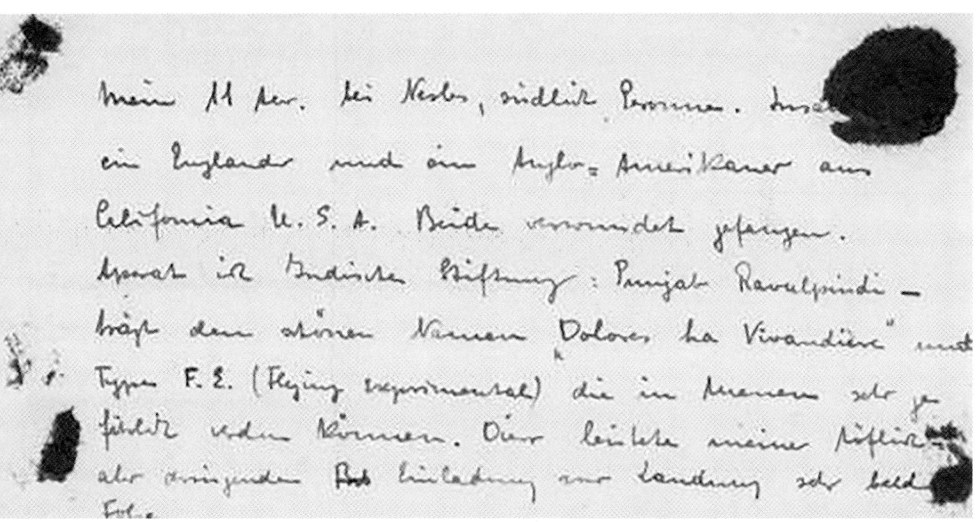

mein 11 ter. bei Nesles, südlich Peronne. Insa[illegible]
ein Engländer und ein Anglo=Amerikaner aus
California U.S.A. Beide verwundet gefangen.
Apparat ist Indische Stiftung: Punjab Rawalpindi –
trägt den schönen Namen „Dolores la Vivandière" und
Type F.E. (Flying experimental) die in Massen sehr ge-
fährlich werden können. Er leistete meiner höflichen
aber dringenden Einladung zur Landung sehr bald
Folge.

Note hand-written by Buddecke on the back of the picture of the F.E. 2b. Translation: "My 11th. At Nesles, south of Peronne. Inmates an Englishman and an Anglo-American from California. Both wounded and captured. Apparatus is Indian foundation Punjab Rawalpindi – bears the beautiful name Dolores la Vivandiére. Type F.E. [Flying Experimental], which can become very dangerous in masses. He soon accepted my polite but urgent invitation to land." (Photo and translation courtesy of Tobias Weber)

Buddecke's visit to *Jasta 4* at the end of October 1916. His older brother Senior Lieutenant (navy) Hartmut Buddecke on the left and Hans Buddecke on the right. This picture was taken several months after Hartmut had been injured at Jutland. (Photo courtesy of Tobias Weber)

Turkey 1917

Hans Joachim Buddecke

k. o. Hauptmann u. Chef der Flieger auf Gallipoli u. Klein-Aſien

Oberleutnant d. R.

im Leibgarde-Inf.-Reg. (1. Gr. Heſſ.) Nr. 115

Conſtantinopel Gr. H.-Qu. Abt. 13

Hans Buddecke's calling card.

Smyrna in 1917. Captain Buddecke in helmet greets General Otto Liman von Sanders, German Commander of the Turkish Army. Buddecke's aircraft is a Halberstadt. (Photo by Heinz Herbst, courtesy of Tobias Weber)

Captain Buddecke in helmet and General von Sanders inspecting the Halberstadt. (Photo by Heinz Herbst, courtesy of Tobias Weber)

It was a joyous occasion when Hptm.d.Res Hans Joachim Buddecke arrived at *Jasta 18* to help his old friend. Seen at the reception at Avelin Airfield were, from bottom left: Vfw Hermann Margot, Ltn Hugo Schäfer, Ltn Hans von Buttlar, Ltn.d.Res Josef Veltjens, Berthold (with his arm in a sling) talking to Buddecke, Ltn Johannes Klein, Ltn Olivier Freiherr von Beaulieu-Marconnay, and Ltn.d.Res Arthur Rahn. Top row from left: Ltn George von Hantelmann, Ltn Paul Lohmann, Oblt Ernst Wilhelm Turck, Ltn Walter Dingel, Ltn Walter Kleffel, and Vfw Theodor Weischer (Arthur Rahn Album via NMUSAF).[2]

Among this collection of pilots, Hans Buddecke (thirteen confirmed kills), Rudolf Berthold (forty-four confirmed kills), Josef Veltjens (thirty-five confirmed kills), George Hantelmann (twenty-five confirmed kills), Olivier Freiherr von Beaulieu-Marconnay (twenty-five confirmed kills), Johannes Klein (sixteen confirmed kills), Hugo Schäfer (eleven confirmed kills), and Arthur Rahn (six confirmed kills) became aces. Berthold, Veltjens, Hantelmann, Klein, Schäfer, and Rahn survived the war.

2. Photo courtesy of Peter Kilduff. Caption from Kilduff, p. 108.

Above: 'C' Flight pilots, 203 Sqn, May 1918. Canadian pilot Arthur Whealy, the ace who shot down Hans Buddecke, is in the center. (Picture is courtesy of his grandson Chris Whealy at whealy.com)

Below: This is the Sopwith Camel flown by Arthur Whealy. (Picture is courtesy of his grandson Chris Whealy at whealy.com)

Hans Buddecke

Left and below: Gravestone for Hans Joachim Buddecke at the *Invalidenfriedhof* Cemetery in Berlin, designed by Christoph Natter in 1918. (From Wikipedia, photo by Jörg Zägel, taken 2008).

(Photo courtesy of Tobias Weber)

There is some confusion over who and what planes were shot down by Hans Buddecke from 6 to 12 January. There were only four documented British planes shot down between 6 and 12 January 1916.[268] There was also one French pilot killed on 6 January. An annotated list of Buddecke's confirmed and unconfirmed kills can be found in Appendix I, but some of them deserve more detailed discussion.

Buddecke claims that on 6 January he shot down one of a group of Farmans that was bombing his airfield and which with only a forward-firing machine gun and unsupported by the other aircraft in the flight, went down and crashed near the Narrows of Chanak. This was his fourth credited kill. He then describes a second kill that same evening, which went unconfirmed.

Another secondary source claims that the first plane shot down this day was "Maurice Farman MF.11 number 942 of Escadrille MF 98 T piloted by *Ltt* Jules Charles Lecompte."[269] It does not appear that Lecompte was flying with an observer, which was often the case with bombing raids early in the war. Considering Buddecke's morning opponent "spun into the ground," and that his grave was later marked at Seddülbahir, it is clear Buddecke is describing the downing of Lecompte.[270]

It is stated in a British account that Flight Commander Hans Acworth Busk took off at 3 p.m. from Imbros, meaning Buddecke's "evening" kill on 6 January probably would have occurred between around 3:30 to 4:30 in the afternoon. At this time of the year in Gallipoli, twilight occurs between 6:30 and 7:40 p.m. Of course, the British operating in the Mediterranean were probably still operating on Greenwich Mean Time (GMT) while Istanbul and Gallipoli are at GMT +3 hours. This then indeed appears to have occurred in the evening according to local time. While Buddecke talks about the second plane shot down in the evening after another enemy squadron came, it appears that Busk was downed while conducting a solo bombing run without an observer. His description that this second kill of the day "vanished from sight" almost certainly describes Busk, who disappeared and probably crashed into the sea. One British compatriot notes that Busk "was last seen about five miles by air from the Galata Aerodrome (German)."[271]

The interesting aspect here is that Busk probably should have known better than to be out without an observer. There were multiple aircraft from the French squadron that attacked Buddecke's base in the morning. Considering that they lost an aircraft to his Fokker and Schüz also shot at one, they probably now knew that there were Fokkers in the area. Apparently, this knowledge was not transferred to the British. Up until late July, the British No. 3 Squadron was co-located with the French squadron at Tenedos; they then moved to Imbros. If they were still located together, then it is possible that the British would have known of the Fokkers and Busk would not have conducted a mission without an observer.

A Turkish book published in 2003 claims:[272]

> On 6 January, the Allied aeroplanes raided Galata airbase but they failed to cause any damage to the camp. Air Lieutenant Buddecke responded promptly and took off from the airbase and shot down one French Farman aeroplane under the control of pilot Leconte [*sic*]. She crashed on the Asiatic side between the Ozbek and Karacaviran district. Leconte died in the crash. On the afternoon of the same day, Buddecke again shot down another Allied aeroplane in the Burhani area with his Fokker.

While Buddecke claimed two planes on the 6th, and two planes in the subsequent days, some listings record him with three claims, one on the 9th, the 11th, and the 12th.

While not conclusive, there is some supporting evidence for the claim on 9 January. The *Kriegs-Chronik der Leipziger Neuesten Nachrichten* states: "9 January 1916. One of our airmen attacked an enemy Farman-type biplane that went down, enveloped in flames, near Seddülbahir."[273] The *Leipziger Neuesten Nachrichten* was a conservative daily newspaper published in Leipzig from 1892 to 1945. It was the largest daily newspaper outside of Berlin and during the Great War regularly published a war chronicle recording the events of the day. It also reports: "12 January 1916: Our aircraft piloted by Lieutenant Buddecke and Chonos shot down a fourth enemy airman on 9 January. He crashed into the open sea near Seddülbahir."[274]

This is probably a case of two reports of the same engagement. The mention of "Chonos" may well be a reference to Theodor Croneiss, who may or may not have been with the 6th Squadron that Buddecke commanded. It also notes that this was the fourth enemy airman shot down. Considering that Buddecke shot down two planes on 6 January, and it is claimed that Croneiss shot down planes on 7 and 8 January, this would be a separate, fifth kill.

This unconfirmed victory is usually credited to Buddecke and has not been credited to anyone else.[275] There is no evidence of a French or British plane going down on the 9th, although a British Voisin flown by F.D.H. Bremner went down on the 8th as previously described. One wonders if this is delayed evidence of Theodor Croneiss' kill, although Bremner, who survived the war, was not in flames and did not crash into the open sea. He did land in Cape Helles, where Seddülbahir is located. Evidence of French planes being shot down are hard to locate for MF-98T.[276] As the claim is not mentioned in Buddecke's account, and not otherwise supported by the records other than these two newspaper reports, it seems prudent to dismiss this unconfirmed claim. It could have been an aerial encounter that did not result in a downing (and these occurred more often than not).[277]

For the claim that would have occurred on either the 9th or the 11th Buddecke reports:

> A few days later, as the sun shone down on the empty English trenches, where Turkish soldiers were having a go at the mountains of abandoned provisions, two Fokkers hung over the yellow land. Schütz flew a hundred meters behind me.

> Below me I spotted a colorful gentleman. In no time I was on his tail. We went around in three spirals, and my aim was good … he flipped … plunged … fell into the sea. English torpedo boats came to pick him up.

This appears to have been the Henry Farman shot down on 11 January that was flown by the Australian Flight Lieutenant Cecil H. Brinsmead. The observer was Lieutenant Noel Henry Boles.[278]

The next victory Buddecke discusses appears to be his kill on 12 January. He states:

> I was getting closer to him. When he turned back homeward, he noticed that I was already in front of him. Skillful and determined, he took his advantage and attacked me from above. With an evasive movement I could have avoided his fire, but I knew that a thousand heads were waiting below for me to run him over the houses.
>
> So I flew sideways to his course, let him come close in order to fire, then I slewed my muzzle around to point at him, jerked the machine up as high as it could go, and fired until he was over me. We lay flat on our backs for twenty meters, pointing straight up.
>
> The Fokker only barely held up in the subsequent U-turn since it had lost all its momentum in the climbing maneuver. But then I saw that my opponent had already had enough. In spirals, with a few warning shots, I accompanied him downstairs, where the pilot landed his machine in the tangle of trenches and broke his neck in the rollover.
>
> A few minutes later, Enver Pasha and his staff arrived to inspect the plane, whose death struggle they had been observing. Back on the Alçitepe I noticed that my opponent had inflicted on me a shot in the center of the propeller. The bullet had ricocheted off and hit the engine, damaging it a little.

> … For months there were no more enemy planes over the peninsula.

The victims were Flight Junior Lieutenant James Sydney Bolas of the No. 2 (Naval) Wing, and his observer Midshipman Douglas Montagu Branson who was wounded and taken prisoner.[279]

The end result is that Buddecke is credited with two confirmed kills and three unconfirmed kills at this time. Of those three unconfirmed, two look highly probable. The claim for the 9th, which is not addressed by Buddecke in his book, is very questionable. It is based upon the report in the 12 January *Leipziger Neuesten Nachrichten*; which probably shouldn't be given much credence.

It is claimed that Hans Schüz shot down a plane on the 11th, but this is contradicted by Buddecke's account. Buddecke describes his encounter on the 12th:

> Schütz took off first … **At first I thought: I want to let Schütz take this enemy, since so far he has only had bad luck.** But then other considerations prevailed.

This would strongly argue that on 12 January, Schütz had yet to shoot down an airplane, so couldn't have downed one on the 11th. It appears that Buddecke had at least two, and probably four, kills from 6 to 12 January and six to eight planes by the end of the month. The crews of the three British planes Buddecke is credited with downing have been identified by name, as has the one French plane, which maximizes the likelihood that they are verified victories. In one of the oddities of nature, every British plane shot down was flown by a pilot whose name began with a "B'. This was also the case with the observers.

At the same time, between 7 January and 4 February 1916, Theodor Croneiss was credited by some with three kills and Hans Schüz with one.[280] If all these claims were true, it would appear that twelve enemy planes were shot down between 6 January and 4 February, adding up all of the claims credited to Buddecke (of which only four are fairly certain), the one for Hans Schüz (which probably did not happen) and the three for Croneiss (of which only one is certain). Croneiss is never discussed in Buddecke's account.

It seems clear that seven of these claims are not correct and the real count from 6 to 12 January is probably five aircraft downed (four by Buddecke and one by Croneiss).

In 1958 Major Serno wrote an account that says:

> Besides this, the new Fokker fighter squadron now distinguished itself. The squadron leader was Lieutenant Buddecke who had already attained several combat victories on the Western Front. The squadron came into action at Galata in an extraordinarily successful way. In air battles Captain [his Turkish rank] Buddecke shot down four airplanes, Captain Schüz two, Lieutenant Meinecke two, and Lieutenant Muhra one. A hard departure had been prepared for the enemy aerial opposition. The medal of the Great Golden Imtiaz was presented to Buddecke by Enver Pasha on the battlefield of Gallipoli itself. The operations of the squadron over the Dardanelles forms a counterpart to the sensational success that the great German fighter pilots Immelmann and Boelcke attained with the Fokkers on the German Western Front, at about the same time. After his eighth victory Buddecke was also awarded the highest German combat decoration, the *Pour le Mérite*.[281]

It is a nice confirming report, although it clearly covers the period through at least April 1916 and was written over forty years after the fact from memory and whatever notes Serno had. Buddecke had four confirmed kills between 6 January and 27 January, even though we discount the last two. He was awarded the Blue Max in April. Hans Schüz was credited with three kills in April obtained during the siege of Kut al-Amara in Mesopotamia, in addition to the claim sometimes credited to him on 11 January 1916. Emil Meinecke had been in Turkish service since autumn of 1915 but was not transferred to the 6th Squadron until April 1916. He is not credited with any victories until 1917.[282] Eric Muhra had one unconfirmed claim at this time according to some sources. Of interest, Major Serno does not mention Theodor Croneiss.

This account appears to confirm our narrative that Buddecke shot down four aircraft, Muhra was in his unit, and Croneiss was not part of the 6th Squadron during this time.

Hans Acworth Busk:

Flight Commander Hans Acworth Busk was probably Hans Buddecke's victim on 6 January 1916 (Buddecke's fourth confirmed kill).

Busk was born 9 January 1894 and died on 6 January 1916, only 21 years old at the time of his death. His older brother, Edward Busk, an early British aviator who was largely responsible for designing the B.E.2c, had recently been killed on 5 November 1915 while testing a B.E.2c at Farnborough.

Hans Busk started his flight training in December 1913 and joined the Royal Naval Air Service in January 1914. He was assigned to the Gallipoli Campaign, deploying to the island of Imbros in late October 1915.[283] He was with the No. 2 (Naval) Wing.

On 6 January French and British aircraft were bombing the Turkish Galata airfield. As recounted by Flight Lieutenant Theophilus Chater Vernon, Busk was flying a Henry Farman with a 130-hp engine, carrying a 500-lb bomb and, to save weight, no observer (or machine gun). He took off from Imbros at 3 p.m. and was last seen about five miles by air from the Galata Aerodrome.[284]

The Blue Max:

An informal standard was established that the medal would be awarded to any pilot who had shot down eight planes. This was later changed to sixteen planes in early 1917, and towards the war's end to thirty planes. It was, however, sometimes awarded to other aviators without such kill claims. The *Pour le Mérite* was widely awarded outside of the aviation community, having been a medal for bravery and service for the Kingdom of Prussia since 1740.

Other famous German aviators so honored included Kurt Wintgens and Rudolf Berthold.[285] In fact, every German ace with thirty-six or more claimed victories had a Blue Max. Ernst von Hoeppner, the command General of the air service, was also awarded one even though he did not fly.

The war in Europe was well into its second year, but America was still officially neutral, so the exploits of Hans Buddecke continued to be recounted in the Indiana press. One such article was in the *Palladium* of Richmond, Indiana, published on Tuesday, 18 January 1916:

HERO OF GERMAN AERIAL CORPS WELL KNOWN IN INDIANAPOLIS

> Lieut. H.J. Buddecke, hero of the German aviation corps, now cooperating with the Turks in the Dardanelles, who yesterday, according to dispatches brought down his fifth allied aeroplane after a battle in the air, is well known in Indianapolis. Lieut. Buddecke, a nephew of Albert Lieber, president of the Indianapolis Brewing Company, came to Indianapolis in 1914 and prepared to start a school of aviation here. He had several aeroplanes and balloons, but before his plans were completed war was declared and Lieut. Buddecke started for Germany and joined the aviation corps. He served on the western front during the first part of the war, where he made a reputation as one of the most daring of all of the Taube pilots. Later he was sent to the Dardanelles, where he has sustained his reputation.

The article included a rather large picture of him (see photo section). While downing a fifth aircraft meant that Buddecke was now an "ace," that word was not used in the article as it was still not in general use. Of interest here is the claim that that he had been preparing to establish a school of aviation in Indianapolis and owned "several aeroplanes and balloons." These are new claims not seen before, and are not substantiated by any other sources.

Subsequent claims for January – February:

Buddecke is credited with the following claims for the rest of the month:

Kill/Claim	Date	Aircraft Type	Location	Notes
6	25 Jan 1916	Farman	Near Dardanelles	Not discussed.
Unconfirmed	26 Jan 1916	Farman	Near Dardanelles	Not discussed.
7	27 Jan 1916	Farman	Seddülbahir	Not discussed.

There is also the claim that Croneiss shot down a plane on 4 February 1916. None of the four claims made between 25 January 1916 and 4 February (three by Buddecke and one by Croneiss) can be confirmed. No British planes are reported to have gone down between 25 January through 4 February.[286] Searches of records of the No. 2 Wing and HMS *Ark Royal*'s operation report do not reveal any lost planes.[287] Escadrille MF-98T left Tenedos on 13 January and was no longer active in the area.[288] Still, French aircraft could reach Gallipoli from Lesbos but first flew operations from there to Smyrna on 7 February 1916.

All indications are that none of these three kills are valid, nor is the claim on 4 February credited to Croneiss. Clearly there were air operations and engagements in the area, but no British or French planes were shot down.

Air Superiority?

The final question concerns the Allied use of their armed scouts. The Germans sent three or four Fokkers down to Gallipoli. They quickly established air superiority and stopped the incursions of British and French planes at a cost of at least four Allied aircraft.

Why didn't the Allies make an effort to re-establish air superiority? They had more single-seat armed scouts than the Germans did. In particular, No. 2 Squadron was reinforced by the end of December with five or six Bristol Scouts that may have been armed with a forward-firing machine gun.

The Bristols first arrived at Imbros in September with No. 3 Squadron, so they were certainly operational by the time the Fokkers arrived. It is unknown if they were armed, and if they were, there may have been some concern about the use of the Garros-like firing arrangement, minus any metal plate protection for the propeller. Still, if they were armed, it is surprising they did not make their presence felt in January, when the three or four Fokkers were wreaking havoc on their countrymen. As the British pilots had shown no lack of courage throughout the campaign, it seems likely that the Bristols were not armed.

The Bristol Scout was almost a match for the Fokker Eindeckers. The Bristol Scout D (the British also employed very similar Cs and F.D.H. Bremner flew them) were biplanes with an 80-hp Le Rhone 9C nine-cylinder air-cooled rotary engine. Its maximum speed was 94 mph, and it could climb at about 540 ft per minute. It was armed with one Lewis or Vickers machine gun.

In contrast, the Fokker E.III had a 100-hp Oberursel nine-cylinder rotary engine. Its maximum speed was 87 mph, its rate of climb was 650 ft per minute with a time to 3,000 meters (9,843 ft) of thirty minutes. Its armament was one 7.92 mm LMG 08/15 machine gun. The Fokker E.II was statistically similar, except its gross weight was 1,102 lb, compared to 1,345 lb for the E.III and 1,195 lb for the Bristol.[289]

On the other hand, the Fokkers had two experienced and proven pilots, Buddecke already with three kills and Schütz with one (if he is granted the 11 January claim).

Escadrille MF-98T had three Morane Parasols. These apparently were Morane-Saulnier two-seaters armed with a rear-firing St. Étienne machine gun. They were often assigned at Tenedos to be on call and these planes were involved in at last three engagements around Tenedos as a result. They did not appear to be used offensively. In the second half of 1915, the French did have forward-firing Morane-Saulniers, based upon the modifications done by Roland Garros, but it does not appear that any of these were deployed with MF-98T.

The Fokker was a design derived from the Morane-Saulnier and not significantly better in performance. The Allies clearly had up to a half dozen scouts that could contest the skies with the three or four German Fokkers, and most of their two-seaters were armed with machine guns. In the case of the Voisins and Maurice Farmans, these were forward firing. So the Allies at Gallipoli certainly had some capability to vie for air superiority over Gallipoli, yet it does not appear that they tried. One wonders why?

Another article appears in *The Muncie* (Indiana) *Morning Star*, Monday, 13 March 1916 edition. Like others, it appears to have been placed at the instigation of Albert Lieber. It reads:

> **Albert Lieber's Nephew Has Brought Down 13 Air Craft**
>
> Indianapolis, March 12 – A picture of Hans Buddecke, a nephew of Albert Lieber and well known in Indianapolis, appears in a recent issue of *Die Woche*, a weekly magazine published in Berlin. The magazine was sent to Mr. Lieber by his son Rudolph, who is attending Handel's High School at Cologne. Buddecke, who left Indianapolis to join the German aviation Corps, is a captain. He has thirteen hostile airplanes to his credit, and has been awarded the coveted Iron Cross and also a gold medal by Turkish officers. Accompanying the magazine was a letter from young Lieber that threw some

> interesting sidelights on life in Germany during war times. He declared that the Germans have never wavered in their attitude of optimism with regard to the ultimate outcome of the struggle, and that the fact that thousands of recruits are being drilled in preparation for going to the front shows that there is no shortage in the material for soldiers. Food prices, Lieber said, were rather high, but restaurants, theaters and other places of amusement are running and life goes on much as usual.

The claim of thirteen kills is inflated. According to some tallies, by 12 March 1916 Buddecke had seven confirmed killed and four unconfirmed kills.[290] By his own account, by 12 March 1916 he had shot down seven enemy aircraft. By our count, he had shot down seven aircraft (including the two unconfirmed kills of 6 and 11 January and excluding the two confirmed kills of 25 and 27 January 1916).

Buddecke's Final Claims for Turkey, 1916:

Kill/Claim	Date	Aircraft Type	Location	Notes
Unconfirmed	30 Mar 1916	Farman	Seddülbahir	See Chapter 12.
Unconfirmed	04 Apr 1916	Farman	E of Feahie, Gallipoli	Not discussed.

One of these two claims appears to be the one he describes as a "fun battle," in which he brought down his opponent even though his gun jammed after firing just twenty-five rounds.

The *Kriegs-Chronik* reports:

> 1 April 1916. On 30 March, two of our aircraft under the command of Hptm. Boedge attacked enemy airmen that flew over Seddülbahir. During the air combat, one of the

enemy airplanes fell into the sea while the others fled toward Imbros.

And:

8 April 1916. On 4 April eight enemy aircraft flew over Gallipoli peninsula[.] Hptm. Buddecke attacked them with his airplane, and during the course of the air battle caused one enemy plane to crash outside of Kumdere.[291] The plane immediately sank into the seas. Investigating enemy torpedo boats, which rushed to help, were unsuccessful.[292]

The reference to Captain "Boedge" appears to be Buddecke. It's not clear which of his two unconfirmed kills are discussed in his account. Buddecke claims he was awarded the Blue Max for his eighth victory, even though these last two claims are listed as unconfirmed in many accounts.[293] Immelmann and Boelcke were both awarded after eight confirmed kills. It appears that Buddecke was awarded his after only seven confirmed kills, as it seems that neither of these last two kills were ever confirmed. The French had clearly withdrawn from the area by this point and MF-98T was conducting operations on the Salonica Front. The British report no planes lost in the Mediterranean between 30 May and 4 June 1916.[294]

On 1 May 1916 there were three papers in Indiana that published articles about Buddecke. *The Indianapolis News* reported:

Kaiser Decorates Aviator.

BERLIN (by wireless to Sayville, N.Y.), May 1. – Emperor William has conferred the military order "Pour le Merite" on First Lieutenant Buddecke, a German aviator in the Turkish

> service. The lieutenant has distinguished himself in bringing down several hostile aeroplanes.

In this case, the article may not have been "planted" by his uncle Albert. The same report was repeated in *The Fort Wayne Journal-Gazette*, and on 5 July 1916 in *The Journal*, Scottburg, Ind.

These would be the last articles published in Indiana on Hans Buddecke. The United States joined the war on 6 April 1917, and supporting Germany or reporting on the exploits of its heroes was no longer acceptable. Some people, and even some towns, changed or modified their German names to be less Germanic. People played down their ties to Germany or their German heritage. Obviously, Albert Lieber either felt it was impolitic to publish articles about the exploits of his nephew, or the Indianapolis papers themselves would no longer publish such accounts. Regardless, accounts of Hans Buddecke disappeared from the American press, and his death in 1918 went unreported in the papers that had once lionized him.

Buddecke's Furlough (May 1916):

It appears that shortly after being awarded the Blue Max, Buddecke travelled back to Germany. Photographic evidence confirms that he was with FFA 23 at Vaux on 7 May.[295] In a letter dated 9 May 1916 Boelcke writes: "Yesterday we [he and Althaus] went to Charleville together to visit the chief; we also met Buddecke there, who flies in Turkey. He told some very interesting tales. To go and see Turkey – that would be a most attractive idea to me."[296] Buddecke also apparently visited with Anthony Fokker in Schwerin during this time and is shown standing with Fokker in front of what was probably a Fokker D.I prototype.[297] He is not referenced in Fokker's autobiography. As Schwerin is around 130 miles northwest of Berlin, where Buddecke's family lived, it is assumed he also visited with his family during this visit. In the photographs taken at the time, Buddecke is wearing his Ottoman uniform with the rank of captain, sporting his Kalpak hat, and his Golden Liakat Medal, his Iron Cross, 1st Class, his Prussian Pilot's Badge, and his *Pour le Mérite.* The exact start and end dates of this furlough are not known, but he did return to Turkey for a short while at its conclusion.

Boelcke's Visit to Turkey (July 1916):

In July 1916, Oswald Boelcke was sent to visit Turkey. This was his only significant break from combat operations since the beginning of September 1914.[298] At this point he was the most famous German airman, with nineteen kills to his credit. In comparison, Buddecke had seven confirmed kills at this time, while Immelmann was credited with seventeen kills before he died on 18 June 1916. Boelcke arrived in Vienna on 10 July 1916 and in Constantinople on 14 July.

Boelcke mentions Hans Buddecke in a letter dated 20 July 1916. They had previously met on 8 May 1916 and had at least one acquaintance in common (Ernst von Althaus). His letters and diary in the official biography tell the story:[299]

> 20.7.16. Woke up after passing Akhissar.[300] Very pretty country and well cultivated, many herds. Camel caravans, each headed by a donkey who leads the beasts. After Magnesia vegetation became more luxurious, though only in the plain – many stones on the mountains, not much bread there. Wonderful view of Smyrna on the slope of a hill. Buddecke and others met us at a station. I am put up in the Hotel Krämer, close to shore – I have a view over the whole Gulf of Smyrna from my balcony.
>
> Lunched with Excellency Liman von Sanders, who was very nice and had his photo taken with Buddecke and myself. Strolled through the bazaar in the afternoon; not as large as the one at Stambul. In the evening big dinner at Buddecke's; present Liman von Sanders, Colonel Kiasim (chief of staff), Count Spee, the German consul, etc.; after the meal the

Austrian, Dutch and Swedish consuls came along with their ladies. A very nice evening.

On the 21st I went out with Faller, my old instructor at Darmstadt in August, 1914, to Sevdi-köi aerodrome, south of Smyrna. We rode from the Station to the aerodrome. The Turkish soldiers make a good impression, but their officers – pilots and observers – not so good.

In the afternoon I called on General Trommer, who spoke his mind about the rotten state of things in Turkey. Then went to station to say goodby to Excellency Liman, who was going back to Panderma. All the bigwigs there – lot of fuss. Spent evening with Count Spee in Sporting Club, where there is a wonderful view over the Gulf of Smyrna.

22.7.16. Went bathing with several ladies and gentlemen in Kordilio, where Buddecke came for us with a yacht. Glorious! The view of the surrounding mountains and Smyrna is wonderful. In the evening we went to tea with the Austrian consul and met all sorts of people. Conversation carried on in ever so many languages.

The account of this trip continues with the narration of the author Johannes Werner:

Boelcke originally intended to return to Constantinople with Major Serno on the 22nd. When he was making up his mind to stay on, the gay society in which he found himself exercised a strong influence on his decision; on the other hand, he also speculated on the possibility of flying to the Dardanelles, his next destination, from Smyrna in a few hours, thus eliminating the twenty-six hours' railway trip to Panderma as well as the further journey from Constantinople to the Dardanelles.

And so he spent the next three days in Kordilio, enjoying the yachting parties and the gay society there.

> But his plan of flying to the Dardanelles did not materialise. On July 25th he wrote in a somewhat humble strain: "I now have to go the long way round to Constantinople to the Dardanelles. I could have been there in two and a half hours in an aeroplane, but Buddecke will not let me have one. He gave me a thousand reasons why it was impossible, but I believe he received instructions from the air chief or even from G.H.W., that I must not fly here either." On the 26th he therefore left beautiful Smyrna.

Oswald Boelcke arrived at Chanak in Gallipoli midday on 29 July. He flew back to Constantinople on Sunday, 30 July and left Turkey on 1 August. Travelling through Bulgaria and Austria, he arrived at Berlin on 18 August and at Dessau on 20 August.

Chapter 14

Back in the West

By Hans Buddecke

In the afternoon sun, the mosques and minarets disappeared behind the walls of the Seven-Towered-City. Tired and glassy, the Sea of Marmara lay, unresponsive, as if she had no more life in her.

A week before me, Boelcke had returned from his visit to Smyrna to organize a fighter squadron on the Somme. I followed after him and thus returned to Roupy and Vaux.

We were reunited with the incomparable Franconian, as we called Berthold, the only one of the old gang still there. He had been through a lot while we were away. After Althaus he inherited my Fokker and, like the latter, brought down some opponents with it. Then he got another aircraft and had a serious accident.

He had been in Quentin for over a month. When they wanted to send him home to recuperate, he instead drove out to Roupy, got back into his machine, and resumed his work.

He had already prepared everything for me and brought together the most capable pilots. When we again pitched our tents in Vaux to prepare for the arrival of a dozen planes, I counted five gentlemen with the *Pour le Mérite.*

Now we could go to work together to wrest superiority from the enemy.

Wintgens and Höhndorff flew together according to their custom. Masters of their trade, neither of them ever returned from a flight to the front without claiming one, two, or three victories. Lack of space compelled them to stay in Roupy for the time being. Whenever they returned across our airfield, we would hear Wintgens giving a sign with his rotary motor: Brr…brr…brr…brr…brr…. The sign that he had downed one. Unfortunately his machine, which had carried him from the first to the sixteenth victories, soon became his undoing. When a Nieuport surprised him with an attack from above, he quickly dove away. As with Immelmann, the long lever arm of the fuselage of this type of aircraft could not withstand the force of the movement and broke. They were a magnificent pair of pilots. A year later, Höhndorff was to follow him in a machine he had built himself.

Not all the men were together in Vaux when we took off for the first time. Berthold was in the lead, the rest of us staggered behind and above: Stehle, Bernert, me.[301]

We went over the lines and were shot at – poorly, because of the clouds. After ten minutes, Berthold had caught a small Nieuport far below me. We all dove down at a frantic rate to be quite close to the crash site, so we could confirm the kill. But the Nieuport somersaulted into a cloud and disappeared.

One after another we pulled our machines out of their dives and regained altitude. The row of airplanes made a beautiful picture. Berthold lay so far below me that I could hardly keep an eye on him or see him when he threw himself downward. You just stuck to the tail of the plane in front of you and followed his movements.

We resumed our flight up and down the front for half an hour. Here and there a little dot appeared in the west, but it quickly disappeared at the first sight of our string of aircraft on the German side. Then Berthold took off in a different direction and we flew into enemy territory. He tipped over and dove on some tethered balloons; we all fell in behind him, and soon I saw that I had burst into a long line of "Groß-kodriger" [big Caudrons][302] who were practicing how to handle their flock of fat balloons. Immediately I pivoted on one wing to dive on the first one I came across. He misunderstood this movement and tried to turn in pursuit of me, but instead got right in front of the muzzles of my guns. I hammered the two machine guns and he plummeted downward, smoking.[303] Next to me – the altimeter showed 900 meters – floated a balloon decorated with cockades. I flew below it, turned and unloaded into a second "big Caudron" in the same way.

The same thing was repeated a third time when I turned away from that one. The rest of the remaining ones were sent falling to Earth by my comrades.

When my last prey had disappeared into the darkness of the clouds, I turned to make my way home. The Nieuports would be arriving soon; there was nothing to be done about the balloons without the ammunition intended for that purpose.[304] During the fighting I had lost track of our front man [Berthold]. I saw Bernert, faithful to the end, behind me in his brown double-decker. Ever efficient, he concluded that the moments when I was weaving my way through a sea of shrapnel clouds of enemy artillery were the perfect time to do combat exercises on me. He came at me from above, peeled off, moved to the right, to the left.

Once behind our lines, we started climbing. Bernert noticed that I flew a stubborn southerly course. He thought I wanted to see whether there was anything going on there; it didn't occur to him that I had actually lost my orientation and was looking for recognizable shapes of forests and cities between the clouds. It wasn't until we were over Roye, from a mighty height, that I recognized Ham, where I had been every day a year earlier.

With empty tanks we came home to discuss our experience. Then and later, we enjoyed tackling these big Caudrons. You could always spot them from a distance, engaging in their sinister occupations. We considered them to be dark gentlemen, who, if possible tail forward, would fly out to the front to spy on something, to adjust the fire of the heavy artillery, and to try to appear quite harmless. If one dove on them, they at once had their tails up and immediately stretched their wings in the form of four colorful side-slips away from the attacker. You could almost say that before you even thought about diving, they had already smelled your idea. It was possible for them to drop vertically like little single-seaters when danger threatened.

That evening I took off again with Bernert. Above the trenches at Péronne an enemy squadron of large planes passed below us. Since I had climbed faster, I was behind Bernert, who was now in perfect position to pounce; but he did not attack. I fidgeted with impatience behind him. What is he doing? I didn't know, of course, that he hesitated because he was waiting to get into a position where the sun was directly behind him. So I dove on a chap well above average size with a very long fuselage, took aim, and fired.

A rattling sounded above me. I turned around. A bang … A blow to the chest and cheek … My pressure gauge was missing. Fearing that I would run out of gas, I broke off my attack while the two Nieuports rattled behind me. Then, when I noticed that my scarf was getting wet, I flew home. It was nothing and yet something. My opponent's bullet from below had passed through the middle of a steel tube of the aircraft's frame and the pressure gauge and, together with the rest of the instrument, penetrated partly into my leather jacket and partly into my neck.

The big chap with the long fuselage was a new apparition in the sky over the Somme. He interested us, and we were to have more dealings with him and his colleagues of the same type. Strangely, we always succeeded in quickly silencing their fire, but never in bringing one down.

Frankl once emptied his whole supply of ammunition on such a fellow – three thousand rounds in all – but the enemy did not fall. So we donated a silver victory cup as a prize for the first long-tailed man. But a gentleman from a neighboring fighter squadron brought it down much later with a single lucky hit.

We eventually found out what had caused our difficulties. Both engines and the pilot's seat were well armored. In the back and front, an observer sat outside the armor behind double machine guns. Everyone saw that this machine could only have been constructed by a cruel man.

There followed days and weeks of uninterrupted take-off, fighting, and landing, a period when one experience followed another in a blur.

Berthold had shot down his eighth that morning and had taken off again when another of us came in to land and announced, breathlessly, that he had seen Berthold fall.[305] We didn't know what to say, and were still standing out on the airfield and discussing when there was a brief hum above us. A machine spiraled down through the haze to land. Thank God – we rushed at him. "What, me dead? Not so fast!" Then he told the story. Two Nieuports had attacked him from behind in a dive, ran together, and streaked downwards past him, missing their wings.

The morning was usually discussed at lunch. Not everyone liked to hear that someone else had shot down another one, and such news did not shorten the length of the meal of those who had no comparable victories to talk about.

Then came a day that was as beautiful as it was sad for the squadron. We received a telegram saying that His Majesty had awarded Berthold the *Pour le Mérite* and given him a fighter squadron in Alsace.

Next day at noon, two of us circled over the station in Quentin, from which a train was just pulling out, taking our loyal companion to a new adventure.

Chapter 15

Air Battle

By Hans Buddecke

And the hunt went on. The main operation was always located above the St. Vaast forest, where the so-called elegant world united at ten o'clock in the morning, at twelve noon and at five in the evening.

The constant shifting of the front lines around that forest north of Péronne required special aviation operations on both sides. Everyone who had the stick in their fists patrolled here during this time to wait for prey. Unfortunately, to get there we had to fly out of the zone assigned to us.

Opposite us lay M. Guynemer with his own. One saw only Nieuports waiting for us behind their lines, while English aircraft of every category were gathered over that forest. Early in the morning, both parties gathered.

We came across reconnaissance and artillery spotters, a few Halberstadts[306] roamed around further forward, then for a while we encountered nothing else.

In the distance we could see small profiles gathering. Once the enemy's squadron had assembled, they came over towards us. The first moments of what followed were pretty messy. Immediately we were in the middle of the dogfight, and after barely half a minute it was finished. The thick clouds of smoke were evidence of exploding petrol tanks. It was seldom that an enemy had to be followed down to the ground to verify a kill; even more seldom that an enemy reached his home ground again. Then you resumed waiting for more targets to approach, or intruded on their side yourself.

The moment he shoots down an enemy plane is the most precious thing in a fighter pilot's life. It is based on observing the whole sea of air, often for hours. Your neck is rubbed raw against your scarf because of the constant turning and swiveling of your head; your eyes water from looking and searching. Just as a bird's life and survival depends on the air, the whole organism of the airplane depends on the eye, which works strenuously. In second place comes the thinking, the imagination and cunning, trying to lure your opponent into battle. Finally comes your flying prowess, your technique, which the men of today, like the birds, do subconsciously.

When the moment came that everything had been scanned again, considered, calculated when this or that Nieuport would be at the optimal place at the optimal time; then when mechanically your little bird turned vertically downwards, and the physical exertion of this radical maneuver gave you vertigo; if you fell on your enemy with a height advantage of several hundred meters; to see all of this through – that was a moment, perhaps more beautiful than the victory afterwards. The uncertainty as to whether your own wings would hold against the violence of the maneuver only increased the appeal.

There were some real hunting days. When at noon the clouds gathered over the country and formed gorges and ridges like the wildest mountains, then we crawled around in the peaks and valleys, searched the corners, and if there was nothing at 4,000 meters above sea level, we drifted down to 3,000, 2,000, then 1,000 meters. Usually we could find someone somewhere, and we immediately closed on them and checked for a cross or cockade.

So the ordinary days of mild weather passed. We hunted alone, in twos, threes, or fours.

The days of major battles were more serious.

Our soldiers' operations on the ground brought the entire air force into action. The first major air battle took place at the end of November 1916 over Biache Maisonette,[307] just south of Péronne.

At 3 o'clock in the afternoon orders went out for an assault to recapture the manor. Three hours earlier, the artillery barrage had begun. From 3 o'clock to 4:30 my fighter squadron was to patrol at high and medium altitude to secure the activity of the artillery and infantry spotting aircraft over the troops.

It was a perfect November afternoon. By the time we got to the front – Frankl was leading the flight of six aircraft above me, I another six at a height of 2,500 – many of our planes were already assembled and busy directing the artillery. We flew through them and took the point. Behind us everyone turned to move the action forward with us.

In front of us a few Caudrons, covered by a few Nieuports, pushed away from the fighting. By following them we got behind the line of the enemy balloons, without having actually come to attack. We stayed there. Frankl sometimes appeared high above me with his six loyal companions, only to quickly disappear into the haze, while I tried to inconspicuously approach a Caudron and a Nieuport. We stayed in this area for about twenty minutes until the first Nieuports intruded and brought life to the operation.

The eye has seldom had to work so hard as in these hours. There were a hundred machines in the air on either side, and often the encounter only revealed at the last second whether one was friend or foe. The whole thing turned into two large rollers that roll together. You drove against the enemy, the enemy pushed back, all the while entangled as both sides dove for speed, only to disengage and seek to regain altitude.

This showed the superiority of the fast climber. He could perform this tour twice, in the time it took the slow one to do it once.

Within a short time after the battle began, I only had one companion with me; the others were busy, attacking targets of opportunity. When a Nieuport dove on me and I banked towards it, a Fokker who hadn't paid attention flew through the line of fire between us and immediately plunged past me to the ground, out of control. The Nieuport, who quickly realized that I was doing everything I could to get hold of him, sped away quickly to the west.

Wherever one looked in those free moments when one could take a breath, one could see the dots and crosses approaching with the movements of great birds of prey, as they forced each other into the depths or dragged each other to the left and right.

After about half an hour the enemy had to be fully alerted. The hunting ground was teeming with cockades, all of which belonged to fighter planes. It took a lot of energy to keep the upper hand over the enemy, especially since we were forced by our machines to always catch them from below so as not to let them break through to the artillery- and infantry-reconnaissance planes.

In the course of the action I encountered members of my flight again, who immediately attached themselves to me. We reformed, then hurled ourselves into the enemy again. Again and again the big biplanes, which our brown rats knew well, turned and twisted with us.

It was a great feeling to advance against the enemy at the head of this innumerable mass. I felt the power and energy of the thousands of horsepower that we were throwing against the enemy. If only we could have blown past those enemy planes like we used to give people rides over the housetops. But again and again there was only circling, and falling.

After an hour and a half, there was a slackening on both sides. No wonder, after so long a period taking a toll on nerves and physical dexterity, keeping the steering constantly in motion, not half a minute in which one could fly straight. One's eyes begin to stare, and no longer pass their messages on to the brain.

Then the first Albatroses[308] of another squadron arrived to relieve us. To my delight, everyone returned safely and allowed the fur jackets to be pulled from their depleted bones by the mechanics, who had followed the fighting with binoculars as best they could.

We had held our ground, and even if it hadn't gone so well for the other squadrons, we hadn't suffered any losses ourselves. Some of us had worked long and hard that day, but could not report any victories. Who wanted to pursue an enemy into that maelstrom?

But for the first time, we realized, there had been a mass engagement in which the attack of our infantry was supported and mirrored at the highest altitudes, and into which both sides had thrown whatever forces were available in the sector.

As with later air battles, not much came of it. Losses were about 2 per cent. That low number is explained by the constant support of each plane by others, which did not give opponents time to zero in on their targets.

For the next few days, delegations with wreaths went to neighboring units. In poor, small village churches there were one or two coffins, flowers, soldiers on either side. The comrades came together quietly. A silent greeting, a handshake.

Thoughts wander, until the clergyman bids them hearken to his words. His Mass is not very successful, though. What is there for him to say to these people, he who cannot know what the world of war looks like from above? The listener tires and dreams his own thoughts. It is a relief when a comrade approaches the crypt to speak to the dead words that affect the living.

Chapter 16

The Western Front, 1916

Hans Buddecke was deployed to Turkey from late December 1915 to around mid-August 1916 (excepting his brief furlough home in spring 1916).[309] He was then recalled to the Western Front, which at the time was dominated by the terrible Battle of Verdun that dragged on for almost ten months, from 21 February 1916 until 18 December 1916. This was the longest and bloodiest battle of the war, with the Germans taking advantage of France's exposed positions to the north and east of Verdun. The German plan was simply to draw the French into battle, attacking them continuously for the sake of running up French casualties and maybe causing the French Army and population to lose their will to fight. This was a brutal attrition strategy that counted on the French, with their smaller population[310] and lower percentage of young men among their population, to run out of soldiers and be too exhausted to continue the war. Of course, an attrition strategy against the French also applied to a lot of young German men.

Increasing the bloodshed, the British conducted a series of bloody offensives in Belgium from 1 July to 18 November 1916, known today as the Battle of the Somme, to try to take the pressure off their French allies.

Buddecke returned to Vaux towards the end of this unprecedented war of attrition in late August 1916 and stayed on the Western Front only until early December, when he was sent back to Turkey.[311] During that time, he shot down three planes in September – two F.E.2bs and one B.E.12. These were his eighth through tenth kills. As of the end of September 1916, he was the sixth highest scoring German ace, exceeded only by Boelcke with twenty-nine kills, the late Max Immelmann with seventeen, the late Kurt Wintgens with nineteen, Wilhelm Frankl with thirteen, and Walter Höhndorf with twelve.[312]

Jagdstaffel 4:

On his return to France, Buddecke took command of *Jagdstaffel 4* (a fighter squadron, also called informally *Jasta 4* or *Staffel 4*). The first of this type of unit, *Jagdstaffel 2,* was established on 10 August and placed under command of Oswald Boelcke, who was still in Turkey at the time. Buddecke was ordered home around 18 August,[313] and his friend Rudolf Berthold was transferred to the squadron. *Jasta 4* was officially established on 25 August 1916 in Darmstadt. While Buddecke was still en route from Turkey, Berthold took over the initial management of the squadron. This is discussed in Berthold's dairy:

> At the beginning of September … I assembled the new *Jagdstaffel 4* for Buddecke. My *Abteilungsführer* [Hptm Hermann Palmer] provided personnel, as he could spare them. They were good sound people, who I knew and could rely upon. Our airfield was again at our old Vaux, which, for us, invoked many beautiful memories. The old spirit of FFA 23 was carried over to *Staffel 4.*[314]

Berthold had had a dramatic run as a fighter pilot since Buddecke had left FFA 23 in December of 1915. Berthold began flying the second Fokker in FFA 23 in early December. He then transferred and took over command over what became a unit of five Fokkers called *Kampfeinsitzer*[315] *Kommando (KEK) Vaux*. He shot down his first two planes in February and three more by 16 April 1916. He was injured in a plane crash on 25 April 1916, suffering serious head injuries and a badly broken leg. He was in the hospital for the next three months, then checked himself out to return to duty, even though he was far from fully healed and had difficulties walking. He continued serving as head of *KEK Vaux* despite not being fit enough to fly. He finally returned to flying on 24 August and claimed his sixth kill on his first flight since his injuries. He still had to be helped into and out of his plane.

The *Jagdstaffel* was a new German organization that created a proper-sized fighter squadron. The former arrangement was of field flying sections (FFAs) that consisted of only six planes, with there being at best only two Fokker Eindeckers per unit. *Jagdstaffel 4* consisted of a dozen aircraft. They were all fighter aircraft.

Berthold remained with the *Jasta 4* until 10 October when he was transferred to take command of *Jasta 14*. During the month of September he claimed four kills; two were confirmed, two were not.[316] At the same time, Buddecke was getting his three confirmed September victories. Berthold was awarded the Blue Max on 12 October 1916 with a total of eight confirmed kills.

Berthold's departure from *Jasta 4* is described in his diary:

> When I left my old unit on 10 October in order to head east to a new unit in Alsace, the day was foggy, damp and cold; my mood was dismal and melancholy. All of my comrades, who were very close to me, saw me off on the train. Many furtive tears were wiped away. From time to time Buddecke shook my hand. Above us was the sound of aeroplane engines – a farewell gesture. The train was ready to pull out. Quick handshakes from my faithful comrades in arms, and then I no longer looked back. I headed out on a dark journey.[317]

Hans Buddecke continued as commander of *Jasta 4* until early December. The squadron was active in September with fifteen kills, but their level of activity declined in the subsequent months, with only four kills in October, three in November (none by Buddecke) and none at all in December.[318]

During Buddecke's tenure, some other German pilots staked their claim to the Blue Max. From 6 September to 9 November, Otto Bernert claimed six kills; he had one kill before he arrived. From 7 September – 22 October Wilhelm Frankl claimed six kills, giving him a total of fifteen. He had already been awarded the Blue Max on 12 August 1916. Wilhelm Frankl was the top ace in the squadron at this time. By the end of 1916, he was one of the two top scoring living aces (tied with Manfred von Richthofen).

Kurt Wintgens:

Kurt Wintgens was the first person to shoot down a plane using a Fokker Eindecker, either on 1 or 15 July 1915. He was one of the five original Eindecker pilots.

He had been born in August 1894, making him the youngest of the early German aces. He joined a communications battalion (*Telegraphen-Bataillon Nr. 2*) as an officer cadet in 1913 and was still in military school when the war began. He went to the Eastern Front as a lieutenant and won the Iron Cross 2nd Class there. He then transferred to the air service, flying as an observer. In early 1915, he underwent his pilot training at the Fokker School in Schwerin. Exposed to the new armed Fokkers during his training, he was selected as one of the first five pilots of the Fokker. He was one of the few German pilots allowed to wear corrective glasses.

His first victory on 1 July 1915 was not confirmed. It likely occurred and was probably a Morane-Saulnier L two-seater from Escadrille MS-48, flown by Captain Paul du Peuty with Junior Lieutenant de Boutiny as the observer. The French aircraft was armed only with a carbine, while Wintgens' aircraft had, of course, a machine gun. Both Frenchmen were wounded in the encounter, but managed to land their aircraft in French territory. Wintgens then downed another Morane-Saulnier L three days later under similar circumstances. It was also not a confirmed kill.

On 15 July, he obtained his first confirmed kill, the first official victory by an Eindecker. He scored two more confirmed victories in 1915 and an unconfirmed victory in January 1916. Sidelined for a while by the flu, he again began scoring kills in May 1916 and on 24 June 1916 achieved his seventh confirmed kill when he shot down a Nieuport 16 flown by American Lafayette Escadrille pilot Victor Chapman, the first American pilot to die in combat. Wintgens scored his eighth victory on 30 June 1916 and on 1 July was awarded the *Pour le Mérite*. He was the fourth German pilot to be so awarded, after Hans Buddecke.

Wintgens was shot down in combat flying alongside Walter Höhndorf, possibly being the eighth victory claimed by French ace Alfred Heureaux. When they recovered his body, it showed no bullet wounds but the plane had a severed elevator spar. At his death, Wintgens had nineteen confirmed kills to his credit and three unconfirmed kills; this made him the second highest scoring ace in the German air force at this time, after Boelcke (with twenty-eight kills) and ahead of the late Max Immelmann (with seventeen kills). He was 22 years old when he died.

Walter Höhndorf (Hoehndorf):

Walter Höhndorf (Buddecke spells it Höhndorff) was born in 1892 and learned to fly in Paris in 1913. He then qualified for the German pilot's certificate at Johannistahl airfield. He was involved before the war in aerobatics and helping design and produce airplanes for *Union Flugzeugwerke*, the developer of the pre-war Union Arrow Biplane that set world altitude records in 1913.

Höhndorf was commissioned a lieutenant in March 1915 and served most of that year as a test pilot for *Siemens-Schuckert*. In late 1915 he was assigned to FFA 12 and got his first two kills in January 1916. In April 1916 he was transferred to *KEK Vaux*, where he began flying with Wintgens and scored one more kill. In June and July of 1916 he scored six more kills and received his *Pour le Mérite* on 20 July 1916, then scored two more kills in July. His twelfth and last kill was claimed on 17 September 1916 while serving with *Jasta 1.* He was with Kurt Wintgens when his friend was shot down on 25 September 1916. He then returned to test pilot duties and flight instruction and died in an accident on 5 September 1917 flying one of his own designs, the AEG D.1.

Otto Bernert:

Fritz Otto Bernert (usually called Otto) was born in 1893 and was commissioned in the German Army in 1912. He was wounded four times before the end of 1914, the last wound being inflicted by a bayonet, which severed the major nerve in his left arm, leaving it useless. He was invalided out of the infantry.

Bernert then transferred to the air arm and trained as an observer. He wore glasses, but astonishingly this and his crippled arm did not prevent him from serving on the Western Front in 1915 and early 1916. In March 1916 he obtained his pilot's license and was assigned to *KEK Vaux.* He scored his first victory on 17 April 1916 flying a Fokker Eindecker.

He continued scoring, becoming an ace on 9 November 1916 when he shot down his fifth, sixth, and seventh victories on the same day. He was awarded the Blue Max on 23 or 24 April 1917 after having claimed nineteen victories. On 24 April he shot down five planes in one day, the first pilot on the Western Front to do so. His total kills for April 1917 alone were fifteen.

On 1 May 1917 he was appointed commander of *Jasta 6.* He scored three confirmed victories in May 1917 and an unconfirmed victory on 19 May. This increased his total count to twenty-seven confirmed victories and one unconfirmed. These were his last victories, although he continued in command positions and continued flying.

Bernert was severely wounded on 18 August 1917. This wound, which hospitalized him for three months, took him off flight status and removed him from command. He was also diagnosed with *Kriegsmüdigkeit* (war weariness, similar to "battle fatigue"). He was promoted to a senior lieutenant, but ended up back in hospital care in May 1918, probably due to lung problems. He died from the Spanish flu on 18 October 1918.

Rudolf Berthold (continued):

In December of 1915 Rudolf Berthold inherited Buddecke's Fokker when Buddecke was transferred to Turkey. In October, Buddecke had received a Fokker E.II with a 100-hp engine. Buddecke took over this new machine and the old machine was passed to Ernst Althaus. Althaus then flew that plane to a nearby aviation facility and exchanged it for a new Fokker.[319] Berthold accompanied Althaus when he shot down an enemy plane on either 3 or 5 December 1915. Berthold started claiming his own victories in February 1916 and by the time he had reunited with Buddecke in France in late August or early September, had claimed six victories.

Berthold continued to score with notable proficiency between injuries. The first serious injury to put him in hospital was on 25 April 1916. He returned to his unit to command, even though he was still unable to fly because of his wounds. By the end of September 1916, he had eight confirmed victories and two unconfirmed. He was awarded the *Pour le Mérite* on 12 October 1916 and the following day was made commander of *Jasta 14*. He was the tenth aviator to be so honored.[320]

Berthold resumed scoring in March and April 1917 with four victories, but was injured in combat again on 24 April. By August he was again certified fit to fly, and scored fourteen more victories in September 1917. By early October he had twenty-eight confirmed victories. On 10 October he was injured again in combat. He returned to command of *Jagdgruppe 7* on 6 March 1918. On 8 March he arranged for his friend Buddecke to transfer to his unit; Buddecke was killed in action two days later.

Berthold then took over command of the newly formed fighter wing *Jagdgeschwader II* on 18 March 1918. Between May through August 1918 he increased his tally to forty-four. He was flying even though he had not fully healed and was using narcotics to control his pain. He was shot down again on 10 August and seriously injured. He would never fly again.

Having survived the war with forty-four claimed victories, he was tied with Bruno Loerzer as the seventh highest scoring German ace of the war, and the third highest scoring living ace (after Ernst Udet and Josef Jacobs). He returned to duty in 1919 and then independently formed a *Freikorps* militia in April 1919 based upon his reputation. They moved into the Baltic states to fight the Bolsheviks. They joined the right-wing Kapp Putsch in March of 1920 and moved to Hamburg. There they got into a fight with local workers that resulted in the death of thirteen workers and three *Freikorps* combatants; eight captured *Freikorps* members were executed by the workers. Berthold and some of his men ended up besieged in a Harburg school. Berthold negotiated a safe passage in exchange for disarming, but as they left they were attacked by an angry mob which overpowered Berthold. They took his handgun from him and fatally shot him six times with it. He died on 15 March 1920.

Because of his organization of a *Freikorps* unit and support of the Kapp Putsch, Berthold's memory was later honored by the Nazis.

Buddecke's three claimed kills on the Western Front in September 1916, all confirmed:

Kill/ Claim	Date	Aircraft Type	Location	Notes
8	06/16 Sep 1916	F.E.2b	Chaulnes	See Chapter 14.
9	22 Sep 1916	F.E.2b	Combles	Not discussed. Sergeant T. Jones and 2nd Lieutenant F.A.A. Hewson wounded and captured. Jones died of wounds.
10	23 Sep 1916	B.E.12	Sailly	Not discussed. Lieutenant J.M.J. Kenney wounded and captured. Died of wounds.

Buddecke's eighth "confirmed" claim cannot be confirmed from the available historical record. The date of the kill is given as either 6 September or 16 September. The British lost one F.E.2b on the 6th at Loos and lost five F.E.2bs on the 16th.[321]

His ninth confirmed claim appears to have occurred, but various sources disagree as to who the British victims were (see below).

Buddecke's tenth claim, confirmed at the time, has also been confirmed from the historical record. This was the first single-seat airplane that he shot down.

His total confirmed claimed kills were now ten, with five unconfirmed claims. Two of the unconfirmed victories were most likely occurred on 6 and 11 January 1916, while three of the confirmed claims cannot today be verified from the historical records, and two of those almost certainly did not occur.

Hunt and Law, or Jones and Hewson?

Some accounts have identified Buddecke's ninth claim on 22 September 1916 as being 2nd Lieutenant K.F. Hunt (pilot) and Corporal L.O. Law (observer), of No. 25 Squadron flying F.E.2b number 6993.

Others have identified the downed plane as F.E.2b 4937 from No. 18 Squadron.[322] Almost certainly the victims were Sergeant T. Jones and 2nd Lieutenant F.A.A. Hewson of No. 18 Squadron, flying F.E.2b aircraft no. 6937, *Punjab 29 Rawalpindi.* Both crewmen were wounded and captured, as was the plane; Jones later died of his wounds. There is a picture of Buddecke standing in front of the aircraft at *Jasta 4*'s airfield at Roupy. Pilot Hewson was British, while his observer Jones was an Anglo-American from California.[323] Photos of the aircraft and Buddecke's note are in the photo section of this book.

Buddecke claims in his note that this was his eleventh victory. It appears to have been his ninth confirmed victory and that he is counting two planes from his time at Gallipoli as verified victories (30 March and 4 April). The German authorities did not confirm these claims.

Caudron:

The "big" Caudron was most likely a French-built Caudron G-4, which was a twin-engine bomber first flown in March 1915. It still used wing warping for lateral control. It was the first widely used two-engine aircraft. Some 1,421 were built, including twelve built in the United Kingdom by the British Caudron company. The observer/gunner was in the nose of the aircraft, able to fire forward (but not to the rear). It carried a bomb load of 100 kilograms (220 lb). In November 1916, the plane set a new altitude record of 7,950 meters (26,083 ft).

Wilhelm Frankl:

Wilhelm Frankl, who was Jewish, was born 1893. He learned to fly at his own expense in 1913. He joined the German Army at the start of the war and scored his first victory in May 1915 as an observer using a carbine to shoot down a French Voisin.

Switching to Fokkers, he got his first solo kill on 10 January 1916, became an ace on 4 May, and was awarded the *Pour le Mérite* on 12 August 1916 after nine kills.

He was credited with twenty kills by the time he died in combat on 8 April 1917. His Albatros D.III lost its lower wing under the stress of combat maneuvers.

He converted to Christianity in early 1917 in order to marry his Austrian fiancée. Still, his Jewish heritage resulted in his name and exploits being omitted from the German accounts during the 1930s until after World War II.

Georges Guynemer:

Georges Marie Ludovic Jules Guynemer was a top French ace in September 1916 with fourteen claimed kills as of the end of August.

Born in 1894 to a wealthy noble family, he was repeatedly rejected for military service because of his frail appearance. Finally joining the French air service in November 1914 as a mechanic, he became a pilot in April 1915. He scored his first victory on 19 July 1915 and became an ace on 3 February 1916 with two kills that day. He was made a *Chevalier de la Légion d'Honneur* (a Knight of the Legion of Honor) on Christmas Eve 1915.

He spent his entire flying career with Escadrille No. 3, the famous Stork squadron (*Les Cigognes*). Made an *Officier de la Légion d'Honneur* (an Officer of the Legion of Honor) on 11 June 1917, he died in combat 11 September 1917. He had fifty-three claimed victories, making him the second highest scoring French ace of the war.

Chapter 17

The Travelling Circus

By Hans Buddecke

After a four-month guest role in the West, it was back to the Dardanelles!

It was a long drive to get my travelling circus back out there. At last the orderlies, mechanics, and soldiers reached the small Anatolian town by sea with petrol barrels and storage equipment, camouflaged to hide them from enemy destroyers, and they set up my little tent in a meadow, a fertile valley between the mountains, on a riverbank overgrown with willows. I arrived a bit later. My plane's tail skid broke on a stone when I landed, and a wide club of willow wood replaced it.

The little biplane looked very sad. It was a different kind of fighting here from that in France. Everything was always available there, and one word was enough to get a new machine. Soon after I arrived, both tires went to hell; we had installed an axle for very heavy aircraft. Then the oppressive heat required double cooling apparatuses. My craft had endured these hot days, and the cold nights with rain showers, uncovered, which is why the wings wobbled worryingly against the fuselage when he was in the air.

My orderly had chosen the lovely spot for camp and was now brewing tea and toasting some bread. There was butter here, which seems to me worth mentioning. Eggs too, but that was all. This was how dinner was made, followed by a pipe of my personal blend. The kerosene lamp was quickly transformed into one for gasoline. We cut a hole in the glass with a file and then let it burn a little low; a contrivance that helped us above all else. The jackals could be heard screaming in the distance.

I had some concerns about the location of the place on the river. I expected that there would be a bunch of mosquitoes here, but nothing of the sort had shown up yet.

By half past ten I was sacked out. Our lights were out. I woke up for the first time at one. I don't remember whether it was from the screaming jackals, which now sounded like an army of baby carriages full of screaming babies, or from the burning of one half of my face. Mosquitoes.

The weather was very bad the next morning, even though the sun was shining. I could see nothing with one eye and little with the other. So I rode off to find a better camp.

The good peasants in their sky-blue trousers, their red belly scarves, and their little blue jackets must have taken me for the Devil incarnate.

Here, too, I was too far from the enemy and the route they probably had to fly to get to Smyrna.[324] My hunting area, however, extended 100 km to the north. So I got the circus moving again. I found a dried-up swamp across from the enemy's island, nicely hidden by mountains. I settled there. For days I watched the sky and hoped for my salvation on the telephone, which also belonged to the circus and was simply hooked on to the next line.

But in vain.

Thick clouds came up, rain flooded the land and washed the make-up from the face of my new location. It reverted into a swamp and the danger threatened that I would no longer be able to take off at all. In rain and storm I took off and returned to Smyrna.

When the sky there cleared, reports of my opponents started coming in again.

In the north, they had "visited" a small town; a telegram ordered the circus there. Two days later I landed on a small peninsula. It was a nice place, and not badly prepared.

A hollow carved into the stone, then a tent stretched over it as a roof. Over there a deeper trough for my plane and around it the tents for the personnel. The whole thing by the sea, and above all an observation post at the front of the beach, a shed from which my opponents could be spotted.

It took three days for him to report for the first time: "They are coming!" Ten minutes later, I saw five dots heading towards me at 2,000 m. I was happy – finally, after all the effort. Out of habit, my hands worked the levers of my plane.

The dots grew larger – a lattice tail in front, lower than me; a Nieuport behind it, also lower; and above me, another small plane.

Funny, I had no interest in the two below me; a dive would have been enough – perhaps – to bring them into my hand. I was sure that, if I could force an agreement with the gentleman above, I could politely invite him to land. I could have separated them, by fire, from the rest of their squadron. I could have taken them all.

But as it always is: if you get too cocky, you never succeed.

I left the two beneath me to proceed in peace as I rejoiced in all the colorful cockades; then I looked the gentleman above me in the eye.

He arced over and attempted to come at me from behind; but I also banked around to come at him as well.

We flew towards each other, firing head-on. One of my machine guns jammed, but I continued with the other.

Just before we collided, I pulled sharply away to control our movements. I was just thinking "So, my boy ..." when there was quite a surprise! My bird, as if seized by an unknown force, pointed sharply upwards, head over its wings, and falling, spun twice around.

I was speechless with anger (I like to talk to myself in air battles) – this was the effect of the sun, rain, and hard maneuvers.

After a fall of 200 meters, I regained control.

My opponent, who probably thought he had hit me, dove on me again; but I matched him, and we began to separate, flying in a widening circle.

Then my second MG also jammed.[325] As we wheeled about, I tried to clear first one, then the other.

Our battle became the epitome of hopelessness. Even apart from my trouble with my guns, it was not possible for me to hold my apparatus at my opponent's altitude and at the same time to get momentum, to throw myself onto his neck through a lightning-like curve. But over and over we bent apart and ran against each other again until we finally flew past each other at two meters distance.

I had become so indolent, I looked out at my wing to see if it would strike the enemy, thinking it was inevitable and of no more importance than just bumping into a passer-by in the street. Not even the slightest bit of excitement.

My opponent flashed past me like a ghost. Our combined speed meant that he was only a blur to my eyes. Like two passing trains.

Lo and behold, my friend flew home. Why? Did he have a meeting to attend?

A ray of hope. He left me his comrades who had dropped their bombs somewhere. I did not fly after him, but immediately started working on my rifles until they fired. My fingers – I couldn't get my gloves on in the rush – were bleeding from the sharp edges on the corners of the guns' sheet metal barrel shrouds.

Down on the landing field was an arrow. In its direction I saw the Nieuports and the lattice tail.

As I drove closer, one of the Nieuports turned – towards me. I was on his tail – both my guns jammed – he pulled up sharply – I banked – my aircraft turned – spun – there I was under him.

I was no longer angry. Now I was getting very sad. I barely reacted to the attack from above. I felt like this defense was beneath my dignity.

The levers of both machine guns were jammed solid. Nothing more to be done. I prevented the Nieuport from getting on my tail, and when he gave up to fly home with the lattice-tail, I flew a little ways over the sea with the two of them. One of them shot at me eagerly – I didn't care.

When I landed at the airfield, I tore the metal shrouds off the machine and behold, the configuration of the guns made shooting impossible. Which friend did this to me? The next day I worked on the bird from sunrise to evening, checking, tightening, oiling and testing. Faller, who was still here, had made telephone calls to request a new tail skid be brought by air. There was none. So I had to continue with the willow stick. We stood in the small tent, thickly covered with seaweed and beach plants, and complained about our fate. The ram he had brought with him on the plane bleated hungrily. My orderly simmered in a pan some fish that he had caught himself. To refresh ourselves we drank Dusiko, the drink of the country; became a little more fun again, enjoyed life and the beauty of the landscape and ended up with the conclusion that things couldn't be bad as long as one still has a plane with gasoline.

As there is sunshine, there is also rain. How many unsuccessful battles preceded the successes in France, how many times were there when you couldn't keep up, couldn't get close, when the guns wouldn't fire?

The deliveries of new aircraft by the various industries were noticeable every month, or every six months. Sometimes we had superior numbers, sometimes inferior. This explains the periods in which we suffered enormous losses of planes, though this was also in part because of mass deployments by the English (though not by the French, who always stayed behind their own lines).

So be patient. If you are a target today, you can be a shooter the day after tomorrow.

An urgent telegram called me to Smyrna. "Aircraft over the city."

I landed on the golf course early in the morning and stayed hidden. I used all means to keep my bird ready for action. I lurked like this for two days.

In the evening, when the threat was over and the light of the setting sun shone through a thousand windows far at the back of the mountain, I hunted jackals on horseback with my rifle across my saddle or stood under a mighty, isolated tree in the wide alluvial plain to look for eagles.

After three days Hassan came running over with a message: "Three planes at Smyrna."

The otherwise phlegmatic blood of these people became electrified. Mohamed George, the efficient old sergeant who had taken part in the Italian and Balkan wars and who had received the Iron Crescent from me for his medals, carefully took my pipe from the plane. Let's go.

Below me the white arrow lay on the green grass, pointing towards the city. Now there would be a battle over the city, which I did not want. Who could know the outcome of such a fight, which was to take place on the stage of a theater full of people of all nationalities? But when you get aloft you quickly forget the people down there.

I searched.

A speck – on my binoculars, or in space?

The point moves – in space. I open my eyes wide so as not to lose him. Getting bigger; come up here to me. Quite calmly, he bores on towards me. As if I were his friend. Is there anything under me? The lattice tail.

He realized his mistake too late. Immediately I got into position and fired. He defended himself by speeding up and slowing down, and banking until his engine stalled.

There's a rattling behind me. I spin around. A Nieuport, from above. I dive down, come back up against him. He breaks off his attack, wants to move on. I turn in his direction, line him up in my sights – over there you shoot for your life.

I calmly push the small plate on the wheel. My guns are working.

My opponent's right wing breaks away and he falls.

Instinctively, I kick the rudder and the wide expanse of the wing fills my view.

Above me, a third one I hadn't seen turned for home. It wasn't Lady Luck who let him survive to report on what he should have thwarted.

Chapter 18

Anatolian Images

By Hans Buddecke

February in southern Anatolia. The caravan moves slowly forward. These weak little horses beneath us have trodden this way a thousand times already, carrying a thousand different riders in their saddles. Our people and their luggage follow behind us in two wagons. Far behind are the ten camels dragging camp beds, tables, chairs, and storage equipment. The short day's march will soon be over.

On the right is a poisoned lake; all around us, chains of desolate mountains, behind which there rise mighty, massive, snow-capped peaks. It's not cold so we have left our furs on the wagon. We are just exiting a village of mud-walled huts when an eagle of a rare breed circles over our heads. We don't shoot at it. Why burden ourselves with unnecessary booty at the beginning of the journey?

The area to the left is also beginning to become barren. Mountains emerge that look like a child's beachwork. White sand – no bushes, no trees, no grass – nothing.

The city lies where a river emerges from the mountains in the wet season. The river floods the streets and flushes away the rubble of houses that an earthquake collapsed years ago, licking across the majestic churchyard, where stones pile up in colorful tangles.

On the right is the dead lake, in which neither fish nor worm lives; the roads avoid this area, bypassing miles to the north. What fool could have built this city? Nobody can tell us, not even the Bey with whom we stop to have a bite, who is the head man in town.

He can hardly read and write. His house, however, smells of rose oil, his coffee tastes like it, and in his gardens the roses shine in the most wonderful, richest colors...

Roses wherever you look. In one fell swoop we are back a millennium. There is a Turkish bath in the village. We walk through streets just wide enough for three men to walk abreast. A gutter in the middle serves as the sewer system.

Ahead of us a boy is carrying a large lantern, whose glow flits whimsically through the night.

In the anteroom of the hammam[326] we undress on white towels. There are only men here, but everyone is undressing, full of shame, as if women are watching. Before one's shirt falls, a bathing attendant has a red towel ready to quickly wrap around his hips, and a yellow sheet to drape around his shoulders.

A domed room with glass portholes extends above us. In the four corners of the square room, thick walls separate small washbasin niches.

Under the dome is an octagonal yellowish marble podium. It's hot from the hissing steam. We do not follow the example of the natives who stretch out here for hours to dream, but instead go into a washroom.

Two taps dispense hot and cold water into a basin where we crouch. The yellow cloth is thrown off the shoulders. There are two bowls at the edge of the pool. They are old but clean. Incidentally, they are very similar to those that are used to wash our hands with a little warm water and lemon after dinner. Exactly the same shape, the same material.

We draw the water and wash ourselves. The movement of scooping, the hot water and the warm air warms us up pleasantly.

Cautiously inquiring, the bath boy approaches, whipping foam with a small brush. He shyly pushes up the red towel to soap up the lower part of the body and then quickly rearranges it. Then we rinse ourselves with the bowls.

A little tired, but pleasantly clean after the days of driving through the Meander plain,[327] where at every small station we had to have a word with the station master and a stroll up to the locomotive, riding crop in hand, in order to shorten the train's stop.

Then we clatter on the wooden bathing shoes with their cothurn-like[328] construction through the vault into the anteroom, where a new, clean bed awaits us.

Wrapped up tightly, with turbans on our heads, we lie across from each other, give ourselves completely to the feeling of peace and cleanliness.

The house of the Bey has bare woodwork and whitewashed walls. We abide in the main room. He thinks the carpets and window coverings, both of which are disgustingly screaming colors, are beautiful. All around are cushions that invite you to sit up and lie down. They are covered in white; underneath red plush with gold embroidery comes to light. The hand towels and table napkins are also embroidered with gold.

Then we seat ourselves at his tables on old-fashioned upholstered chairs.

The Bey brings soup. It's good. After a while he carefully opens the door, brings a rice dish with meat, brings a bean dish, numerous other dishes, and finally brings in a sweet semolina dish that tastes like roses. Everything smells and tastes of roses.

We stretch out to rest from the exertions of the meal. But now comes the main meat course: spare ribs. It is only with great effort that we get through this course, believing we are finally free when the door opens again to admit the jewel of the meal, the mutton with rice. But it's still not enough. Poultry meat with nut sauce follows, a sweet dish made from puff pastry, sugar, fat and water. Then two small cups of coffee. He expresses his regret that there is no more.

Seldom, and only with great effort, does a word fall, to tear apart the comfortably sluggish silence. On thick mattresses, covered in white and red, embroidered with gold, which the Bey has spread out on the ground, we lie down and dream…

The drivers have already moved ahead. The area where we hunt is beautiful. There are no deer, but there are supposed to be a lot of pigs roaming the country. We have been on the road for a fortnight now. We have moved through bushes, half resembling forests so lush was their vegetation, through mountains, valleys, over wild shaped rocks and rich meadows.

The eye sees tracks everywhere. An old man leads us. The clothes of the people here are mostly white. They have beautiful, brown, well-proportioned faces, honest eyes, good character. He assigns us our posts and gives each man an escort.

I get myself set up. My companion pulls a piece of flat bread from his belt, tears off a piece, sprinkles cheese and nuts on it, clumps the whole thing into a cube and devours it.

High above me, not far from a rocky platform, the old man stands, well covered, on the mountain above. About half an hour has passed when I see the drivers moving down their respective slopes with their white, long-haired dogs. Noise and yapping fill this silent valley at the end of the world.

My Turk points to something in front of me that I neither see nor hear: "*Domus*!" ("Pigs!")

A native appears on top of the rock platform. He too is clothed completely in white, with an endlessly long, ancient blunderbuss. Next to him is Allianack,[329] the interpreter. The two excitedly point behind our line. The man lifts the gun to his beard. A mighty bang roars through the silence. Nothing else. Nothing stirs or moves.

Later we meet up with the drivers and have breakfast. They bring the piglet that the Turk shot. The brown, open faces above the gray and white flowing beards gather in a circle. One eats balls of bread, nuts, and cheese, looks calmly straight ahead, and keeps silent.

Then we ride on out of the silent valley over mountains, valleys, meadows, and towering rocks. For three days.

*

A little story flew to me here that I want to tell.

One of the crusaders who crossed the Hellespont and built castles in the ancient times came here. He recruited Seljuks[330] who had run away from the wild mountains, who lived by raiding the caravans of other robbers. He won land for his people and at last found his army arrayed before a strongly fortified city.

Before they stormed the city, they agreed to share the spoils among themselves. They had to think of their sustenance, because the land around them was deserted and empty. The captain approached the crusader-leader, clasped his hands, bowed humbly, and said, "Beyim, what do you want to be brought to you?"

The land was desolate and empty, and for a year he had seen only rocks and steel, so he, the infidel, said: "Bring me the most beautiful woman."

They took the city, looted all that was in it, and now had enough to eat until the next battle. And the centurion came and said:

"Bey, I bring what you desire."

And as he spoke he laid a pale head with black hair at his feet, and a torso by Phidias.[331]

*

The camels squat in the yard. Inquisitively, they turn their long skulls with the big clever eyes and haughty, superior noses, now to the right, now to the left, willing to be laden with the burdens of their lives, in order to carry them silently on felt-soft feet across the globe.

The Bey stands with his brothers at the gate. We give them amber pens and silver pencils as thank-you gifts.

Our route goes along the poisoned lake to the four sources of the Meander. There a Greek woman takes us into her clean hotel and roasts the wild boar that we captured in the south a week ago.

In the evening a local expert comes up to us and explains excitedly, as if the life and death of the whole country depended on it, that there are a lot of pigs here that have to be killed. He shows us how to defend ourselves in close combat.

The following day we are in the swamp. The reeds all around us are infested with pigs. They set fires and the flames are crackling. Dark smoke rises straight up to the sky, which flickers blue with the heat.

After an hour we go home. We haven't seen a single pig. That's how they are. The "expert" may have known for himself that none of the animals were here, but he thought a hunt would please us.

High above us, the snow peak of the Akdach[332] raises its head to the sky. There, in autumn, the deer call to each other.

*

We pitch our tent deep down on the vast plain. All around the spikes of mountaintops protrude into the blue sky. Ancient round towers of the infidels stand against the sea breeze that rushes up from the valley against them like the host of the descendants of Mohammed once did.

Hands and knees ache from climbing. The big bird whizzes past me as fast as an arrow around the edge of its eyrie. I hold my breath, don't move, press myself close against the wall. The fist clasps silently around the neck of the rifle.

Now he's nearby … I hear the rustle of his wings … past me … I shoot. The glowering giant peaks around me echo, their heads swimming in the blue of the sky. He falls hundreds of meters in a descent as fast as an arrow.

Too bad for him.

Chapter 19

Turkey, 1917

This last chapter in Buddeke's memoir is interesting because it shows that he liked to write. It is a series of descriptive and observational anecdotes, most which have nothing to do directly with the larger story of his military service. These episodes appear to have been recorded for their own sake. It is one of the few chapters that give us some insight into Buddecke's personality. Throughout his memoir, that is the challenge: his notes describe what he did, but they do not really describe who he was. This can be determined to some extent by certain passages and a little "reading between the lines."

First, it is clear that he was loyal to family and friends. His repeated references to Berthold show this, as does his hiding in the early text exactly who his uncle was, possibly to keep him from persecution in America.

Second, he seems to have had a sense of humor. This is shown by his rather sarcastic description of his female cousin and of the other flyers at Cicero Airfield.

It appears that Buddecke was a little arrogant or cocksure of himself. This is not particularly surprising for an ace fighter pilot; but it also shows up in his descriptions of his workmates at the car factory, his associates Orr and Linn, and his descriptions of the occupants of hangars 2–8.

His high-handed, caustic descriptions of Americans may have had a lot to do with when he wrote his passages, although they were probably not all written at the same time. We gather the book was compiled from his notes by his father, an effort which was completed in early 1918 (and it's reasonable to assume he intended to write more). The United States had joined the war on 6 April of 1917 and now was his enemy. It may have been an issue if he only said complimentary things about the people who were now their enemy, and he may have felt a need to go out of way to make negative remarks about Americans because of his background of having lived there and having family there. Still, one does not see any real negative remarks about the British and only one negative remark in passing about the French (mainly that their aircraft "always stayed behind their own lines," which, to be fair, was an order under which the Germans frequently operated as well). With a couple of exceptions, he does not say anything particularly negative about most of the Turkish people he interacts with although he does make some condescending references to some of his poorer Turkish associates as "sheiks" and "beys." Of course, there is nothing really negative about any Germans.

Still, a reader of his notes gets the sense that he sometimes looks down upon, or negatively evaluates, people he encounters. An example is his description of some of the Turks at Gallipoli in 1915 and of the Bey he met during his hunting trip in southern Anatolia in 1917. So, it does appear to be that there was some arrogance there and a certain sense of Euro-centric superiority, which shows up in spades with his description of his cousin as a "dollar-princess." This obvious slur on his American-based uncle's daughter was not going to help his family relations. Perhaps he never intended to return to America after the war was over, or if this was his first draft, it may have been edited out if he had been able to finish his book.

It is not known if Buddecke had actually assembled his notes in final form, or if this was done after his death by his family. If this was his first draft, then perhaps these passages would have been toned down or revised in the final draft. Still, it is odd that he would openly slur the daughter of his American-based uncle with whom he was obviously close, and who had helped him considerably in getting established in the United States – so established that he was able to launch an airplane construction business with a number of well-established investors. This is not access available to most people, especially not foreign newcomers.

One cannot rule out that German censors insisted upon a few anti-American statements and that they were inserted grudgingly by his father when the book was published, but the sarcastic descriptions of Orr and Linn and the occupants of hangars 2 through 8, not to mention his condescending depictions of most Turks, tend to argue that this was all part of his own writing and plan for the book. He notes his uncle turns into "a sober American businessman, interested only in numbers," and later provides a more extended description of Americans:

> The American is a courageous, intrepid man; he is tempted by danger. On the other hand, it seems incomprehensible to him, who only has a sense for his family, that there are noble families in Germany whose sons are aviators or who drive torpedo boats, although they don't need to put themselves in that danger. The first folk song the Americans came out with during the war was "I Didn't Raise My Boy to Be a Soldier."

This last observation is made by a German officer who grew up in a very militarized Germany.

Operations in Turkey:

It is not known why Buddecke returned to Turkey. Was it at his request or the request of Major Serno, or someone else? The Ottoman Empire, with the help of the Germans and at the request of Enver Pasha, was expanding its air force to 100 aircraft in 1917. Apparently his return to Turkey in December 1916 was part of that effort. While based initially in Smyrna (now called Izmir), he reported directly to Major Serno's headquarters in Constantinople and was in charge of all airmen in Gallipoli and Asia Minor, according to one of his calling cards.[333]

In 1917 Buddecke requested and was granted a full reinstatement in the military. He previously was on reserve status.[334] This is a strong indicator that he had decided that his future was going to be spent in Germany, as opposed to returning to Indianapolis after the war. He was now a German officer, following in the tradition of his father, and not an enterprising American businessman.

Buddecke's two claimed kills in second trip to Turkey, both confirmed:

Kill/ Claim	Date	Aircraft Type	Location	Notes
11	30 Mar 1917	Farman F.27	Smyrna	See Chapter 17. Junior Lieutenant B.A. Trechman (pilot) and Leading Midshipman W.A. Jones captured.
12	30 Mar 1917	Nieuport 12	Smyrna	See Chapter 17. Lieutenant J.E. Morgan (pilot) and Junior Lieutenant A. Sandell killed.

End of Turkish Service:

There is not much recorded as to what else Buddecke did in his sojourn of over a year in Turkey. He apparently gambled and at fairly high stakes, and was given a railway freight car in Smyrna in settlement of a gambling debt. This railway car operated on the rail from Smyrna, where Buddecke was based, to Panderma (now Bandirma) on the Sea of Marmara, around 180 miles away. He sold the freight car to a Jewish merchant and this apparently got him into trouble with Turkish authorities in early 1918.[335] It's not known whether the issue was that he sold it to a Jewish merchant, or if it was because they were using train cars for private business in the middle of the war. It was probably the latter, which is likely why it came to the attention of the Turkish high command. Operating such rail cars also required conducting other illicit activities, like bribing Turkish officials. Our knowledge of this incident comes from Major Serno's 1958 memoir, in which he says Buddecke "adapted to the Turkish custom" of bribery. As his previous business adventures in America were not always completely honest, this is not particularly surprising. This incident created a scandal that offended the Turkish high command. Major Serno was required to travel to Smyrna to deal with it. Buddecke then requested a transfer to the Western Front, which removed the "troublemaker" from Turkish service.[336]

Although the Ottoman Empire was a majority Muslim country, gambling was tolerated there. The penal code stated that gambling was punishable by six months of imprisonment and a fine, yet it appears that wartime Smyrna had at least one casino operating in the city that was probably visited by Buddecke, the president of the rail company, and the "Polish prince" he met while crossing the Atlantic incognito in August 1914.

The only reference to gambling in Buddecke's own account was of him and his fellow passengers playing poker during the crossing of the Atlantic to Italy, and the mention of his friend "the Polish prince." As Buddecke described his shipboard acquaintance with this man, and their encounter "two years later" (probably in 1917, but possibly 1916) at a club in Smyrna:

> The Polish prince intended to have a real prince's suit and boots made in Italy for the time being, and he would play it by ear from then on. For the time being, all his income came from the money he took from Mr. Noradungian at poker, as he told me two years later at a club in Smyrna, where he suddenly sat down across from me at my table one fine evening.

Indications are that Buddecke was a fairly serious and regular gambler. One can envision from his account he had become reacquainted with the Polish prince in an encounter in the Turkish casino.

Buddecke had certainly already taken a lot of risks in his life with acquiring a plane and teaching himself how to fly, making the Atlantic crossing in August 1914, and of course, becoming a famous ace. Risk-taking was in his nature. It is not that surprising to see him gambling or getting into trouble with authorities because of his activities. It is also not that surprising to see him involved in some questionable business practices in light of his entrepreneurial activities in the United States.

Chapter 20

The Western Front, 1918

The "Final Victory":

The foreword to his memoir by Buddecke's father refers to Germany's "final victory" with the statement that: "Death has taken the weapon and the pen out of his hand, and just as his burning desire to witness the German final victory remained unfulfilled, so will he no longer be able to enjoy the fruit of his spiritual work."

This was written in the spring of 1918. The "final victory" is certainly his perception of what the outcome of the German Spring Offensive, or the *Kaiserschlacht* (Kaiser's Battle) of 21 March to 18 July 1918, would be It was also known as Ludendorff's Offensive, named after General Erich Ludendorff, the First Quartermaster General of the German Staff.

On 8 November 1917 Vladimir Lenin, the head of the new Bolshevik government of Russia, signed a Decree of Peace stating their intention to end the war in the East. On 15 December 1917 an armistice was concluded between Soviet Russia and the Central Powers (Germany, Austria-Hungary, Bulgaria, and the Ottoman Empire). However, negotiations – and fighting – dragged on until the government of Russia signed the Treaty of Brest-Litovsk on 3 March 1918 with the Central Powers. Germany had already begun the transfer of troops from the Eastern Front to the Western before the permanent peace treaty was agreed to.

The German Spring Offensive was their chance to unleash the full force of their army against the weary British and the French before the full might of the fresh American army arrived on the Western Front.

This kindled the idea in the minds of many Germans that they could now finally win the war. This appears to have been what Buddecke's father thought.

In fact, the offensive stalled surprisingly quickly. The main prong, a hook to the north that was supposed to go all the way to the English Channel, stalled first. The Germans then shifted their focus to where they were making progress, which turned into a drive to the southwest. This had some tactical success but was strategically irrelevant. By June the German offensive had ended, having been stopped entirely by the British and French. The newly arriving American forces were beginning to deploy along the line, but had been held back from the fighting so that the could be employed offensively in a knockout blow.

Hans Buddecke returned to the Western Front in early 1918 (probably the first half of February) and was initially assigned to *Jagdstaffel 30*. *Jasta 30* was located in Phalempin, in French Flanders about fifty miles (eighty kilometers) north of his previous area of operations around Vaux. This unit was still using Pfalz D.IIIs in early 1918. *Jasta 30* was commanded by ace Hans Bethge, who scored his nineteenth kill on 19 February 1918 in conjunction with Buddecke. He scored his twentieth confirmed victory on 10 March 1918 and had been recommended for the Blue Max. He was killed in action on 17 March 1918 before receiving the medal.

Buddecke began service at *Jasta 30* on 15 February 1918.[337] Even though he had previously been a squadron commander in both Germany in 1916 and in Turkey in 1916–17, he was not brought back to command the squadron. Instead, he was just one of the pilots. This may have been a result of the controversy over his run-in with Ottoman authorities over the winning and sale of the freight car. He had twelve confirmed kills, had held command positions since

December 1915, and was the longest serving airman holding the Blue Max, all of which would seem to have made him a natural choice for command at the squadron level at least.

Buddecke had been the third pilot to be awarded the Blue Max, way back in April 1916. The first two pilots awarded the Blue Max (Immelmann and Boelcke) had been killed before the year was out, as was the case with the next three pilots who earned the award after him. Of the thirteen pilots awarded the Blue Max in 1916, only Buddecke, Althaus, and Berthold remained alive by early 1918. Over three-quarters of his peers were dead.

Buddecke was credited with one kill in February 1918. Four days after his return to the Western Front, he and his squadron commander, Bethge, engaged at least three Sopwith Camels from No. 80 Squadron. They each took down one and damaged a third plane, giving Buddecke his thirteenth victory and Bethge his nineteenth. Buddecke's victory is reported to have occurred at 1400 at Neuve Chapelle while Bethge's was Sopwith Camel B9185 at 1405 north of Lorgies. These locales are within two kilometers (1.4 miles) of each other. Buddecke's thirteenth kill ended the life of either 2nd Lieutenant S.R. Pinder or 2nd Lieutenant E. Westermoreland. They were both No. 80 Squadron pilots that went down that day.

Some sources claim this encounter occurred while Buddecke was attached to *Jasta 18*, but it was in fact while he was still with *Jasta 30*.[338] He does not discuss this period of his life in his book. He then transferred to *Jasta 18*, which was commanded by Senior Lieutenant Ernst Turck. Rudolf Berthold was in command of air wing *Jagdgruppe 7*, to which *Jasta 18* reported.

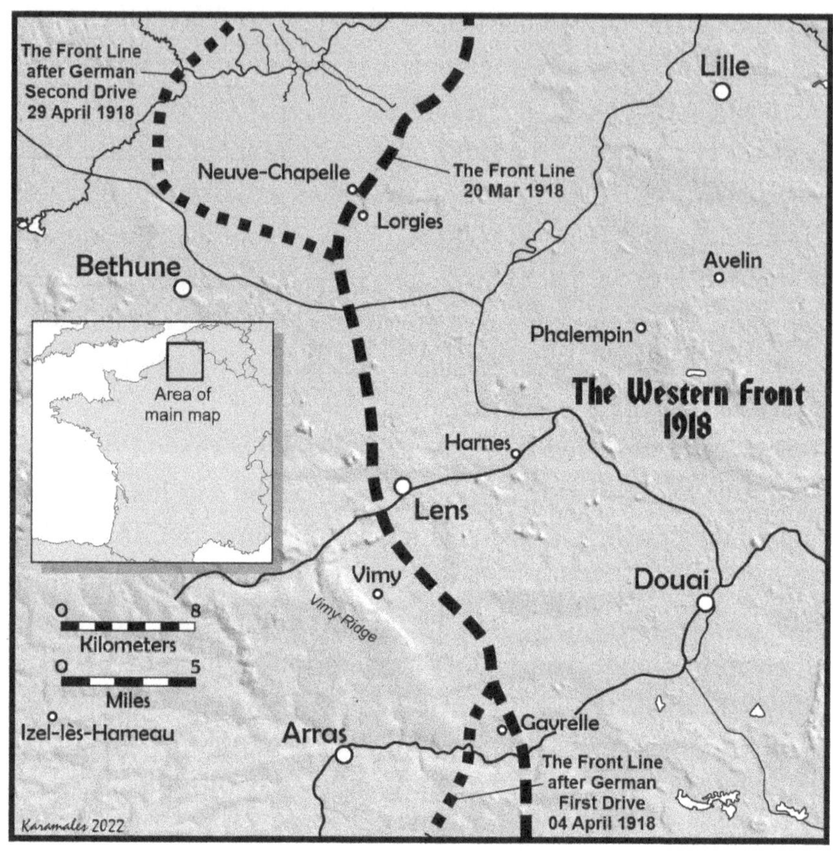

Buddecke's final claimed kill on the Western Front in February 1918:

Kill/Claim	Date	Aircraft Type	Location	Notes
13	19 Feb 1918	Sopwith Camel	Neuve Chapelle	Not discussed.

While Buddecke was still on his second tour in Turkey, Rudolf Berthold had commanded *Jasta 14* and was wounded again on 24 April 1917. After hospitalization and rest, he remained in command of the *jagdstaffel*, but was not cleared to fly. He was then transferred on 12 August to command *Jagdstaffel 18*. This unit was located in

Flanders, where the fighting was much more intense. It was decided to combine the four *Jagdstaffeln* in the Fourth Army area under a newly formed *Jagdgruppe 7*. Berthold took command of this fighter group, which consisted of *Jastas* 18, 24, 31, and 36, on 6 March 1918.

When Berthold returned to flying in August 1917 he had a dozen confirmed kills, and in a seven-week period scored another sixteen victories. Having been deployed continually in combat now for over three years, Berthold had run a score by early October 1917 of twenty-eight confirmed kills, half of them made in September 1917. He was then wounded once more on 10 October 1917 and did not fly again until May 1918.

In contrast, Buddecke's total was twelve confirmed kills. On 23 September 1916, Buddecke scored his tenth confirmed kill while Berthold had scored his eighth confirmed kill three days later on the 26th. In 1917 Buddecke scored two kills, while Berthold scored twenty. Now the two aces were reunited.

Two days after taking command of *Jagdgruppe 7*, on 8 March 1918, Berthold arranged for his friend Buddecke to transfer to his old unit, *Jasta 18,* also in French Flanders. At that time, Berthold was listed in the German *Luftwaffe* magazine as Germany's third highest-scoring living ace,[339] but he was still not cleared to fly because of his injuries.

The plan was for Berthold to lead *Jasta 18* on the ground (in addition to commanding the *Jagdgruppe*) while Buddecke led them unofficially in the air.[340] This was probably an arrangement by Berthold because his friend Buddecke was not allowed to actually hold a command at this time. The arrangement did not last long.

On 10 March Buddecke led a patrol of Albatroses south of the airfield at Avelin towards Lens. The weather was good but hazy, and visibility was poor. At around 1:00 p.m. to the east of Lens, Buddecke's patrol was surprised by a flight of Sopwith Camels from the 'C' flight of No. 3 (Naval) Squadron. To quote from the combat report made by 24-year-old Canadian Flight Lieutenant Arthur Treloar Whealy:[341]

> I dived down with my flight on about seven or eight enemy aircraft. After pulling out of a dive on one enemy aircraft I saw another to my left about 500 ft. below, heading away from me. I immediately dived on his tail and opened fire at about 100 yards, firing a burst of about forty rounds from each gun. The enemy aircraft turned half over onto its back and went down in a series of stalls and spins. I watched it till it was about 3,000-4,000 ft. above the ground and then lost sight of it on account of the haze, but I feel fairly certain that I hit the pilot. Other pilots of the patrol observed the enemy aircraft crash.

Whealy's own personal diary has this version:

> Sun. March 10 1918
>
> Went out on an Escort and O.P. at 12:00 a.m. [presumably he means noon.] B & C Flights were to go together. C as a close escort & B as a high escort. Six machines each. B flight failed to pick us up, so we (C flight) went along with the R.E.8. He took us nearly to Douai, about seven miles over at 5,000 ft. It was too low to be comfortable. On the way out a Hun dived on us, but didn't come close enough for me to get a good shot at him. I was leading the top three machines in our flight and had a new chap, SMITH, with me. The Hun kept diving & firing on SMITH's tail and I knew SMITH didn't see him, so I had to S turn as hard as I could to keep SMITH S turning, so that the Hun could not get a good shot at him. After escorting the R.E.8 back to the line we carried on an O.P. Met 'B' flight scrapping with about ten Huns back of Lens. We joined in the scrap and I feel sure that I did in one of the Huns, an Albatros scout. (Decisively).[342]

Hans Buddecke crashed on the German side of the lines at Harnes, northeast of Lens. He was 27. His father states in this book that "a stray bullet struck him in the heart."

He was shot down by Captain Arthur Treloar Whealy, the "C" Flight commander of the No. 3 (Naval) Squadron, who claimed an Albatros D.V two miles east of Lens. The new No. 3 (Naval) Squadron to which Whealy belonged, had been recently renamed on 17 February 1918 as the 203rd Squadron (RFC), and was not the same squadron that was deployed for so long in the Gallipoli Campaign at Tenedos and Imbros. That squadron (wing), one of Buddecke's opponents in Turkey, had been disbanded in early 1916 and a new squadron formed on 5 November 1916.

A memorial service was held near Avelin, *Jasta 18*'s base; afterwards Hans-Joachim Buddecke's remains were transported by train to Berlin and buried on 22 March at *Invalidenfriedhof* Cemetery.[343]

Invalidenfriedhof Cemetery in Berlin is the traditional resting place for the Prussian Army. The cemetery includes such notables as Gerhard Johan David von Scharnhorst (1813), Alfred von Schlieffen (1913), Helmuth Johannes Ludwig von Moltke (1916), Buddecke's good friend Rudolf Berthold (1920), Karl von Bülow (1921), Ludwig von Falkenhausen (1936), Ernst Udet (1941), and a number of unsavory characters from World War II.

Hans-Joachim Buddecke's gravestone was designed by German artist Christoph Natter. His name on the stone is given only as Hans-Joachim, even though his full name was Adolf August Hans Joachim Buddecke. He left behind no children that we are aware of. There is no record of him ever being in a relationship, although such things are not always reported in the biographies and autobiographies of the time.

Arthur Treloar Whealy:

Arthur Whealy was born in Toronto, Canada, in 1895. He was a medical student at the University of Toronto before the war started.

He learned to fly at his own expense, receiving his aviator's certificate on 5 February 1916 at the Atlantic Coast Aeronautic School (also known as the Curtiss Flying School) in Newport News, Virginia. He was commissioned in the Canadian Army on 29 February 1916.

On 24 August 1916 he was posted to the No. 3 (Naval) Wing, and served in the both the new No. 3 and No. 9 (Naval) Squadrons in that wing. His first victory was on 12 April 1917; he became an ace on 7 July 1917, having scored his first five victories flying a Sopwith Pup. He claimed two subsequent kills flying a Sopwith Triplane, and then flew Sopwith Camels for the rest of the war.

Hans Buddecke was claimed as Whealy's tenth kill, an Albatros D.V two miles east of Lens. Whealy would later be credited with twenty-seven kills (five were shared), most of which were fighters.[344] He was posted to the Home Establishment on 24 September 1918.

Whealy would survive the war, logging 521 hours of flight time before Armistice Day. He worked in the family paper box manufacturing business after the war and passed away from a heart attack in 1945 in Canada at the age of 50.

List of Aircraft Flown by Hans Buddecke:

May-July 1914: U.S. built Nieuport IV monoplane copy
September – November 1914: Albatros B.I[345]
November 1914 to before June 1915 (with FFA 27): LVG B.I[346]
Before June to July 1915 (with FFA 23): Albatros B.I.,[347] Rumpler B.I, and Albatros B.II
July – December 1915: Fokker E.I (2/15 or 4/15 or 15/15 and occasionally 36/15)
December 1915 – August 1916: Fokker E.III (96/15 and perhaps 108/15)
August – December 1916 (*Jasta 4*): Halberstadt D.V[348]
1917 (FA 5): Halberstadt D.II or D.III, Halberstadt D.V[349]
Early 1918 (*Jasta 30*): Pfalz D.IIIa
March 1918 (*Jasta 18*): Albatros D.V.

Buddecke's final count:

Hans Buddecke was officially credited with thirteen kills. In Appendix I he is listed with thirteen confirmed kills and six unconfirmed kills. Two of those unconfirmed kills, on 6 January 1916 and 11 January 1916, almost certainly occurred; the others probably did not. There is a strong reason to doubt his confirmed kills of 25 and 27 January. His confirmed kill on 6 or 16 September has also not been clearly established as correct, but there is no strong reason to doubt it. Of his thirteen victories in three years, eleven were two-seaters and only two were single-seat fighters (a B.E.12 and a Sopwith Camel). Three of the two-seaters did not have an observer (i.e., someone who could fire back at him). A total of eleven men have been identified as killed in action by him; with an additional five wounded and captured, of whom two died of wounds, and three were possibly captured uninjured. Six men survived being shot down by him, thirteen did not. Possibly another two men were killed in the confirmed kill on 6 or 16 September, whose occupants have yet to be identified. Hans Buddecke himself was also shot down one time before his death, but that time he was not injured.

Chapter 21

Afterword

As in the original book

Adolf August Hans Joachim Buddecke was born on 22 August 1890 as the son of the then-lieutenant in the 1st Grand Ducal Hessian Infantry (Life Guard) Regiment No. 115, Albert Buddecke, during his command of the War Academy in Berlin. He attended the grammar schools in Potsdam, Strasbourg in Alsace, and Charlottenburg, and joined the Cadet Corps in the spring of 1904, where he went through to the Selekta. He passed the officer examination with the grade "good" and in the spring of 1910 became a lieutenant in the Life Guard Infantry Regiment 1st Grand Ducal Hessian No. 115, but retired from military service in the spring of 1913, when he was transferred to the regiment's reserve officers, in order to create a new career in the United States of North America. With an iron diligence, he succeeded there in quickly working his way up, opening up the prospect of a happy future, when the war broke out. In August 1914, he enthusiastically rushed back to his homeland to protect the severely endangered Fatherland. Despite all the dangers, he was able to reach European soil with other comrades on a Greek steamer which landed in Italy, which was still neutral at the time, and made himself available for aviation service at his old garrison in Darmstadt at the end of August, bringing with him the skills he taught himself in America to now put into practice in the service of a larger cause. After a short training period, he was sent to the Western Front in September 1914 and soon became energetically and successfully active in reconnaissance and combat flights. When we acquired the first aerial combat capability with the Fokker aircraft, he was, along with Immelmann and Boelcke, the one who most successfully demonstrated the superiority of this weapon. By 1915 his victories in aerial combat had already won him both Iron Crosses,[350] the Knight's Cross with Swords of the Hohenzollern House Order,[351] the Royal Saxon Military St. Order of Henry,[352] and other war decorations. Transferred to the German military mission in Turkey at the end of 1915, he was allowed to take a decisive part in the heavy fighting on Gallipoli. Almost without any support, he succeeded, with boldness and technical superiority, in beating the English who, appearing in squadrons and completely dominating the airspace, were inflicting tremendous damage on our Turkish allies every day by dropping bombs, driving them from the field in a short time and robbing them of their ability to conduct aerial reconnaissance, thus contributing to the liberation of the country from the English invasion. For this act his Imperial Commander-in-Chief rewarded him with the order *Pour le Mérite*, which he received in May 1916,[353] while His Majesty the Sultan bestowed on him his highest war award, the Great Golden Imtiaz Medal.[354] From September to December 1916 he was, at his request, transferred back to the Western Front in France and won several aerial victories as the leader of a fighter squadron. In January 1917 he returned to Turkey and was the faithful guardian of the skies over the Dardanelles for a year. Just the presence of the German fighter pilot, to whom the Turks gave the honorary name *Shahin* (falcon), was enough to keep away the enemy planes stationed on the occupied islands. But if they dared to attack, he struck them a couple of heavy blows, as last year when he shot down two English planes in one flight over Smyrna. The city thanked its protector by awarding him a precious gold plaque. In the meantime, he was also reactivated by his old regiment.

In response to his ardent desire to serve the fatherland directly again and to lend it his tried and tested strength in the coming decisive battles, he was transferred to the Western Front in early 1918. After a few successful battles, he took to the air on March 10th of this year in the Lille area as the leader of a fighter squadron of only seven aircraft, to oppose an English squadron of eighteen aircraft which had advanced over our lines. In the victorious flight close behind our infantry lines, a stray bullet struck him in the heart and ended the young, hopeful life of the aviator hero. His burial took place on March 22nd in his native soil in the *Invalidenfriedhof* Cemetery churchyard in Berlin.

Chapter 22

Final Comments

All the early Fokker pilots were like bright meteorites, flashing briefly before falling to earth. Of the initial five pilots who were made famous because of the "Fokker Scourge," Max Immelmann (seventeen kills) was the first to go, killed in action or, ironically, by a failed synchronizer gear on 18 June 1916 at the age of 25. Otto Parschau (eight kills) was next, shot down on 21 July 1916 also at the age of 25. Kurt Wintgens (nineteen kills) went down on 25 September 1916 at the age of 22. He was followed to the grave by Oswald Boelcke (forty kills) on 28 October 1916, at the age of 25. When Buddecke died in spring 1918, he was credited with 13 confirmed and six unconfirmed kills.

Buddecke's close friend, Rudolf Berthold (forty-four kills) survived the war, only to be killed by fellow Germans on 15 March 1920 at the age of 28 in Hamburg, as described elsewhere.

Ernst Freiherr von Altaus lasted much longer. He is credited with nine confirmed aerial victories before his failing eyesight caused his removal from aerial combat in July 1917. He then took command of an infantry company at Verdun, where he was captured by Americans on 15 October 1918. Repatriated to Germany in September 1919, he became a lawyer after the war, even though he had a total loss of vision by 1937. During World War II he was the director of the County Court in Berlin. He passed away due to illness in 1946 at the age of 56.

Hans Buddecke was in America, setting up a business, when the war began. One wonders what would have become of these shooting stars if the Great War had not taken over their lives. Would Buddecke have become a successful and established Indianapolis businessman like his uncle? Would he have taken a German-American wife and remained an American for the rest of his life? Would there be generations of Buddecke children, grandchildren, and great grandchildren in the American Midwest? Would he have remained in aviation the rest of his life? How would he have dealt with Prohibition and the Great Depression, which gutted his uncle's and his cousin Kurt Vonnegut's businesses?

If war had not come, would Max Immelmann have become a successful engineer? Would Oswald Boelcke help lead the German Modern Pentathlon team to an Olympic medal in 1916? What of the rest of these pilots and pioneers? Would we have ever heard of them if the Great War had not occurred?

As the authors of a book on Hans Buddecke, we still do not understand him or really know who he was. He was confident. He may have been arrogant. He appears to be straightforward but not always honest, as his entire business plan in America was based upon a series of outrageous lies. He served Germany with honor, even making an extraordinary effort to return home when the war started, but his business dealings were not always honest, even in wartime. He protected his American uncle, hiding his name, but then insulted his cousin Sophie. He had no hesitation in insulting and putting down some people, but was highly supportive of others. He clearly had some good friends, like Rudolf Berthold, but he doesn't seem to have had a lot of friends. He was hardworking, ambitious, and driven; and was a man with considerable talent in several fields.

Still, there are elements of his story that are troubling. For example, he states early in his book:

> Twice before, I had been interested in military ventures. The first time was when I wanted to set up a volunteer machine gun unit with some acquaintances and go kill Mexicans. The other revolved around an island on the Mexican coast that belonged

> to a Chicago family. The Mexicans had occupied and looted this patch of earth. When diplomacy failed, the family set about trying to raise a private force to exact some justice. But nothing came of it.

We assume both of these adventures were tied to his time in America, so it appears he arrived in America and began immediately toying with the idea of going on filibuster expeditions or contracting himself out as a mercenary. This indicates that he really was drifting around trying to find his purpose in America. Apparently that purpose may have included killing Mexicans if it were convenient and profitable.

As noted earlier, he apparently was a high-stakes gambler, and his gambling got him into trouble. The nature and extent of the trouble was probably more than just gambling, he may have been involved in illicit business. One could argue that his gambling led directly to his death.

Perhaps his father, a lieutenant colonel on the German General Staff, felt the need to publish a book on his son quickly, so as to preserve and protect his reputation. Considering his position, he was probably aware of some of the problems in which his son was involved.

We don't really have a good feel for the person though. He certainly was adventurous and brave. He was not always honest. Was he someone likeable? Was this someone we would like to have a beer with?

The Survivors:

Hans Buddecke did not survive the war, although his wartime notes did. Many of the friends and associates he flew with also did not survive. Those who did survive include Rudolf Berthold, Ernst Althaus (both Blue Max winners in 1916), Hans Schüz, and Erich Muhra. There were a number of survivors among the aces in *Jasta 18*, although it appears they only worked with Hans Buddecke for three days. They include Josef Veltjens, Georg von Hantelmann, Johannes Klein, Hugo Schäfer, and Arthur Rahn.

Hugo Schäfer (eleven confirmed kills) was the first of these Great War survivors to die, dying in a flying accident on 3 February 1920. He was 25 years old.

Rudolf Berthold (forty-four confirmed kills), as we have seen, died in postwar political violence.

Georg von Hantelmann (twenty-five confirmed kills) was killed 7 September 1924 on his farm in Prussia by Polish poachers. He was 25 years old.

Johannes Klein (sixteen confirmed kills) died in 1926. His age and the circumstances of his death are not known.

Hans Schüz (ten confirmed kills) died in a plane crash in 31 August 1941 flying over the Mediterranean Sea. He was a major general in the Luftwaffe at the time and was probably under 50 years old.[355]

Theodor Croneiss (five confirmed kills) may never have met Hans Buddecke. As we have seen, he died at age 47 of natural causes, as did Ernst Freiherr von Althaus at the age of 56.

Josef Veltjens ended the war as the 11th highest scoring surviving ace (and 18th overall among all German aces, tied with four other pilots). He was wounded in 1919 while fighting German communists in Bremen. He joined the Nazi Party in 1929 and resigned from it in 1931. He then worked as an arms dealer between the wars. On 6 October 1943 he died in plane crash flying in a Junkers 52 that crashed into Monte Cervellino in northern Italy. He was a lieutenant colonel in the Luftwaffe at that time, despite having left the Party. He was 49 years old.

Arthur Rahn (six confirmed kills) migrated to the United States in 1928 and almost made it to retirement age, passing away in Redford, Michigan, on 27 April 1962 at 64.

Dr. Erich Muhra lived to a ripe old age of 76. He served as a lawyer both during and after World War II, in addition to holding some command positions. He was an officer in the Luftwaffe during the World War II, with the rank of major as of 1943. He passed away in 1972.

Arthur Treloar Whealy, the man who shot Buddecke down, passed away from natural causes in 1945 at the age of 50.

Appendix I

List of Hans Buddecke's Kill Claims

Kill/Claim	Date	Aircraft Type	Location	Notes
1	19 Sep 1915	B.E.2c	Near St. Quentin	See Chapter 7. Lieutenant W.H. Nixon killed and Captain J.N.S. Stott captured.
2	23 Oct 1915	B.E.2c	St. Quentin	See Chapter 8. Captain C.H. Marks and Lieutenant William G. Lawrence killed.
3	11 Nov 1915	B.E.2c	Near St. Quentin	Not discussed. Lieutenant W.A. Harvey wounded and captured.
4	06 Jan 1916	Farman	E of Cape Narors	See Chapter 12. Probably was Maurice Farman MF.11 number 942 of Escadrille MF-98T piloted by *Ltt* Jules Charles Lecompte
Unconfirmed	06 Jan 1916	Farman	E of Jalova	See Chapter 12. Probably was Flight Commander Hans Acworth Busk, who was killed.
Unconfirmed	09 Jan 1916	Farman	Off C. Helles	Not discussed.
Unconfirmed	11 Jan 1916	Farman	Jalvari, C. Helles	See Chapter 12. Australian Flight Lieutenant Cecil H. Brinsmead and British Lieutenant Noel Henry Boles killed.
5	12 Jan 1916	Farman	Galata	See Chapter 12. Flight Junior Lieutenant James Sydney Bolas killed; Observer Midshipman Douglas Montagu Branson wounded and captured.

Kill/Claim	Date	Aircraft Type	Location	Notes
6	25 Jan 1916	Farman	Near Dardanelles	Not discussed.
Unconfirmed	26 Jan 1916	Farman	Near Dardanelles	Not discussed.
7	27 Jan 1916	Farman	Seddülbahir	Not discussed.
Unconfirmed	30 Mar 1916	Farman	Seddülbahir	See Chapter 12.
Unconfirmed	04 Apr 1916	Farman	E of Feahie, Gallipoli	Not discussed.
8	06/16 Sep 1916	F.E.2b	Chaulnes	See Chapter 14. Buddecke refers to the plane as a "Caudron" in his text, and the text implies that he shot down three of them on this day.
9	22 Sep 1916	F.E.2b	Combles	Not discussed. Sergeant T. Jones and 2nd Lieutenant F.A.A. Hewson wounded and captured. Jones died of wounds.
10	23 Sep 1916	B.E.12	Sailly	Not discussed. Lieutenant J.M.J. Kenney wounded and captured. Died of wounds.
11	30 Mar 1917	Farman F.27	Smyrna	See Chapter 17. Junior Lieutenant B.A. Trechman (pilot) and Leading Midshipman W.A. Jones captured.
12	30 Mar 1917	Nieuport 12	Smyrna	See Chapter 17. Lieutenant J.E. Morgan (pilot) and Junior Lieutenant A. Sandell killed.
13	19 Feb 1918	Sopwith Camel	Neuve Chapelle	Not discussed.

The "confirmed" kills were verified by the German command or reported by German newspaper accounts during the war. They may not have actually happened. The unconfirmed kills are those claimed by the pilot that could not be confirmed by German witnesses during the war.

There is a strong reason to doubt his confirmed kills of 25 and 27 January. His confirmed kill on 6 or 16 September has also not been clearly established as correct, but there is no strong reason to doubt it. Two of those unconfirmed kills, on 6 January 1916 and 11 January 1916, almost certainly occurred. The rest of his unconfirmed kills probably did not occur.

Some tallies of Buddecke's victories include a claimed, but unconfirmed, kill for 6 December 1915. It is not listed above, as it clearly could not have happened.[356] Of these nineteen kills, Buddecke only discusses ten of them in his account.

Appendix II

Timeline of Hans Buddecke's Account

Buddecke's memoir does not always provide a rigid timeline. Examining the events he describes, and cross-referencing them to other sources, makes it possible to assemble a timeline of events in and around his life.

Date	**Event**
22 August 1890	Hans-Joachim Buddecke is born in Berlin.
Spring 1904	Buddecke joins the cadet corps.
Spring 1910	Buddecke is commissioned a Lieutenant in the 115th Life Guards Infantry Regiment.
Spring 1913	Buddecke leaves service.
22 November 1913	Edith Sophia Lieber is married to Kurt Vonnegut Sr.
Late 1913–early 1914	Buddecke moves to America.
22 February 1914	*The Indianapolis Star* publishes its first story on Hans Buddecke.
6–7 March 1914	Articles of Incorporation and the formation of the Aerial Advertising Company of America are reported in *The Indianapolis News* and *The Indianapolis Star.*
May – mid-July 1914	Buddecke at Cicero Field.
20 May 1914	Buddecke buys his Nieuport-like monoplane.
25 May 1914	*The Indianapolis News* reports that the Indianapolis Brewing Company purchased a plane.
28 June 1914	Archduke Franz Ferdinand is assassinated in Sarajevo.
22 July 1914	*The Indianapolis Star,* in an article on Buddecke, reports that he returned to Indianapolis about a week ago.
23 July 1914	Buddecke mentioned in *The Indianapolis Star.*

Date	Event
28 July 1914	Austria-Hungary declares war on Serbia.
30 July 1914	Russia orders general mobilization.
31 July 1914	Article in *The Indianapolis News* about Buddecke flying over the city.
1 August 1914	Germany declares war on Russia.
3 August 1914	Germany declares war on France.
3 August 1914	Buddecke and his uncle attend a meeting of Germans in Indianapolis.
3 August 1914	Buddecke starts his trip to New York City.
4 August 1914	Germany declares war on, and invades, Belgium.
4 August 1914	The United Kingdom declares war on Germany.
4 August 1914	Both *The Indianapolis Star* and *The Indianapolis News* report on German reservists.
7 August 1914	*The Indianapolis Star* has another article on German reservists.
Late August 1914	Buddecke returns to Germany by ship.
End of August	Reports to old garrison in Darmstadt.
29 August 1914	Bernard Vonnegut is born.
2 September 1914	Buddecke assigned to FEA at Darmstadt.
27 September 1914	Assigned to FEA 3.
20 October 1914	Assigned to training camp (EFP 2).
November 1914	Meets Berthold in training camp.
2 November 1914	Russia declares war on Turkey.
11 November 1914	Ottoman Empire declares war on the Entente.
15 November 1914	Article mentioning Buddecke in *The Indianapolis Star.*
12 January 1915	Assigned to FFA 27.
11 April 1915	The first wartime article on Buddecke is published in *The Indianapolis Star.*
25 April 1915	The Allies make the first amphibious landings at Gallipoli.
10 June 1915	Buddecke assigned to FFA 23.
1 or 15 July 1916	Wintgens shoots down first enemy plane using a Fokker.
27 August 1915	*The Indianapolis News* reports on Buddecke receiving the Iron Cross 1st Class.
September 1915	One Fokker monoplane arrives at Canakkale.

Date	Event
19 September 1915	Buddecke scores his first victory near St. Quentin in northern France.
19 September 1915	Boelcke shoots down his third aircraft.
21 September 1915	Immelmann shoots down his third aircraft.
23 October 1915	Buddecke shoots down William Lawrence (it was his second victory).
11 November 1915	Buddecke scores his third victory.
3 January 1916	Three Fokker monoplanes arrive at Gallipoli.
6–12 January 1916	Buddecke claims two confirmed and three unconfirmed kills around Gallipoli.
8 January 1916	Theodor Croneiss shoots down a Farman at Gallipoli.
9 January 1916	The British withdraw from Cape Helles.
12 January 1916	Immelmann and Boelcke awarded the Blue Max.
18 January 1916	Article on Buddecke in the *Palladium* of Richmond, Indiana.
25–27 January 1916	Buddecke gets two confirmed victories and one unconfirmed victory around Gallipoli.
13 March 1916	Article on Buddecke in *The Muncie Morning Star.* This appears to be the last article planted by his uncle.
30 Mar – 4 Apr 1916	Buddecke gets two unconfirmed victories around Gallipoli.
14 April 1916	Buddecke is awarded the Blue Max.
1 May 1916	*The Indianapolis News* reports about Buddecke being awarded the Blue Max.
18 June 1916	Immelmann dies in combat.
1 July 1916	Kurt Wintgens is awarded the Blue Max.
20 July 1916	Boelcke first mentions meeting Buddecke in Smyrna, Turkey.
21 July 1916	Otto Parschau is shot down.
25 July 1916	Buddecke prevents Boelcke from flying home.
Mid-August 1916	Buddecke leaves Turkey.
25 August 1916	Assigned to *Jasta 4.*
6–23 September 1916	Buddecke gets three confirmed victories on the Western Front in northern France (eighth through tenth victories)
25 September 1916	Kurt Wintgens is killed in action.

Date	Event
28 October 1916	Oswald Boelcke is lost (mid-air collision during combat).
Early December	Buddecke leaves Western Front
3/5 December 1916	Berthold is using Buddecke's old Fokker.
January 1917	Returns to Turkey.
30 March 1917	Buddecke gets two victories at Smyrna, Turkey.
6 April 1917	The United States declares war on Germany.
15 February 1918	Assigned to *Jasta 30.*
19 February 1918	Buddecke shoots down a Sopwith Camel at Neuve Chapelle. This was his 13th and last victory.
8 March 1918	Buddecke transfers to *Jasta 18* at Berthold's instigation.
10 March 1918	Hans Buddecke is shot down and killed near Lille, France.
21 March 1918	The beginning of the German Spring Offensive, the *Kaiserschlacht.*
22 March 1918	Hans-Joachim Buddecke is buried at *Invalidenfriedhof* churchyard cemetery in Berlin.
Spring 1918	Buddecke's book, *The Hunting Falcon* is published.
11 November 1918	Armistice ends the Great War.
11 November 1922	Kurt Vonnegut, Jr. is born.

Endnotes

1. The book was found at website for Eberhard Karls Universitat Tübingen, Universitatsbibliothek. See: http://idb.ub.uni-tuebingen.de/opendigi/Kg3461#p=2
2. A Life Guard regiment is one that was intended to serve as a bodyguard to the royal or ducal families. The two German Army Life Guard units were the 115th (1st Grand Ducal Hessian) Life Guard Infantry and the Royal Bavarian Infantry Life Guard Regiment.
3. This is the foreword to the original memoir of Lieutenant Hans Buddecke. It was written by his father after Buddecke's demise in combat. The book is called *El Schahin (Der Jagdfalke) Aus meinem Fleigerleben*, or the *Hunting Falcon: from my life as a flyer* by 1st Lieutenant Hans Joachim Buddecke (deceased). "With nine illustrations. Printed and published by August Scherl LLC, Berlin." It is not dated, but is assumed to have been published in April or May 1918. The actual book had only nine photos in it and no other illustrations.
4. The reference to the "final victory" is almost certainly because of the ongoing German spring offensive of 1918. See the discussion on this in Chapter 20.
5. The *Siegessäule*, or Berlin Victory Column, is a monument completed in 1873 to commemorate Prussia's victory in the 1864 Danish-Prussian War. The monument itself is now much more well-known than the all-but-forgotten war.
6. "Häns" and "Ämörrikä" are deliberate misspellings probably intended to make fun of his cousin's American-English accent when she spoke German.
7. His uncle was Albert Lieber (1863–1934). His female cousin was Edith Sophia Lieber (1888–1944).
8. "Dollar princess" was a disparaging term used by Europeans around the turn of the twentieth century to refer to American girls from wealthy families, particularly those who would visit Europe in hopes of meeting

and marrying men with land and/or titles. It was the title of a famous German operetta first performed in Vienna in 1907. The English language version ran in London and Broadway in 1909 and was quite popular at the time. There are four references to the play in *The Indianapolis Star* in 1913. It seems odd that Buddecke would use this term to refer to his cousin Edith, for whom he otherwise seemed to have tender feelings.

9. Mignon is the title of a poem by Johann Wolfgang von Goethe first published in 1797. Franz Schubert wrote several songs, or *lieder*, based around the character Mignon. One was titled *Kennst du das Land?* (Op. 62/D 321), composed in 1815. It was later made into a waltz by Johann Strauss Jr. (*Wo die Zitronen blühen*, Op. 364, 1874). In 1866 there was also an *opéra comique* called Mignon done by Ambroise Thomas based upon Goethe's novel. The original opera was done in French, but the German version was given a different and more tragic ending to be more in line with Goethe's writings. The versions of the opera performed outside of France were usually conducted in Italian.
10. Buddecke wrote this phrase, "damned German professors," in English rather than German, indicating it's a direct quote.
11. "The Chicago airfield" was Cicero Flying Field, which was in operation from 1911 to 1916. See Chapter 5.
12. The Blackstone Hotel is still in operation as of early 2023. It is located at 636 S Michigan Ave in Chicago.
13. The Gnome 7 Omega was a French 7-cylinder air-cooled aircraft engine, designed by the Seguin brothers and first flown in 1909. It was the first rotary engine for airplanes that was ever produced in large quantities. See Chapter 5 for more detail.
14. "Miss Stinsson" was Katherine Stinson, a pioneer of female aviation. Buddecke's comment about her being a 17-year-old is not accurate. Stinson billed herself as "the Flying Schoolgirl" at airshows in which she performed; her age was deliberately misstated by promoters and Buddecke may have been taken in by that. For more information, see Chapter 5.
15. Which would be the princely sum of about $11,500 in 2023 dollars.
16. This would be Elmer Partridge, who with his partner Henry Keller built a number of prototype aircraft. See Chapter 5 for more information.
17. The nearest "Luna Park" was the Chicago amusement park from 1907 to 1911 at 51st & Halstead Streets. It was a "trolley park" (located on a trolley line to make it easy to get to) that did indeed feature a roller coaster; however, the park was closed and most of its attractions

moved to make room for a food market by 1912 – at least a year before Buddecke's arrival at Cicero.

18. After Buddecke replaces the original 35-hp engine with the more powerful 50-hp Gnome, he starts referring to his "bird" as "he" rather than "she" as heretofore.
19. William "Billy" Robinson was a notable early aviator and long-distance air mail pilot who regularly flew out of Cicero. He was known to operate a Nieuport-type monoplane; some sources say Buddecke bought his "bird" from Robinson and not Orr and Linn, as Buddecke himself claims.
20. "I Didn't Raise My Boy to be a Soldier" by Al Piantadosi and Alfred Bryan, was a song that arose from the strong American pacifist movement in the period before the *Lusitania* sinking. It was a popular, recently written song, rather than a folk song.
21. Eugène Adrien Roland Georges Garros was a pioneering French aviator and famous pre-war air racer and performer. He became famous for his 1913 flight from France to Tunis across the Mediterranean and was awarded the Legion of Honor. When the war broke out he became one of the first fighter pilots. In August 1914 a story began circulating that he had been involved in the very first aerial combat in history, flying his plane into a Zeppelin (actually, an observation balloon) and killing himself and the German crew; it was later determined that no aspect of the story was true, though papers across the world reprinted it with great sensationalism. Garros helped develop the concept of putting metal bullet deflectors on a plane's propeller, allowing the pilot to fire a machine gun forward through the spinning blades. Fittingly, he achieved the first-ever aerial victory over another aircraft by firing through his propeller on 1 April 1915. Garros was shot down and killed on 5 October 1918, just five weeks before the Armistice; he outlived Buddecke by seven months.

    Due to a stadium being named after him which hosts the annual French Open tennis tournament, he may be the second most famous aviator from the Great War.
22. They faced the possibility of being intercepted at sea by a British warship and being interned or imprisoned at the British base at Gibraltar.
23. Most likely he was a member of the 7th (1st Rhenish) Hussars "King William I," which was first raised in March 1815 to fight against Napoleon.
24. Gabriel Efendi Noradunkyan (alt. Noradounghian; 1852–1936) was an Ottoman statesman and bureaucrat of Armenian descent. He had

been the Ottoman Minister of Foreign Affairs from 22 July 1912 to 23 January 1913. Buddecke is implying that this passenger was indeed the former minister himself.

25. Switzerland has had a President of the Confederation since 1848, so the companion's assumption that Switzerland was ruled by a Kaiser, as Germany was, betrays the fact that he was not in fact Swiss.
26. The Triple Alliance was forged (largely by Bismarck) in 1882 and consisted of Germany, Austria-Hungary, and Italy. Its primary purpose was to offset the perceived threats from France and Russia. At the time of Buddecke's story, Italy was considering withdrawing from the Alliance because it considered Austria-Hungary the aggressor in the rapidly widening war, and the Alliance was supposed to be a purely defensive arrangement.
27. The Capuchin catacombs of Palermo ("Catacombe dei Cappuccini") date from the seventeenth century and contain over 9,000 skeletons and mummified corpses in various crypts and galleries.
28. One newspaper article quoted below specifically states that he migrated to Indiana in 1914 while other articles say that he was in Indiana for almost a year by then, which could mean as early as August 1913. In light of the number of errors and contradictions in these articles, it is difficult to choose one set of dates over another. Most likely he arrived in Indianapolis around November 1913 for the marriage of his cousin, or around January 1914 in the company of his uncle.
29. Birth date is from Lance J. Bronnenkant, PhD, *The Blue Max Airmen: German Airmen Awarded the Pour le Mérite, Volume 2, Buddecke, Wintgens, Mulzer* (Aeronaut Books, 2012), page 4; https://www.findagrave.com/ memorial/141235532/albert-buddecke; https://erster-weltkrieg.dnb.de/WKI/Content/EN/Persons/02-buddecke-en.html; and https://www.ancestry.com/genealogy/records/albert-wilhelm-friedrich-heinrich-august-buddecke-24-9nq36l. His full name is given as Albert Wilhelm Friedrich Heinrich August Buddecke. His parents were Wilhelm (August Friedrich Wilhelm) Buddecke (1832-1864) and (Christine Wilhelmine Luise Henriette Karoline Amalie) Fanny Döring (1836–1924). Wilhelm Buddecke's early death may be explained by the fact that it was in the same year as the Second Schleswig War (Prusso-Danish War).
30. These included *Tactical Decisions and Orders: A Study in Troop Leading, Based on the Operations of an Independent Division, for Individual Instruction* (1908). See: https://www.anobii.com/en/books/tactical-decisions-and-orders/9781120991690/pi07ffe08f0d80bc64. This book was translated by Captain A.L. Conger in 1906 and republished in

2010. A copy is available at https://babel.hathitrust.org/cgi/pt?id=hvd.hwra54&view=1up&seq=7. His works also appear to include *Die Literature über den Felddzug 1864* (1915) and *Bibliographie der neueren deutschen Kriegsgeschichte* (1915).

31. See https://erster-weltkrieg.dnb.de/, op cit.
32. For example, see Walter Goerlitz, *History of the German General Staff 1657–1945* (Lucknow Books, 2015, first published in 1953) and Trevor N. Dupuy, *A Genius for War: The German Army and General Staff 1807–1945* (Lume Books, 2018, first published in 1984). Bronnenkant, page 4, notes that Albert Buddecke published several military treatises.
33. Full name was Karl Albert Wilhelm Werner Buddecke.
34. Full name was Max Robert Franz Hartmut Buddecke.
35. Bronnenkant (pp. 5, 26) notes that a U.S. patent was awarded to him in 1929.
36. See Bronnenkant, pp. 4–5. The genealogy website gives his full name as August Hans Joachim Buddecke, see https://www.ancestry.com/genealogy/records/albert-wilhelm-friedrich-heinrich-august-buddecke-24-9nq36l.
37. Much of this is from Bronnenkant, pp. 4–5.
38. According to the U.S. census in 1880 his birth year was 1864, in 1910 it was 1865, in 1920 it was 1862 and in 1930 it was 1864. The family history says he was born in 1863 (see Kurt Vonnegut, *Palm Sunday* (Belacorte Press, New York, 1981).

    His 1880 census records show him as 16 years old, ethnicity as "American," and his occupation as "Clerk in Brewery." His 1910 census records show him at age 45 living with his wife, Ora D., his daughter Edith, 21, his son Peter, 19, and his son Rudolph 14. Albert and his three children are listed as having been born in Indiana, while Ora D. is listed has having been born in Ohio. His profession is given as president of a brewing company. The census indicates that he and his three children all spoke both English and German. Ora D. is listed as an English speaker.
39. The birthdate of Sophia St. André is reported as 1839 in the Vonnegut genealogy website: https://www.geni.com/people/Edith-Vonnegut/6000000002729648070. The newspaper reports her three years older than that in November 1914.

    In the 1920 census Albert Lieber's father is listed as born in Germany and his mother tongue is listed as German but his mother is listed as born in France and her mother tongue is listed as French. In the 1930 census both of Albert Lieber's parents are reported as being from Germany.

40. https://oldmainartifacts.wordpress.com/2015/01/08/indianapolis-brewing-company-indianapolis-in/
    This is taken from Bob Ostrander and Derrick Morris, *Hoosier Beer: Tapping Into Indiana Brewing History.*
41. See https://notesfromgreatbookssyntopican.com/2020/02/.
42. Kurt Vonnegut, *Palm Sunday*, op cit. The account is drawn from a manuscript by Kurt Vonnegut Jr's uncle John G. Rauch (1890–1976) entitled *An Account of the Ancestry of Kurt Vonnegut, Jr., by an Ancient Friend of His Family.* It is a particularly caustic and critical account of Albert Lieber. It is not footnoted or sourced, and its accuracy is unverified. Still, as it was written by a contemporary relative of Albert Lieber and included in Vonnegut's book, it is worth noting. (http://legacy.owensboro.kctcs.edu/crunyon/Eng262/05-Contemporary/Vonn/albert_lieber.htm)
43. https://www.geni.com/people/Edith-Vonnegut/6000000002729648070
44. Vonnegut, *Palm Sunday*, op cit. Unfortunately, there is no account that provides Ora D. Lane's life story. Despite any faults she may have had, Albert Lieber does not appear to have been the perfect husband or family man either.
45. *The New York Times*, 28 December 1928, quote from Carl Snyder of the Federal Reserve Bank of New York. Note that in 1914, a million dollars was equivalent to over 27 million in 2023 dollars.
46. For example, it is claimed that the average height of a British recruit in 1914 was 5'5" (see https://www.tommy1418.com/wwi-facts--figures--myths.html).
47. Kurt Vonnegut, *Fates Worse Than Death: An Autobiographical Collage* (Berkley Books, New York, 1991), pages 28, 33–34, 36 and 187.
48. Sources include: "Air of mystery: Photos offer clues to trace life of 'Prof. Bumbaugh'" by Rick Steelhammer, *Charleston Gazette-Mail*, Jan. 28, 2017 at https://www.wvgazettemail.com/news/air-of-mystery-photos-offer-clues-to-trace-life-of-prof-bumbaugh/article_40b160e0-22a8-5869-b249-6845f3c37dc2.html.
49. There's no direct evidence for this belief, but it is assumed it is the case from the newspaper reports and Buddecke's description.
50. The Wikipedia page states that "By saving his earnings, on May 20, 1914 he was able to buy his own aircraft (a Nieuport monoplane) and he immediately taught himself how to fly. On the day Buddecke started his own aircraft production company, war was declared and he abandoned his business plans and returned to Germany, with the American-built Nieuport monoplane he had purchased at the Cicero aerodrome."

The sources for these claims is given as the website CICERO FLYING FIELD (lincolnbeachey.com), and the books *Early German Aces of World War I* and *Above the Lines: The Aces and Fighter Units of the German Air Service, Naval Air Service and Flanders Marine Corps, 1914–1918.*

On the Cicero Flying Field page (see http://lincolnbeachey.com/cicart.html), it says "On May 20, Hans-Joachim Buddecke flew 'Billy' Robinson's Gnome-powered Nieuport-type monoplane and apparently enjoyed the experience, for he purchased it from Robinson. He flew the monoplane at Cicero on several occasions from late May to early July, where he had an accident while landing … In August 1914, as war began to rage in Europe, Hans-Joachim returned to Germany with his Nieuport-type monoplane": On page 18 of *Early German Aces of World War I* it states that Buddecke purchased his plane with his own funds.

There are three problems with these statements. First, it appears that the plane was purchased by either his uncle, his uncle's brewing company, or by the new company that they founded in March 1914. *The Indianapolis News* article on 25 May 1914 states the Indianapolis Brewing Company purchased the plane. This is different from the claim that Buddecke purchased the plane "by saving his earnings." Buddecke in his memoir does not state the source of his funds.

Second is the claim that "on the day Buddecke started his own production company war was declared." The Aerial Advertising Company of America was incorporated in March 1914, war was declared in August 1914. So unless Buddecke had founded another company, this did not happen on the day war was declared. Buddecke in his book does not state that it occurred on the day war was declared.

Third, Wikipedia states that he travelled to Germany with the American-build Nieuport monoplane. That is clearly contradicted by his account in Chapter 4; it is unlikely that he was travelling with his airplane and didn't mention it later.

The purchase date of 20 May 1914 is provided by Cicero Flying Field website. *The Indianapolis News* on 25 May reports that the Indianapolis Brewing Company (owned by Albert Lieber) had purchased an airplane of French make. The pilot was going to be "Captain Hans Buddecke." This date is assumed to be correct.

51. According to an article in *The Indianapolis Star* on 22 July 1914, Buddecke had returned to Indianapolis about a week earlier.

52. Many accounts say that he went down because of ground fire. In his interview published in 9 March 1918 in *The New York Times*, Garros states he went down because of mechanical problems: "Because of motor trouble I was forced to land on Belgian soil north of Courtrai. I managed to burn the machine but found I was surrounded by enemies."
53. For example, see *The New York Times*, 3 August 1914, front page. The original story is credited to the London *Standard*. As *The New York Times* notes "The *Standard* fails to give the source of its story, and there is no foundation that in any way confirms it in responsible quarters." The story was repeated in dozens of newspapers across the United States.
54. This was by French newspapers after his fourth and fifth kills on 3 April 1915.
55. See transcript of the unpublished book by Harold E. Morehouse, *Flying Pioneers Biographies Collection* at https://edan.si.edu/transcription/pdf_files/24187.pdf. Other sources say it was shut down in 1916.
56. Morehouse, *op. cit.*
57. Some sources state Cicero ceased operations in the fall of 1915, while Wikipedia states it was closed in April 1916. Ashburn Flying Field was in operation in the spring of 1916 according to some sources while Wikipedia says it opened in November 1916.
58. Early in the war, many aircraft used by the French Army and British Royal Flying Corps were built by Farman Aviation Works (*Avions Farman*), a plane builder founded in France by two British brothers.
59. To be clear, since Buddecke's narrative is not: he is not referring to Védrines but to an anonymous victim in a later encounter. Details follow in the next chapter.
60. Vaux-en-Vermandois, about 3 km northwest of Roupy, France.
61. The German word Buddecke uses here, "Pfauenaugen," is the German name for a colorful butterfly with a large round patch on each wing – much like the red, white, and blue roundels on the wings of British and French aircraft.
62. This victory was against 2nd Lieutenant Walter Henry Nixon (pilot) and Capt. John Nowell Stanhope Stott (observer) flying a B.E.2c, No. 2008, from No. 8 Squadron of the Royal Flying Corps. As mentioned in the text, Buddecke was flying a Fokker Eindecker. This event took place on 19 September 1915.

John Stott of the 5th Dragoon Guards was born in 1877 and received his aviator's certificate No. 373 on 21 December 1912.

63. The bashlyk is a traditional Cossack or Turkish headgear, cone-shaped and made of leather or felt.
64. The "lines and dots" description presumably refers to the silhouette of the aircraft from behind, with the two lines being the upper and lower wings and the three dots being the fuselage and two motors.
65. Armand Fallières (1841–1931) was the President of France from 1906 to 1913.
66. Recall Buddecke's days in Cicero when he would turn off his engine and volplane to a landing.
67. The volte was a leaping movement by a fencer to avoid a thrust; or in dressage and classical horse riding, a maneuver in which the horse describes a circle.
68. Refers to a series of British single-engine, two-seat biplanes built by the Royal Aircraft Factory, based on an original design by Blériot. The B.E.2 was reputed to be a good, stable aircraft well suited for artillery observation and aerial photography, which could explain the behavior Buddecke sees here. But its "stability" meant it was not very maneuverable, and another weakness was that the observer, who also manned the defensive machine gun, sat in the front seat, which limited his field of fire. The most common variant at the front at this time was the B.E.2c.
69. Lawrence is William George Lawrence, age 25. He was the younger brother of Thomas Edward Lawrence, who would later gain fame as Lawrence of Arabia. See Chapter 9 for more detail.
70. This was the War Merit Cross (Brunswick) 2nd Class, or *Braunschweigisches Kriegsverdienstkreuz* (aka *Ernst-Augustkreuz*), established 25 October 1914 by the Duke of Brunswick, Ernest Augustus. This may have been the Duke who visited the squadron at Roupy.
71. Exceptions being the French attacks around the Noyon Salient from 20 December 1914–17 March 1915 and the British attack at Neuve Chapelle on 10–13 March 1915.
72. Bronnenkant, *op. cit.*, page 8.
73. Bronnenkant, *op. cit.*, page 8.
74. Bronnenkant, *op. cit.*, page 8.
75. Bronnenkant, page 8. On page 9, Bronnenkant provides a group photo of FFA 27. It identifies the pilots as Buddecke, von Mudra, Captain Alfred Keller, Baur-Betaz, Müller, Volck, (possibly Sr.

Lieutenant Günther) Viehweger, *Rittmeister* (cavalry captain) Anton von Brederlow (wounded 9 May 1917 as CO of *Jasta* 17), Demmel, Captain Kurt Schmikaly (wounded 22 October 1916 with KEK Metz, died next day), Sr. Lieutenant Kurt Drobnig (killed 7 June 1916 with FAA 221), von Sillich, Lieutenant Hans Reitter (killed 8 December 1915), Dr. Fantel, and the dogs Kiwi and Joffre. Joffre was named after the Chief of the Army Staff for the French Army at this time. Buddecke was the only one of these 14 pilots who became an ace.

76. The plane could have been a variation of the AEG B.II or B.III; the Aviatik B.I or B.II; the Euler B.I, B.II, or B. III; the Friedrichshaften FF.33b; the Halberstadt B.I, B.II, or B.III; the LVG B.I B.II, or B.III; the Rumpler B.I; or the Schutte-Lanz D.I or D.II. It was probably not an Albatros C.I, which Boelcke used for his first aerial victory. It was also probably not the Aviatik C.I, which mounted the observer in front of the pilot.
77. See Peter Kilduff, *Iron Man Rudolf Berthold: Germany's Indomitable Fighter Ace of World War I* (Grub Street, London, 2012), p. 47. Berthold notes in June: "I succeeded in having Buddecke transferred to my section."
78. Kilduff, pp. 46–48. The use of a machine gun on an Albatros B.II is reported by Berthold on 8 June 1915.
79. The date of 10 June comes from Bronnenkant, p. 8.
80. Kilduff, p. 47. Some of the German words have been translated from his account: *Abteilung* became section and *Leutnant* became Lieutenant. We kept the German abbreviations from his translation. *Oblt* is a senior Lieutenant, *Ltn.d.Res* is Lieutenant of the Reserves, *Ltn* is Lieutenant, and *Hptm* is Captain.
81. Roughly, "blonde lace," probably a reference to his hair color and obviously a play on his name.
82. Kilduff, p. 30, says 34 FFA and eight EFP (Forward Area Aircraft Staging Depots). Wikipedia says 33 at the start of the war. Greg van Wyngarden, *Early German Aces of World War I* (Osprey Publishing, Oxford, 2006), p. 6, implies that there were 33.
83. For example, on 30 September it is claimed that Lionel Rees and James Hargreaves shot down an Albatros C over Gommecourt flown by Kölpin and Leonhardi of FFA 23. See: http://www.frontflieger.de/2-ffa023.html and http://www.theaerodrome.com/aces/wales/rees.php.
84. http://www.theaerodrome.com/aces/france/gilbert.php.

85. Some sources claim rather specifically that he learned to fly in 1913 at his own expense, qualifying as a pilot in September. See Norman Franks, Frank W. Bailey, Russell Guest, *Above the Lines: The Aces and Fighters Units of the German Air Service, Naval Air Service and Flanders Marine Corps, 1914–1918* (Grub Street, Oxford, 1993), p. 71.

    This does not seem to be supported by the one complete biography of him. See Peter Kilduff, *Iron Man Rudolf Berthold: Germany's Indomitable Fighter Ace of World War I* (Grub Street, London, 2012).
86. See Bronnenkant, p. 9, which states of Buddecke, "During one of them [reconnaissance missions], he barely escaped with his life after French pre-war aviator Jules Védrines attacked him and set the flares that Buddecke carried on board ablaze."
87. In common usage, a "triple ace" is a pilot who has shot down at least 15 aircraft. There was no established norm for what constituted an "ace" until later in the war. The allies tended to count pilots with five confirmed kills as an ace, while the Germans eventually set their standard at ten. Common usage usually sets the standard at five confirmed kills.
88. According to some sources, he had only 15 kills. The figure of 17 comes from "The Aerodrome" website listing for Max Immelmann, which is based upon books by Norman Franks.
89. Many sources say it was a mechanical failure, including Fokker. Marc Dierrikx, *Anthony Fokker: The Flying Dutchman Who Shaped American Aviation* (Smithsonian Books, Washington D.C., 2018), p. 99, states that: "On April 18, however, Garros's luck ran out. The engine of his machine was hit by shots fired from the ground just as he had crossed the German lines. He was forced to land and was taken prisoner before he could manage to set his plane alight."

    Fokker states "As luck would have it, a faulty motor brought the plane down within the German lines. Pilots landing in enemy territory were instructed to burn their machines, but before this one was fully consumed it was captured. The airman proved to be the famous Roland Garros, one of France's greatest stunting pilots before the war." See Anthony H.G. Fokker and Bruce Gould, *Flying Dutchman: The Life of Anthony Fokker* (George Routledge & Sons, Ltd., London, 1931), p. 129.

    Roland Garros himself, in an interview published in 9 March 1918 in *The New York Times*, states he went down because of mechanical problems: "Because of motor trouble I was forced to land on Belgian soil north of Courtrai. I managed to burn the machine but found I was surrounded by enemies."

90. See Marc Dierrikx, *Anthony Fokker: The Flying Dutchman Who Shaped American Aviation* (Smithsonian Books, Washington D.C., 2018), pp. 99–100. He states: "Yet it was known that he had been experimenting in Schwerin with his chief mechanic, Heinrich Lübbe, to develop a synchronizing mechanism since the end of 1914 … Around Christmas time they set to work with a small team. Five months later they had arrived at a reasonably workable solution."

    He also notes that "The basic principle of this idea had been the intellectual property of aviation pioneer August Euler since July 1910. In May 1912 Euler received a patent for his invention."
91. A parasol wing is a wing usually above the cockpit, not directly attached to the fuselage, but held above it. While the L version looked very different from the H version because of the wing arrangement, it was otherwise very similar. They both used the Le Rhone 9C 80-hp engine.
92. Source for this is P.M. Grosz, *Fokker E.1I/II, Windsock Datafile 91*, (Albatros Productions Limited, 2002). It was Fokker factory airframe number 191, accepted by the German Army on 26 May 1914 and shipped on 15 June 1915.
93. It is not known who was assigned E.2/15 and E.4/15. One certainly was the plane Buddecke was flying. Parschau's "green machine" was Fokker A.16/15. According to one source, he used the "green machine" at least until November 1915, when it was replaced by a later production model. See Wyngarden, pp. 9, 12 and 14.

    Bronnenkant identifies his Fokker as 15/15 on page 29 and also notes they he may have flown 36/15.
94. Also credited with three planes by this time was Eugene Gilbert with MS-23. He would shoot down his fourth and fifth planes on 7 and 17 June 1915 with MS-49.
95. The 8mm (.315) Hotchkiss M1909 had a rate of fire of 400–600 rounds per minute with a muzzle velocity of around 2,375 feet per second (this is the muzzle velocity of the Hotchkiss Mle M1914 machine gun). It was fed by strips of 30 rounds that could easily be fed as a continuous stream if being handled by a machine gun crew. This was more difficult to do in the air.

    The .303 Lewis gun had a rate of fire of 500–600 rounds per minute with a muzzle velocity of 2,440 feet per second. It was drum fed, with each drum holding 47 rounds. Changing out the drums was a little time consuming and difficult.

    The French company *Hotchkiss et Cie* was established in the 1860s by American industrialist Benjamin B. Hotchkiss (1826–1885). The

Lewis gun was invented in 1911 by American U.S. Army Colonel Isaac Newton Lewis (1858–1931).

96. The 7.92mm (.312) Parabellum MG 14 had a rate of fire of 600–700 rounds per minute. The 7.92mm Bergmann MG 15na had a rate of fire of 500–600 rounds per minute and a muzzle velocity of 2,900 feet per second. The Spandau lMG 08 was the air-cooled version of the water-cooled MG 08 lightened for use in aircraft and primarily used as a fixed gun. It had a rate of fire of 400–500 rounds per minute and a muzzle velocity of 2,821 feet per second.

    The original five Fokker Eindeckers were fitted with the Parabellum gun. Subsequent production versions of the Eindeckers and many other German fighters were armed with the Spandau. The Spandau lMG 08 used the ammunition belt of the Parabellum MG 14 because of its lighter weight.

    In contrast, the German water-cooled Maschinengewehr 08 or MG 08 weighed 152.1 lb with water. That was 58.4 lb for the gun body, 8.8 lb for the water and 84.9 lb for the tripod. Such a behemoth was clearly unsuited for mounting on an aircraft which itself weighed only 880 lbs empty.

97. The Albatros C.I was the first of the "C-series." It mounted a Parabellum MG 14 and had a 160 hp Mercedes D.III engine. The LVG C.I also mounted a Parabelllum MG 14 and used the 160 hp Mercedes D.III engine but was superseded by the C.II in late 1915. Around 300 were built. Later versions used the Spandau lMG. The Aviatik C.I came into service in April 1915 (according to Wikipedia) or in September 1915 (according to Wyngarden, p. 6). The observer sat in front of the pilot, with the Parabellum MG 14 machine gun clipped on a sliding rail mount that allowed the gun to move to both sides of the cockpit. 548 Aviatik C.Is were built, 402 by Aviatik and 146 by Hannover. It was also powered by the 160 hp Mercedes D.III engine.

98. See Wyngarden, p. 7.

99. *Pfalz Flugzeugwerke* was an airplane manufacturer located at Speyer airfield in the Palatinate area of western Germany. The Palatinate is called "Pfalz" in German. The company was registered on 3 June 1913 and built some of their own aircraft at that time. At the start of the Great War, the company had licenses to produce Morane-Saulnier H monoplanes. They then made the Pfalz E.1, a Morane-Saulnier H with a synchronized Maxim LMG.08 machine gun and a 59 kW Oberursel U.O. seven-cylinder rotary engine.

The first two Pfalz E.I were delivered to the Western Front before the end of October 1915 and as of 31 December 1915, 14 machines were serving at the fronts. A total of 46 were built.

100. Wyngarden, p. 25
101. According to his younger brother Frantz Immelmann. See Frantz Immelmann, *Immelmann: The Eagle of Lille* (Casemate, Philadelphia & Newbury, 2009), originally published in 1934, pp. 191–93.
102. See "The Departure of the R.F.C. Expeditionary Force" on the Royal Flying Corps website: http://www.airhistory.org.uk/rfc/home.html.
103. 54 Fokker E.1s were built. It's unclear whether this figure includes the initial five Fokker M.5K/MGs or the later ten M-5s converted to armed Fokkers. There were then 49 Fokker E.IIs built, with the two production lines running concurrently based upon engine availability. 249 Fokker E.IIIs were built, although this figure may include some of the E.IIs that were upgraded to E.III standards when they were returned to the factory. 49 E.IVs were built. The total Eindecker production run is stated to be 416 aircraft, which is 15 more than reported for each of the models made.
104. The E.IV had a 160-hp Oberursel U.III two-row, 14-cylinder engine, a copy of the Gnome Double Lambda. The E.I had 80 hp while the E.IIs and E.IIIs had 100 hp. This extra horsepower allowed the E.IV to carry the extra weight for two or three machine guns. The final version of the Fokker was fraught with problems and not well loved by the pilots.
105. Kilduff, pp. 48–49. As Berthold was the more senior pilot with two Iron Crosses, it is not surprising that he was offered the Eindecker. The diary entry is probably from August 1915.
106. Kilduff, p. 49. He references a quote from the German 3rd Army air commander, "These aeroplanes go up only to repel [enemy] aircraft that have broken through [our defences]; they have orders to not cross the lines under any circumstances." This was probably the policy across all German armies. FFA 23 was attached to the 2nd German Army. That the order applied also to FFA 23 and the 2nd German Army is reinforced by the next quote from the diary of Berthold.
107. Kilduff, pp. 49–50.
108. The seven-cylinder engine was used on the Fokker M.5. The M.5K/MG was the armed version, of which five were made. The armed version was designated the Fokker E.1. A total of 54 were built. The Fokker E.II was upgraded with the nine-cyclinder Oberursel engine

and the machine gun integrated with its airframe (vice being just bolted on).

109. The list is primarily drawn from the article on Buddecke in the "The Aerodrome" website at http://www.theaerodrome.com/aces/germany/buddecke.php.
110. Bronnenkant, p. 11. Source of this count is not given.
111. Pilot identification was from Bronnenkant, p. 12.
112. For example, see the internet article by Hames W. Thams, "Lawrence of Arabia's Family" at http://stdavidsny.org/lawrence-of-arabias-family/. Also see https://telsociety.org.uk/23-october-1915/ and http://www.theaerodrome.com/forum/archive/index.php/t-30058.html and: https://airwar19141918.wordpress.com/2015/10/23/23-october-1915-sweeter-than-a-small-ladies-handkerchief/.
113. https://www.jewsfww.uk/cecil-hoffnung-marks-1820.php.
114. See https://www.jewsfww.uk/cecil-hoffnung-marks-1820.php and https://theyserved.fandom.com/wiki/Cecil_Marks#cite_ref-cam_3-0.
115. This is the only case in Buddecke's notes where he used the word "Ottoman." The rest of the time he refers to Turkey, Turkish, or Turk.
116. Probably refers to the road from Uzunköprü to Keşan (in German, Keschan) to Bolayır (Bulaiar, Bulayr) and thence to Gelibolu (Gallipoli).
117. The Maritza River, aka Marits, Meriç, Evros, or Euros, is the longest river in the Balkans and forms the border between modern Greece and European Turkey – a result of the Balkan Wars of 1912-1913. From Uzunköprü it is about six miles/10 km to the river.
118. The Battle of Bolayır (26 January 1913) during the Balkan War of 1913 was an attempt by Turkish forces, on the southwest tip of the Gallipoli peninsula, to break through the Bulgarian blockade and relieve the besieged city of Edirne. It failed, at great loss to the Ottoman Empire, so it's unclear where Buddecke learned his understanding of the battle as related in his account.
119. The *Barbarossa*, aka *Barbaros Hayreddin*, was one of two pre-dreadnought battleships Germany sold to the Ottoman Navy in 1910. Built in 1891, while serving in the German Navy it was known as the SMS *Kurfürst Friedrich Wilhelm* of the *Brandenburg* class. It was sunk on 8 August 1915 by the British submarine HMS *E11*; see Ch. 13 for more details. If Major Serno was indeed aboard, he was lucky to escape with his life.
120. Otto Hersing (1885–1960) commanded the German submarine *U-21*, and was credited with the first sinking of a modern warship by a self-

propelled torpedo when his boat sank the British scout cruiser HMS *Pathfinder* off the coast of Scotland in September 1914. In the spring of 1915 *U-21* was transferred to the Mediterranean to support the Ottoman Navy. It sank the British pre-dreadnought battleships HMS *Triumph* on 25 May and HMS *Majestic* two days later. These losses forced the Allies to withdraw all their large warships from the Cape Helles (aka Sedd el Bahr) area at the southwest tip of the Gallipoli peninsula, complicating support for the Allied forces that had already been landed there.

121. The Battle of Aegospotami was a naval confrontation between Athens and Sparta in 405 BC. It resulted in a resounding victory for the Spartans commanded by Lysander and the destruction of the Athenian navy, forcing an end to the Peloponnesian War (431–404 BC).
122. Possibly these were Farman MF.11s, a type that was sometimes used as a light bomber. This model was fairly obsolete by this point in the war, but was still used as a reconnaissance plane or light bomber in some theaters, including the Mediterranean.
123. *Jugend* ("Youth") was a Bavarian art magazine published from 1896 to 1940, featuring the work of German art noveau artists.
124. The "Narrows of Chanak" refers to the area around Çanakkale, which is the narrowest part of the Dardanelles. ("Tschanak" or "Tschanak Kale" in German accounts, and pronounced chon-OCK-uh-lee.) The crossing in 480 BC by Persian Emperor (King of Kings) Xerxes I of Persia (c. 518 bc – 465 BC) during his invasion of Greece is usually considered to have been made around the towns of Abydos and Sestus across two pontoon bridges built from ships. Ancient Abydos is 3-4 kilometers north of Çanakkale near Nagara Point (Nagara Burnu or Nara Burnu).

    The first plane shot down this day is claimed to have gone down east of Cape Narors. It was possibly a Henry Farman from No. 2 (Naval) Air Wing, RNAS, piloted by Flt Cdr Hans Acworth Busk (1894–1916), who was carrying a 550-lb bomb to attack the Turkish airfield at Galata. The plane carried no observer to save weight for the bomb, so therefore did not carry a machine gun. If the other aircraft in the British flight were similarly configured, there was nothing they could have done to assist Busk against Buddecke.
125. Also known as Achi Baba. It is 217m (712 ft) high. The village of Alçitepe, also known at the time as Krithia, is on a plateau at its western base.
126. Muslims.
127. Enver Pasha's official title at the time was Vice-Generalissimo.

128. By using the grand titles "bey" and "sheikh" for these Turkish commoners, Buddecke is clearly being condescending and gently mocking.
129. A Russian swing is a large, floor-mounted swing used in circus acrobatic acts to make high jumps.
130. "Rocinante" was the name of the hero's horse in Miguel Cervantes' 1605 novel *Don Quixote.*
131. This is a fragment of the lyrics from the wartime song "Du kann kein Kaiser und kein König was bei machen" which contains a Berlin dialect pun that doesn't translate well into English.
132. See article in the Quadrant Online for a history of their fate: https://quadrant.org.au/magazine/2013/04/the-ethnic-cleansing-of-greeks-from-gallipoli-april-1915/
133. The Ottoman Empire (1299–1922) or *Osmanli Imparatorluğu* was an Empire established by Turkish people with its capital from 1453 at Constantinople (now called Istanbul). At its peak, from the 1500s to 1812, the areas it controlled included Greece, Eastern Mediterranean Islands, significant parts of the Balkans, Romania, Crimea, the Anatolian Peninsula, parts of Armenia, Azerbaijan, major parts of the Arabic fertile crescent (Syria, Iraq, Lebanon, and Palestine), the west coast of the Arabian Peninsula and parts of the east coast, Egypt, Sudan, Eritrea, Djibouti, and the North African coast (Libya, Tunis and Algeria).

     It had recently lost most of its possessions in Europe, in part because of the Balkan Wars (1912-1913) but at this time still controlled its possessions in the fertile crescent and the west coast of the Arabian Peninsula.

     During the period of Buddecke's service, the nation and people were often called Turkey or Turkish, even though that is not technically correct. Buddecke in his writing almost always used the term Turk or Turkey, using the word Ottoman only once. Its successor nation is the modern country of Turkey, missing most of its holdings in Europe, the fertile crescent and Africa. For all practical purposes, the terms Turkey and Ottoman are interchangeable.
134. There is a claim that on 1 March 1915 Turkish Lieutenant Cemal Bey dropped bombs on the British battleship HMS *Majestic*, causing "substantial damage." The ship was still functional and operational and on 3 March was still patrolling and on 9 March shelled Turkish positions. See http://armsregister.com/articles/articles_documents/nzar_a67_gallipoli_rnas_fighter_aircraft.pdf.

135. See armsregister.com, *op cit.* There is some confusion over this. For example, Pavelec, *Airpower over Gallipoli 1915–1916* (Naval Institute Press, Annapolis, Maryland, 2020) states on p. 36 that: "The Ottoman air force could only rely on the use of one obsolete Blériot monoplane during the initial Allied naval attacks. In fact, in March there were only four German aircraft total in the empire."

Pavelec also states on p. 44 that "Serno dispatched a single seaplane to Canakkale, which arrived on 17 March." It test flew on the 17th and conducted a reconnaissance on the 18th flown by Serno.

136. The French pre-dreadnought battleship *Bouvet* capsized and sank with 643 of its 718 crew lost after being hit by a shore battery and striking a mine. Also sunk by mines were the pre-dreadnought battleships HMS *Irresistible* and HMS *Ocean.* The battlecruiser HMS *Inflexible* was seriously damaged by mines and the French pre-dreadnought battleships *Suffren* and *Gaulois* were damaged by coastal artillery.

137. Pavelec, p. 51, states that by the end of the day, they had landed 19,000 troops.

138. This includes the counterattack on 27 April by Mustafa Kemal's 19th Division. Mustafa Kemal later became the very influential first president of Turkey from 1923 to 1938 under the name of Atatürk.

139. HMS *Ark Royal* started operations with a Short Type 136 (a Short Folder), two Wight Pushers, three Sopwith Type 807 seaplanes, and four Sopwith Tabloid wheeled aircraft. It lost one Type 807 on 5 March due to a mechanical problem (the crew was recovered). The Tabloids were exchanged for a pair of Sopwith Schneider single-seat floatplanes and she received two Sopwith Type 860s, another Wight Pusher, and Short Type 166. This gave her a total of 11 seaplanes, of which 9 were two-seaters. Some were stored on the collier *Penmorvait.* Not all were operational. The "Short Folder" planes (the Short Type 136, one-of design, and Short Type 166) had folding wings for use on ships.

The *Ark Royal* Flying Log, 31 January 1915 to 30 January 1916, National Archives Air 137/2, states that:

"H.M.S. ARK ROYAL sailed from Sheerness shortly before midnight on the 31st January, 1915 … The seaplanes which she carried were rather a heterogeneous collection, consisting of –

two 200 h.p. Canton Unne Wight Pushers

One 200 h.p. Canton Unne Short Tractor which had been through the Cuxhaven raid and had seen her best days.

Three 100 h.p. Monosoupaper, *Daily Mail* type Sopwith Tractors.

In addition she carried four Tabloid Sopwith aeroplanes which were supposed to be able to fly off the forecastle, but which were never used for that purpose."

According to Pavelec, p. 26, these Sopwith Tabloids were armed. They carried a Lewis gun on the top wing that fired over the propeller arc. These planes needed a land base for use.

140. See John Oliver, *The Air War in the Dardanelles* (2017), p. 3. These 18 planes included at least 2 B.E.2s, 10 Maurice Farmans, and 3 Sopwiths (and we deduce 2 other B.E.2s and a Nieuport 10). See Oliver, p. 12, among other sources.

The No.3 (Naval) Squadron upon arrival at Tenedos found they only had five serviceable aircraft – 4 B.E.2s and 1 Nieuport 10 – out of the 30 aircraft that had been crated to them. More aircraft were made operational later.

Pavelec, p. 29, states that they were ready for flights from Tenedos on 27 March. The first complement of aircraft included the B.E.2a No. 50 (Samson's plane), two Maurice Farman MF.11 Shorthorns, and eight Henri Farman HF.20s, for a total of 11 aircraft.

Oliver states on p. 29 that as of 4 April, the No. 3 (Naval) Squadron had unloaded 18 planes, got five of them ready for operations and got working again two abandoned French seaplanes on the beach. The personnel of No. 3 (Naval) Squadron is listed for early April as 17 officers, 2 doctors and 110 ratings for a total of 129 people.

Pavelec, p. 30, states that in the first week of April the rest of the squadron arrived and brought another 11 aircraft. This included a "handful" of B.E.2cs, the two Sopwith Tabloids from *Ark Royal*, a Breguet Bre.4 two-seat bomber, a "Canton Unne Maurice Farman," tail number 1241 (probably a Maurice Farman Shorthorn). He states they had 22 aircraft total, of which five were operational: four Be.2c's and the Breguet. There were 102 men and 18 officers, at least one horse and six mules.

Pavelec, p. 48 states that Samson initially commanded 11 aircraft, a dozen pilots, a half dozen observers, and another 40 men. By the first week of April the rest of the squadron had arrived, adding another dozen aircraft for a total of 22 (including the two Sopwith Tabloids from HMS *Ark Roya*l) and the remaining personnel for a total of 18 officers and 102 men.

141. The Escadrille 524 website (http://albindenis.free.fr/Site_escadrille/escadrille524.htm) gives a date of 23 March 1915. Pavelec, p. 29, states that they were ready for flights from Tenedos on 27 March.

142. Oliver, pp. 35 and 37.
143. The original intention was to base five seaplanes and four pilots at the Dardanelles. The detachment consisted of Nieuports N14 and N17, two experienced French pilots, a petty officer, ten seamen, and two experienced British observers. Their first operational flight was on 11 April. They conducted bombing missions on 17 April on the Asian shore of the Dardanelles and later supported the French landing at Kum Kale on 25 April. See https://aegeanairwar.com/articles/the-french-seaplane-squadron-at-the-dardanelles.
144. Pavelec, p. 17. It is assumed that only refers to planes in the Gallipoli area. He states that they were facing ten seaplanes for the Allies – six British and four French attached to their seaplane tenders. Obviously the first reference is to the planes of HMS *Ark Royal.* The second reference is assumed to be to the planes of the French Seaplane Carrier *Foudre.* While the *Foudre* was operating in the Mediterranean at this time (and Pavelec discusses it on p. 16), it has not been established that it was at Gallipoli.
145. Pavelec, p. 32.
146. Pavelec, p. 47 states that at this time (March or April) the Ottoman forces consisted of one land plane and three seaplanes at Canakkale under command of local naval commander. There was one land plane at Galata under command of Major Erich Serno, and joined by twelve German pilots, 32 mechanics, along with Turkish mechanics and newly trained pilots. Germany shipped one Rumpler B.I and three Albatros B.Is to the air force through Bulgaria.

    It is also stated that Preussner was in charge of seaplanes in March and his command included experienced Turkish observer Captain Hussein.
147. Oliver, p. 24.
148. The base at San Stefano was in existence before the war. It's not clear when the Galata base was established, but it was active by April 1915. The same with the land-based airfield on Canakkale, which was first spotted by the British on 15 April 1915.
149. Oliver, pp. 40–41. It is stated that they destroyed an airplane in its hangar, damaged other buildings, and destroyed the fuel stores, but these claims have not been cross-checked to German or Ottoman records. It is claimed that destruction of the fuel stores greatly restricted German and Ottoman air operations and that: "The Turkish air force was now effectively grounded and would remain so until after the landing on the isthmus of Gallipoli. In one stroke Samson had gained air superiority over the battlefield." Pavelec, p. 48

says the raid was conducted by Samson and two of his pilots, implying that three aircraft were used.

150. Pavelec, p. 58, states that at the start of May they received two replacement land-based aircraft.
151. Oliver, p. 56, gives the date of 29 April for their arrival and a date of 11 May for their first operational aircraft. According to another source, their first flight was on 4 May (see https://aegeanairwar.com/articles/the-french-seaplane-squadron-at-the-dardanelles). Pavelec, p. 57, has the squadron arriving on 2 May. The website http://albindenis.free.fr/Site_escadrille/escadrille524.htm says the squadron landed its equipment at Tenedos on 6 May 1915 and that the first French Farman took to the air on 11 May.
152. See http://albindenis.free.fr/Site_escadrille/escadrille524.htm. It notes that the pilots of the squadron were S/Lt Marcel Saint André, Warrant Officer Pierre de Deausire de Seysell, Sergeants Louis Garsononnin, Guy de Grosourdy de Saint-Pierre, Dumas, Jules Lecompte, Dubois, and Brigadier Fourrier Célestin Sanglier.
153. http://albindenis.free.fr/Site_escadrille/escadrille524.htm.
154. Ibid.
155. Oliver, p. 66, states that the squadron had eight pilots and eight Maurice Farman MF XI aircraft "that were much more reliable and powerful than the British version." Pavelec, p. 16, states that the squadron comprised eight Farman 80-horse power HF.20s. Pavelec, p. 30, states that it had eight pilots and eight Maurice Farman HF.20s. The HF.20 is a refined version of the MF.11 with Gnome Lambda 7-cylinder 80-hp engine.

    Pavelec, p. 57 has the squadron with eight "Maurice Farman HF.20s, with eighty-horsepower Gnome rotary engines." The complement of the squadron was eight officers (in addition to Captain Césari?) and 40 men.

    While many sources identify the planes in question at the MF.11, this was probably not the case. This was an underpowered pre-war plane (the British called it the Shorthorn). Other sources indicate that the French version had more power than the British version. It is clear that the plane had to be a later-developed version of the airplane, like the HF.20, HF.27, HF.30 and F.40.
156. Oliver, p. 25. The exact time frame of this count is not given, but the count of missions attempted versus those completed was based upon an examination of the *Ark Royal*'s records. The actual statement was "They had set out on 75 missions and only managed 25, but only three of these were spotting missions for the Fleet."

Oliver also states on p. 14 that "By the end of March the 'Ark Royal' had been on station for 44 days and had been able to put aircraft in the air on only twenty of those days for a total of 60 flying hours."

In contrast, Oliver notes on p. 31 that "From 19th March to 24th April there were only nine days of bad weather which made flying impossible for 3 Squadron, and a few other days when it was impossible for the seaplanes to even try to fly, but 3 Squadron in this period carried out numerous missions:

42 reconnaissance or bombing flights by aeroplanes during which 65 bombs were dropped.
12 reconnaissance flights by seaplanes during which 15 bombs were dropped.
15 spotting flights by aeroplanes
10 spotting flights by seaplanes
18 photographic flights by aeroplanes
10 evening aircraft patrols by aeroplanes"

Oliver also notes on p. 53 that "During this period of twenty-two days [from 26 April to the middle of May] the RNAS would carry out some 284 missions. The balloon on the 'Manica' went up on thirteen of those days for eight hours per day on average. The 'Ark Royal's' performance had slipped back [compared to the 25th and 27th of April] and it was only capable of sending up on average two flights per day, which was a poor show compared to Samson and 3 Squadron's daily average of ten."

157. Pavelec, p. 59.
158. Oliver, p. 57.
159. Oliver, p. 59. Keep in mind that this is an average of six flights a day from a squadron that on paper had 18 aircraft.
160. Oliver, pp. 59–60. On 17 May, Commander Samson returned to England a number of airplanes that he considered unsuitable for active service in the Dardanelles (see Oliver, page 70).
161. Oliver, p. 61. The British claimed to have killed the observer, but the Ottoman plane landed near Turkish shores and was not taken by the British. The British could not have known for certain the condition of the crew.
162. Oliver, p. 64. He references 22 sorties during "this four day battle," so it's not clear which four days he means. The Second Battle of Krithia is usually considered to have run from 6–8 May.
163. Oliver, pp. 66, 81.
164. Pavelec, page 62.

165. Around 13,000 Ottoman casualties, including 3,000 killed, versus 160 killed and 468 wounded among the Australians and New Zealanders. This was an exchange ratio of over twenty-to-one.
166. Oliver, p. 80. Page 79 gives the dates as from 9 May until June. On page 80 he notes that the No. 3 Squadron made 170 flights over enemy territory in that same period.
167. Pavelec, p. 64.
168. Pavelec, p. 65, says that the British received two additional Voisins at the end of May. Not sure if this was in addition to the six they had already received.
169. Pavelec, p. 64, dates this event at the end of May. Oliver, p. 67, notes during May that a few days into the operation of making bombs in May, a French pilot was killed. On the other hand, the Escadrille 524 website (op. cit.) does not report either such event or any personnel losses in May.
170. Oliver, p. 83, states the ship had four Short Type 184s. Oliver, pp. 89 and 96, identifies the Schneider floatplane by serial number (#1445). He also lists all the planes by serial number (#821, #841, #1841, and #1445). Wikipedia (https://en.wikipedia.org/wiki/HMS_Ben-my-Chree) has the ship arriving at Lesbos on 10 June with only two Short Type 184s. It also (https://en.wikipedia.org/wiki/Short_Type_184) has two prototype Short Type 184s loaded on the ship, which set sail on 21 March 1915.
171. The No. 3 (Naval) Squadron) usually had around six aircraft operational at any one time, out of over a dozen total. HMS *Ark Royal* had perhaps two aircraft regularly operating and maybe had a half-dozen total. HMS *Ben-My-Chree* had four aircraft, all operational. The two kite balloon ships each had one kite balloon, usually operational. There were two Sea Scout airships, with usually only one operational due to there being only one hangar erected. The French air squadron reported 14 planes operational and total on 5 July 1915.
172. Oliver, p. 89: "pushing Samson's men up from 4,000 ft to 7,000 ft."
173. See Oliver, pp. 96–97. "Since the *Ark Royal* arrived in the Dardanelles her seaplanes had suffered a total of 91 engine failures. They were due to carry out a total of 270 missions of various types, but had to date only managed to carry out 139. In June her seaplanes were due to carry out some 44 missions but they only carried out 14, due to engine failures."
174. This temporary airstrip was brought under enemy artillery fire whenever it was in use, resulting in a loss of five airplanes before it was shut down according to Pavelec, p. 57.

175. See Oliver, p. 92, for a more detailed description of the action. Also see Pavelec, p. 68.
176. This is a curious episode, for the objective was not a military target like the air base at San Stefano, but the city of Istanbul in general (Pavelec, p. 68, states: "The intent was to bomb the city directly, hopefully leading to the strategic outcome of knocking the Ottomans out of the war"). The plane was armed with 14 20-pound bombs. The Hague Convention of 1907 included the *Declaration Prohibiting the Discharge of Projectiles and Explosives from Balloons.* This declaration covered the aerial bombardment by all flying craft, but among the major powers, it was only ratified by China, the United Kingdom, and the United States, though it was signed by the Ottoman Empire. Germany was not a signatory to this declaration, but most of the major powers, including the United Kingdom and the German Empire, had signed the convention on *Law and Customs of War on Land.* Article 25 of that convention specifically stated that: "The attack or bombardment, by whatever means, of towns, villages, dwellings, or buildings which are undefended is prohibited." This mission clearly violated that article. The Ottoman Empire had signed but not ratified that convention and also the declaration.

    Now, the German Empire had started bombing the United Kingdom using their Zeppelins in January 1915 and in May 1915 had started the night bombing of London. This bombing was aimed at an occasional military target but mostly killed civilians and the occasional dog. This was clearly in violation of the Hague Convention, which Germany had ratified. If the German bombing of civilians in England was not acceptable under international law, then certainly the bombing of civilians in Turkey also was not.

    As this mission was never completed because of engine problems, this discussion is academic.
177. Pavelec, p. 69.
178. The size of the Ottoman air forces deployed to the Dardanelles in uncertain, but, the claim that at the main Ottoman airfield "all three aeroplanes were destroyed" (see Oliver, p. 102) indicates that there was still only a handful of operational Turkish planes at that point.
179. Oliver, p. 111.
180. http://albindenis.free.fr/Site_escadrille/escadrille524.htm. Also see Oliver, p. 110, where he reports that it was a couple of bombs and 2,500 metal darts.
181. Number from Pavelec, p. 75.

182. There were three main versions of Henry Farmans or Maurice Farmans used by British aviation at this time. Already obsolete was the Maurice Farman MF.7 Longhorn (1913) with 70 hp and the Maurice Farman MF.11 Shorthorn with 80 hp. None of these were deployed in August 1914 to France with the RFC although eight Maurice Farmans were shipped to France in 1914, five to Egypt in 1914 and six more Maurice Farmans were purchased from France in 1914. See http://www.airhistory.org.uk/rfc/EF3.html and subsequent pages at that site.

  The Henri Farman HF.20s (1913) with 80 hp were deployed in August 1914 to France with RFC squadrons 2, 5, and later 6. Although it is often stated that the Gnome Lambda 7-cylinder engine produced 80 hp, its measured output was often lower (around 67.5 horsepower). In general, the Henri Farmans were underpowered.

  Some later variants may have had more horsepower although they continued to use the Gnome Lambda engine (HF.21, HF.22, HF.23, HF.24). Other variants were also developed using different engines (HF.26, HF.27, F.40).

  The commander of No. 3 (Naval) Wing was particularly unsatisfied with the HF.20 with 80 hp engines, and when he received eight of them in early June, he rejected the shipment.
183. Pavelec, pp. 77 and 78. Only one was clearly identified as an HF.24. The HF.24 was the aerobatic version of the FH.210 with a shorter wingspan. It still used the Gnome Lambda engine.
184. Pavelec, p. 78.
185. Pavelec, p 71.
186. Oliver, p. 123.
187. http://albindenis.free.fr/Site_escadrille/escadrille524.htm.
188. Ibid.
189. Another account says it was 140 hp. See https://aegeanairwar.com/articles/gunners-over-gallipoli. This account claims that the target was a Rumpler B.I of the 1st Ottoman Squadron based in Galata.
190. The death of Captain Charles H. Collet is described in Oliver. Also see Pavelec, p 80.
191. One source says they also had Henry Farman F27s. See https://www.greatwarforum.org/topic/250610-aircraft-at-gallipoli/. At this site, Trevor Henshaw is quoting from his book *The Sky Their Battlefield II*. See https://theskytheirbattlefield2.com/. This does not match with the listings provided by Oliver and Pavelec.

According to the diary of F.D.H. Bremner, a pilot that served in No. 2 Wing, his unit while at Imbros had at various times: 1) Avro 504K, 2) Voisin III, 3-4) Bristol Scout C & D 5–6) Caudron G-3 & G-4, 7) Nieuport Gunbus (Nieuport 12, 8) Nieuport Scout (Nieuport 11,9) B.E.2c, 10) Farman HF.20. This is ten different aircraft. See https://bristolscout.wordpress.com/2012/01/21/10-back-to-imbros/. Bremner arrived at Imbros on 19 December 1915.

192. Pavelec, p. 82.
193. Oliver, pp. 132-133. HMS *Ark Royal* recorded 40 attempted flights, of which only 20 were "useful service" for a total flying time of 35 hours and 23 minutes.
194. Seaplane count is from Pavelec, p. 81. Naga most likely was at the western most point of Canakkale where the Military Marine Museum is now located. *The website http://www.tayyareci.com/hvtarihi/canakkale/canak6.asp, in a discussion of August 1915, says that the average strength of the squadron based in Canakkale was around four aircraft.*
195. Based upon British reports for early October (see Oliver, p. 157).
196. Pavelec, p. 81. He also notes on that page that at the time of the Galata raid (after 19 August) there were only three Gotha WD.1 and four Rumpler B.Is in operation at Galata.
197. The website http://www.tayyareci.com/hvtarihi/canakkale/canak6.asp states that it was not until August that they received their first armed aircraft, but the receipt of 4 Albatros C.Is on 13 July, which would have been armed, has been confirmed.
198. Pavelec, p. 86. He says that "these aircraft brought the total force to six land-based aircraft and four sea-based planes for the Ottomans in the campaign." This is lower than our counts. He states that the "total contingent" now included 9 pilots (4 Turkish), 8 observers (3 Turkish), 5 seaplane pilots (all German), and 2 seaplane observers (assumed to be German). See pp. 86–87. This listing does not appear to include planes operating at San Stefano.
199. Pavelec, p. 87.
200. See Pavelec, p. 90.
201. And it seems likely he was not in that staff car. For example, Pavelec on pp. 88–89 recounts the story of the bombing, but then questions whether it actually occurred in his footnote #10 on p. 193.
202. Pavelec, p. 90. Also see p. 86.
203. For example, see the Aerodrome listing for Hans Buddecke: http://www.theaerodrome.com/aces/germany/ buddecke.php.

204. A description of the attack on the Ottoman aircraft is provided at https://aegeanairwar.com/articles/gunners-over-gallipoli. It was a Henry Farman (H.7) flown by Australian pilot Captain Arthur Jopp and the observer was Flight Commander Hans Acworth Busk. The opposing plane is described as a Taube, which was machine gun armed.
205. Pavelec, p. 103. They arrived at Imbros in September 1915 and were assigned to the No. 3 Wing. They were then transferred to the No. 2 Wing in December.
206. Buddecke in his account does not report facing any armed Bristols, there are no other reports of them in action, and there are no German planes shot down in January. These six fighters were probably not yet operational. The Bristols fired through their propeller arc without synchronization or protection. It was done at the risk of damaging the propeller.
207. Plane count from Pavelec, p. 100.
208. Oliver, p. 178, reports two machines lost due to engine failure and on p. 179 records the plane flown by Samson destroyed by an exploding bomb. Pavelec, p. 101, records the loss of the aircraft on 16 December flown by either Heriot and Blackford or Wakeley and Boles (crew was not injured). Other sources report another incident on 20 December, see https://aegeanairwar.com/articles/gunners-over-gallipoli and https://www.wingsofwar.org/forums/showthread.php?19689-100-Years-Ago-Today/page20. The pilot was Jr. Lieutenant Frank Besson and the observer was Australian Lieutenant Shirley Goodwin. Besson drowned while Goodwin was captured. He was questioned by Liman von Sanders. The Senior Ottoman commander, Esad Pasha refused to see him because the air service "had just dropped a bomb on a hospital and killed the wife of the Surgeon General." This is certainly a reference to the death of Anna Schwartz (discussed later in this chapter). Goodwin remained a prisoner for the duration of the war. He was killed in action in New Guinea in 1943.

    While it does appear that they lost five planes in December, no single account picks up all five losses.
209. The downing of the French plane is noted in Oliver, p. 173.
210. Pavelec, p. 102.
211. Pavelec, p. 48 has them arriving in the middle of March, but does not have them taking to the air until 27 March. Oliver in his more detailed account, pp. 21 and 24, says they unloaded on Tenedos on 24 March and flew their first shakedown flights on 28 March. By the end of the month, he says they were flying five missions a day (Oliver, p. 25).

212. See https://bristolscout.wordpress.com/2012/01/21/10-back-to-imbros/.
213. One of Buddecke's claims for 6 January was of a French plane flown by *Ltt.* Jules Charles Lecompte, Maurice Farman MF.11 number 942, of Escadrille MF-98T.

 According to correspondence from Bernard de Broglio, the French squadron departed Tenedos on 13 January 1916. They flew to Mytilene on the island of Lesbos. There they conducted operations against Turkish installations at Smyrna. On 29 February 1916, the French squadron moved to the Salonika Front. He is not aware of any French losses while at Mytilene and suspects there were none.
214. Taken from http://albindenis.free.fr/Site_escadrille/escadrille524.htm.
215. Email exchange with Paschalis Palavouzis dated 26 December 2021 established the date that the planes arrived. He says the unit (6th War Company) was operational on 5 January 1916.
216. Pavelec notes on p. 103 that only one British plane was shot down that day. Due to the lack of records for the Escadrille MF-98T, confirming the French kill has been more difficult.
217. As Buddeke notes: "Two Fokkers hung over the yellow land. Schütz flew a hundred meters behind me."
218. See http://www.theaerodrome.com/aces/germany/buddecke.php and Franks, et al, page 88.
219. Pavelec, p. 104 states: "2 Wing pilot Flight Lieutenant C.H. Brinsmead and his observer Lieutenant N.H. Boles were shot down by two E.Is. The kill was shared by German pilots Schüz and Buddecke." His sources for the shared kills are other secondary sources. We credit this kill to Buddecke.
220. He does note in his account after the discussion of this shoot down that "For months there were no more enemy planes over the peninsula." This is an odd statement in light of the three claimed kills in late January.
221. Wikipedia (https://en.wikipedia.org/wiki/Gallipoli_campaign). Casualties in the entry are drawn from multiple sources, but primarily work done by Edward J. Erickson in his book *Ordered to Die, A History of the Ottoman Army in the First World Wa*r, which provides losses by nationality apart from Allied captured or missing.
222. See https://nzhistory.govt.nz/media/interactive/gallipoli-casualties-country. This site also does not seem to track missing or captured. There are reasons to have more faith in the Wikipedia figures than

those provided by the Government of New Zealand. Both sites give the same casualties for Australia, India, and Newfoundland. The casualties for the French are similar but rounded to the nearest thousand in the New Zealand site. The United Kingdom casualties are significantly lower in the New Zealand site, 73,485 compared to 120,246, and their New Zealand casualties are slightly higher, 7,991 compared to 7,473.

223. They are drawn from the Aerodrome website listing for "Hans Buddecke" and Franks, et al, page 88.
224. https://encyclopedia.1914–1918-online.net/article/pasha_enver is one of the better sources of information on the Web.
225. David Fromkin, *A Peace to End All Peace: The Fall of the Ottoman Empire and the Creation of the Modern Middle East* (Henry Hold and Company, New York, 1989), pp. 119, 152.

    Page 119 states: "Enver had the qualities of a lone adventurer, not those of a general. Though audacious and cunning, he was an incompetent commander. Liman von Sanders, the Prussian Army adviser with whom he frequently found himself at odds, regarded Enver as a buffoon in military matters."

    Page 152 states "Enver bravely planned to remain and defend the city, but his military dispositions were so incompetent that – as Liman von Sanders later recalled – any Turkish attempt at opposing an Allied landing in Constantinople had been rendered impossible."
226. Pavelec, pp. 10–11.
227. Interestingly his surname "Liman" is also a Turkish word meaning "port" or "bay," so many geographical features around Gallipoli may appear to be named after him (e.g. Karanglek Liman, Nagara Liman, Kilia Liman, Ak Bashi Liman, etc.) but this is simply a coincidence.
228. See the Axis History Forum at https://forum.axishistory.com/viewtopic.php?t=123118 and also http://www.tayyareci.com/hvtarihi/canakkale/canak1.asp. Note that this is a count of all Ottoman air sections, although sources disagree as to whether there were three or four seaplane sections. It does imply that Major Serno was involved in setting up all Ottoman air sections during the war.
229. Some accounts claim that the air force was founded in June 1909 with the dispatch of an "inspection council" to the International Aviation Conference in Paris.
230. https://military.wikia.org/wiki/Ottoman_Air_Force.
231. See https://www.liquisearch.com/ottoman_air_force/balkan_wars and https://military.wikia.org/wiki/Ottoman_Air_Force#cite_note-Ordered_228-16.

Data drawn from Edward J. Erickson, *Ordered to Die: A History of the Ottoman Army in the First World War*, Appendix D: The Ottoman Aviation Inspectorate and Aviation Squadrons, p. 228.

Pavelec gives a somewhat different picture. He states (p. 9) that when the First Balkan War erupted in October 1912, only one plane was available for operations at San Stefano and only five were flight worthy in the rest of the empire. All six of their operational aircraft were rendered useless during the conflict through overuse and neglect. He also states: "By the end of the Balkan Wars (July 1913), the Ottomans could only cobble together three serviceable aircraft by cannibalizing the entire fleet. After a severe storm in August that collapsed an aircraft hangar, only one plane remained. When that single aircraft crash-landed at the end of September due to a faulty engine, they were left without any planes" (p. 10).

232. Pavelec, p. 12, gives slightly different figures: "At their disposal, the Ottoman Empire boasted four airplanes, one balloon, and five seaplanes, all based at Yeşilköy." See also https://www.primidi.com/ottoman_air_force/world_war_i_operations.
233. This certainly included the 1st, 2nd, and 6th Squadrons and 1st Seaplane Squadron. Other units may be included in this count. See https://www.primidi.com/ottoman_air_force/world_war_i_operations.
234. See Raul Colon: http://www.aeroflight.co.uk/military/gallipoli.htm.
235. Some sources say in the summer. The date of 13 July comes from http://www.tayyareci.com/hvtarihi/canakkale/canak6.asp.
236. One Fokker monoplane arrived at Canakkale in September 1915 followed by three more in January. These last three were under command of Hans Buddecke. It is also claimed that Hans Buddecke and his fighter pilots Schüz, Meinecke, and Muhra destroyed nine enemy aircraft. See https://de.zxc.wiki/wiki/Fliegertruppe_(Osmanisches_Reich).

Only the kills by Buddecke have been confirmed. He does not report any kills by "Schütz," or by "our youngest" pilot in his account.

The three Fokkers that came down with Buddecke are identified as a Fokker E.III 108/15 Werk number (w.n.) 361 (Ottoman serial F2), Fokker E.III 96/15 (Buddecke's aircraft), w.n. 349 (Ottoman serial F3), and Fokker E.II 93/15 w.n. 346 (Ottoman serial F4). See https://aegeanairwar.com/articles/brinsmeads-unfortunate-distinction; http://www.theaerodrome.com/forum/showthread.php?t=30619; http://www.tayyareci.com/digerucaklar/turkiye/ww1/fokkere1.asp; and https://bristolscout.wordpress.com/2016/01/17/8-jan-1916/.

Bronnenkant, p. 31, notes that Buddecke may have also flown 108/15.

The first Fokker deployed to Turkey in September was a Fokker E.II 36/15, w.n. 286 (Ottoman serial number F1). Since late September 1915 it had been serving with the 1st Squadron at Galata aerodrome (and probably flown by Theodor Croneiss). Its location in January 1916 is not known.

Bronnenkant, p. 31, states that Fokker 36/15 was originally with Buddecke at FFA 23. This was probably not the same plane that was in Turkey. Probably one of the serial numbers is in error.

237. See David Bremner, https://bristolscout.wordpress.com/2016/01/17/8-jan-1916/. He cites Ole Nikolajsen, *Ottoman Aviation 1909-1919*, ole-nikolajsen.com, 2012, p. 70. as his source.
238. See https://www.greatwarforum.org/topic/285180-oblt-eric-muhra-german-pilot/ and https://www.gallipoli1915.de/squadrons-1--6.
239. Emil Meinecke is shown in the Aerodrome website has having claimed six kills and one unconfirmed kill for the war. He became a test pilot for Fokker after the war. Meinecke was also a pre-war pilot. See https://www.gallipoli1915.de/squadrons-1--6 and http://www.theaerodrome.com/aces/germany/meinecke.php.

According to Meinecke, there were three fighter pilots flying with the 6th Squadron: Captain Hans-Joachim Buddecke, Oberleutnant Theo Croneiss, and himself. He was to relieve the squadron commander, Croneiss, as he was on leave in Germany, whereas Buddecke was also being transferred back to the Western Front. So, soon he remained the only Fokker pilot flying in the area. See https://bristolscout.wordpress.com/2016/01/17/8-jan-1916/.

This account further notes that there were two other pilots flying the squad in late December-early January: Ltn Hans Schüz and Ltn Erich Mudra (sometimes reported as Muhra). All of these pilots were credited with aerial victories during the evacuation of Gallipoli: Buddecke with 4, Croneiss with 2, Schüz with 2 [?], and Mudra with 1.

240. Franks, et al, pp. 207–208 and http://www.theaerodrome.com/aces/germany/schuz.php.
241. http://www.frontflieger.de/3-s-f.html#schuezhans and https://www.lexikon-der-wehrmacht.de/Personenregister/S/SchuezHans.htm.
242. https://www.lexikon-der-wehrmacht.de/Personenregister/S/SchuezHans.htm and http://www.frontflieger.de/2-ffa034.html.
243. http://www.theaerodrome.com/aces/germany/schuz.php.
244. http://www.theaerodrome.com/aces/germany/schuz.php and https://aegeanairwar.com/articles/brinsmeads-unfortunate-distinction.

245. Sometimes spelled Chevau-Léger, or "Light Horse."
246. Oddly enough, a couple of major accounts on the air war around Gallipoli also do not mention him. Bronnenkant, page 13, does mention him, but puts him together in the same unit with Buddecke, Hans Schüz, and Erich Murha, with three or four Fokkers. We think this is not the case.
247. https://dehu.abcdef.wiki/wiki/Theodor_Cronei%C3%9F and https://www.staatliche-bibliothek-regensburg.de/fileadmin/regensburg/PDF/Nachlaesse/croneiss.pdf.
248. https://archiv-akh.de/filme/252#1 and https://gw.geneanet.org/croneiss?lang=fr&iz=258&p=gernot&n=croneiss.
249. Sources vary as to whether this was an Albatros C.I or a C.III. See: Thomas P. Iredale, "https://encyclopedia.1914-1918-online.net/pdf/1914-1918-Online-role_of_german_officers_in_the_gallipoli_campaign-2019-12-04-V1.1.pdf#:~:text=month%20before%20the%20Allies%20launched%20amphibious%20attacks%20on,At%20divisional%20level%20there%20was%2-0Colonel%20Georg%20von and Pavelec, p. 90. It appears to have been a C.I.
250. Pavelec, p. 90, states that: "Either Samson, flying Nieuport Number 24 or Davies in Nieuport Number 26 came into contact with the Albatross that morning. The planes flew against each other and shots were fired, but the encounter was indecisive, no damaged sustained."
251. Dates vary across sources; see https://www.gallipoli1915.de/fliegerleutnant-ludwig-preuner and https://www.greatwarforum.org/topic/291937-a-rare-dogfight-over-anzac/.
252. https://forum.axishistory.com/viewtopic.php?p=2290959.
253. Pavelec, p. 90.
254. https://de.zxc.wiki/wiki/Fliegertruppe_(Osmanisches_Reich); https://www.greatwarforum.org/topic/250610-aircraft-at-gallipoli/; https://forum.axishistory.com/viewtopic.php?t=77600; and http://www.tayyareci.com/hvtarihi/canakkale/canak7.asp.
255. http://albindenis.free.fr/Site_escadrille/escadrille524.htm. Pavelec, p. 114, notes that there are no surviving records for French Escadrille MF-98T.
256. https://forum.axishistory.com/viewtopic.php?t=228605&start=45 and http://www.tayyareci.com/hvtarihi/canakkale/canak8.asp. Their source is given as "Karl Stirling Schneide, pages 98-100."
257. http://albindenis.free.fr/Site_escadrille/escadrille524.htm. Pavelec, p. 114, says there are no surviving records for the French Escadrille MF-98T.

258. See Franks, et al., p. 94; https://www.wingsofwar.org/forums/showthread.php?19689-100-Years-Ago-Today/page21; and http://www.theaerodrome.com/aces/germany/croneiss.php. Note that neither detailed account of British operations by Oliver or Pavelec lists these claims, nor notes any British planes shot down 7 January. Neither are any losses listed in Trevor Henshaw, *The Sky Their Battlefield: Air Fighting and the Complete List of Allied Air Casualties from Enemy Action in the First War: British, Commonwealth, and United States Air Services 1914–1918* (Grub Street Publishing, London, 1995). If these claims are valid, then they had to be French planes. There are no records from Escadrille MF-98T that could confirm or refute these claims.
259. https://www.gallipoli1915.de/squadrons-1--6. Also see: Franks, et al., p. 95, and http://www.theaerodrome.com/aces/germany/croneiss.php.
260. There is an excellent account of this encounter from Bremner's logbook at https://bristolscout.wordpress.com/2016/01/17/8-jan-1916/. The author that quoted this logbook, who was Bremner's grandson, claims that there was no way of turning the Voisin quickly enough to return the German fire, so the observer Burnaby took the Lewis gun off its mount and rested in on the top wing and tried to get a bead on the enemy aircraft that way.
261. Bremner (*op. cit.*) met with Paschalis Palavouzis, who provided him additional information claiming that Theodor Croneiss had shot down his grandfather.
262. Interestingly, neither Oliver's or Pavelec's account mention this action.
263. Bronnenkant, p. 15.
264. See Franks, et al., pp. 207–208; https://www.gallipoli1915.de/squadrons-1--6; and https://www.wingsofwar.org/forums/showthread.php?19689-100-Years-Ago-Today/page21. Franks, p. 207, states that the victory "was initially shared with Leutnant Buddecke." Buddecke's account does say Schüz got a kill on the Western Front before 1916, but none of these listings record that.

Dr. Bronnenkant points out in correspondence in February 2022 that the *Kriegs-Chronik der Leipziger Neuesten Nachrichten*, which covered the air war over the Dardanelles, specifically mentioned and described Buddecke's victories on 6 and 12 January 1916. It also gave an account of Buddecke's and Croneiss' joint claim on 9 January (the loss looks like it was actually on 8 January). It also mentions two more Buddecke victories over the Dardanelles in a 29 January report. But it never says anything about a claim on 11 January, which suggests it was not confirmed for him.

He also notes that the *Heeresbericht* report for 6 January mentions Buddecke's French Farman victory. Traditionally, the *Heeresbericht* began mentioning fighter pilots by name only upon their 4th victory and this indeed was its first mention of Buddecke by name. For 9 January, it reported: "*Einer unserer Flieger griff einen feindlichen Doppeldecker vom System Farman ab und brachte ihn zum Absturz, das Flugzeug fiel, in Flammen gehüllt, bei Sed-ul-Bahr nieder.*" The absence of a name strongly suggests the confirmation went to Croneiss, as modern sources relate, since Buddecke would have been mentioned by name at that point. The *Heeresbericht* is completely silent for 11 January. If the kill had been confirmed for Buddecke, one suspects that both the *Heeresbericht* and the *Kriegs-Chronik* would have mentioned it.

265. https://aegeanairwar.com/articles/brinsmeads-unfortunate-distinction. It quotes passages drawn from the British Royal Air Force, Officer's Service Records 1912-1920, the Royal Navy Log Book of HMS *Ribble*, and from HMS *Hibernia*. HMS *Ribble*'s logbook can be viewed at http://www.naval-history.net/OWShips-WW1-10-HMS_Ribble.htm.
266. See http://albindenis.free.fr/Site_escadrille/escadrille524.htm. The author also appears to have not accepted the claim.
267. https://www.gallipoli1915.de/squadrons-1--6 is the source of this claim. Also see Franks, et al., p. 95; http://www.theaerodrome.com/aces/germany/croneiss.php; and https://www.wingsofwar.org/forums/showthread.php?19689-100-Years-Ago-Today/page22.
268. These are as listed in Henshaw, *The Sky Their Battlefield*, page 496. Copies of page provided courtesy of Bernard de Broglio from the 2008 edition. It states: "6th January, 2 Wing RNAS **B of Turkish troops, came down in sea? MIA (FCdr HA Busk KIA). 8th January 8502 Voisin LAS 2 Wing RNAS **Spotting combat near CAPE HELLES 4-30pm shot up engine hit ftl OK (FSLt FDH Bremner/MS HE Burnaby) burnt ac [combat Oblt T Croneiss FAb6]. 11th January Farman RNAS Imbros ** combat with 2 EAs, shot down SEDD-EL-BAHR off HELLES (FSlt CH Brinsmead Aust. KIA/Lieutenant NH Boles KIA) Lt Boles from RFC [met FA6b]. 12th January Farman RNAS Imbros ** shot down off HELLESPONT MIA (TFSLt JS Bolas KIA/MS DM Branson WIA POW) [FAb6]."

The 1995 edition for 11 January (still page 496) lists: "Farman RNAS ** combat with 2EA shot down SEDD-EL-DAHR off HELLES (FSLt CH Brinsmead KIA) [FAb6]" and "Farman RNAS 88 combat with 2EA shot down SEDD-EL-BAHR off HELLES (FLt NH Boles KIA {FA6b]". That he lists Brinsmead and Boles as two separate shoot downs in his 1995 edition is probably why several authors have accepted that both Hans Schüz and Buddecke each shot down a plane this day. There was only one plane shot down this day, and Brinsmead and Boles were both in it.

269. The pilot's full name was Jules Charles Jean Baptiste Lecompte (known as Jean). He was an *Adjudant pilote*, Escadrille MF-98T. Awarded Médaille militaire and Croix de Guerre with one bronze palm. Born 20 August 1891 at Vincennes. Gained his civilian pilot's license on 25 October 1913 in a Blériot, then his military pilot's license on 31 March 1914, joining Escadrille MF-5 (French 1st Army, Battle of Lorraine), where he was promoted sergeant, then Escadrille MF-22 (4th Army, First Battle of Champagne). Lecompte was among the original complement of eight pilots that was dispatched to the Dardanelles with Escadrille MF-98T. He was 24 at the time of his death. He is interred in grave number 2239 at the French national cemetery, Seddülbahir. This research courtesy of Bernard de Broglio.
270. Bronnenkant, pages 14–15 identifies the pilot as Baptiste de Conte, based upon the German inscription in a photo of a grave cross at Cape Helles. A grave marker was later erected at Seddülbahir that refers to the pilot as Jules Le Copte. A photo of this marker was provided by Bernard de Broglio. This name is not correct. His correct name is drawn from his French death record.
271. Drawn from http://www.rudgwickremembers.com/Hans Acworth Busk.html.
272. Cenk Avci, *The Skies of Gallipoli* (Kadikoy, Istanbul, 2003), revised and expanded 2nd edition. This passage was accessed via http://www.rudgwickremembers.com/Hans Acworth Busk.html.
273. Bronnenkant, p. 15.
274. Ibid.
275. The kill is recorded in Franks, et al, p. 88 and in the Aerodrome. Also see Franks, et al., pp. 94–95 (Croneiss) and pp. 207–208 (Schüz).
276. See the discussion of French records in Pavelec, pp. 114–115.
277. For example, Lanoe Hawker in his diary entry of 14 August 1915 records for a three-week period (Sunday, 25 July to Saturday, 14 August) twelve combat encounters resulting in fifteen planes

engaged, of which five were brought down and nine were put to flight (and there was one "defeat"). See Tyrrell M. Hawker, MC, *Hawker VC RFC Ace: The Life of Major Lanoe Hawker VC DSO 1890–1916* (Pen & Sword, Barnsley, UK, 2013), p. 110.

278. https://aegeanairwar.com/articles/brinsmeads-unfortunate-distinction. On the other hand, for 11 January Bronnenkant, p. 15, credits both Buddecke and Hans Schüz with the kill based in part upon two Commonwealth pilots being lost that day, Brinsmead (who he calls Brimstead) and Boles. Boles was the observer for Brinsmead. Either Buddecke or Hans Schüz got a victory this day or shared one. It appears that only one British plane went down this day.
279. https://aegeanairwar.com/articles/brinsmeads-unfortunate-distinction. Pavelec, p. 104, states that: "On the 12th, Flight Sub-Lieutenant J.S. Bolas and Midshipman D.M. Branson were shot down by Schüz; Buddecke also claimed another Allied plane." He references two secondary sources. It seems likely this statement is simply garbled and the only plane shot down that day was by Hans Buddecke.
280. See Franks, *Above the Lines*, pp. 94–95 and 207–208, and http://www.theaerodrome.com/aces/germany/croneiss.php.
281. Copy of translation provided by Lance J. Bronnenkant. Document is stored at the University of Texas at Dallas. It is Box 511/F.5, p. I/24, of the collection that A.E. Ferko donated to them. Ferko had an English transcript of Serno's memoirs that is not complete – only the beginning sections of Serno's memoirs have been translated.

    A complete copy of Serno's account is available at the German archives in Freiburg, but one is only allowed to take notes from it, and is not allowed to make a copy, according to correspondence with Michael Pavelec.
282. http://www.theaerodrome.com/aces/germany/meinecke.php.
283. Oliver, p. 161, has him arriving 17 October, while other sources have him shipping out of England on 14 October and arriving at Imbros two weeks later. See https://airwar19141918.wordpress.com/2016/01/08/6-january-1916–busk-killed-in-gallipoli/.
284. See https://www.winchestercollegeatwar.com/RollofHonour.aspx?RecID=81&TableName=ta_wwifactfile; https://www.findagrave.com/memorial/56005716/hans-acworth-busk; https://airwar19141918.wordpress.com/tag/hans-acworth-busk/; and Oliver, p. 161. While Oliver discusses a number of Busk's other air operations (on pp. 170, 174–175, and 181) he does not discuss the mission of

6 January 1916. Also see http://www.rudgwickremembers.com/Hans Acworth Busk.html.

285. The list of aces awarded the Blue Max includes: Manfred von Richthofen (80 claimed kills), Ernst Udet (62), Erich Loewenhardt (54), Josef Jacobs (48), Werner Voss (48), Fritz Rumey (45), Rudolf Berthold (44), Bruno Loerzer (44), Paul Baumer (43), Oswald Boelcke (40), Franz Buechner (40), Lothar von Richthofen (40), Heinrich Gontermann (39), Carl Menckhoff (39), Karl Bolle (36), Julius Buckler (36), Max Ritter von Mueller (36), Otto Koennecke (35), Eduard Ritter von Schleich (35), Emil Thuy (35), Josef Veitjens (35), Heinrich Bongartz (33), Heinrich Kroll (33), Kurt Wolff (33), Theodor Osterkamp (32), Gotthard Sachsenberg (31), Karl Allmenroeder (30), Carl Degelow (30), Ulrich Neckel (30), Karl Emil Schaefer (30), Walter Blume (28), Walter von Buelow-Bothkamp (28), Robert Ritter von Greim (28), Arthur Laumann (28), Friedrich Ritter von Roeth (28), Fritz Otto Bernert (27), Hans Kirschstein (27), Karl Thom (27), Adolf Ritter von Tutschek (27), Kurt Wuesthoff (27), Oskar Freiherr von Boenigk (26), Eduard Ritter von Dostler (26), Oliver Freiherr von Beaulieu-Marconnay (25), Fritz Putter (25), Erwin Boehme (24), Hermann Göring (22), Hans Klein (22), Rudolf Windisch (22), Friedrich Friedrichs (21), Wilhelm Frankl (20), Otto Kissenberth (20), Kurt Wintgens (19), Max Immelmann (15), Hans-Joachim Buddecke (13), Friedrich Christiansen (13 – but awarded for 21 victories) and Walter Hoehndorf (12). This is a total of 56 aces. Other airmen awarded this order with less than 11 victories are not included in this list.

High scoring aces not awarded the Blue Max include Gustav Doerr (35), Hermann Frommherz (32), Paul Billk (31), Josef Mai (30), Harald Auffarth (29), Otto Fruhner (27), Max Naether (26), Georg von Hantelmann (25), Georg Meyer (24), Hermann Becker (23), Hans Martin Pippart (22), Werner Preuss (22), Karl Schegel (22), Hans von Adam (21), Friedrich Altermeier (21), Fritz Hoehn (21), Friedrich T. Noltenius (21), Hans Bethge (20), Rudolf von Eschwege (20), Hans von Freden (20), Walter Goettsch (20), Oskar Hennrich (20), Wilhelm Reinhard (20) and Otto Schmidt (20). This is a total of 24 aces with 20 or more claimed kills.

286. See Henshaw, pp. 69–70. Bronnenkant, pp. 15–16, also discusses this, noting that Henshaw lists no British losses for 25 or 27 January and the *Kriegs-Chronik* only reports: "29 January 1916: The Mili Agency announces: airman Oblt. Buddecke caused several enemy aircraft to crash on the Dardanelles."

287. According to correspondence with Bernard de Broglio: 'No. 2 Wing RNAS at Imbros:
Unfortunately formal operation reports didn't begin until February 1916. I only have reports from March 1916 onwards. However I checked an airman's diary which has dates, records events of this squadron during the period, and can be considered reliable. No crashes or anything that suggests an aeroplane forced down on these dates.
Ark Royal's report for January and February 1916:
"No losses or crashes noted. On 5 February 1916, a seaplane with Earl of Peterborough at Port Lagos was attacked by a 'German aeroplane' but apparently the enemy's gun jammed."'

288. According to correspondence from Bernard de Broglio, the French squadron departed Tenedos on 13 January 1916. They flew to Mytilene on the island of Lesbos. From there they flew operations against Smyrna. On 29 February 1916, the French squadron moved to the Salonica Front. De Broglio is not aware of any French losses while at Mytilene and suspects there were none. They could still reach Gallipoli from Lesbos.
The website http://albindenis.free.fr/Site_escadrille/escadrille524.htm notes that after arriving at Lesbos, the French were given 15 days of rest and were operational again on 29 January. This implies that the unit was out of action from 13 to 28 January 1916. On 7 February, they conducted a raid on Smyrna, which was more than 200 kilometers away. They were to refuel on Long Island in the Gulf of Smyrna, working with the ethnic Greek inhabitants there. According to accounts, the Greek inhabitants had been massacred before the planes arrived; the French found their corpses in the Orthodox church of the village. A British supply ship arrived the next day and the planes were able to carry out their attack on Smyrna.

289. All stats are taken from Wikipedia. The empty weight for the E.III is given at 880 lb, while the empty weight for the E.II is given as 750 lb. It's not clear what made up the extra 130 lb. The difference in their gross weight is 243 lb.
In an email exchange in February 2022 with David S. Bremner, who rebuilt from scratch and flies his grandfather's Bristol No. 1264, he said this about the relative performance of the planes:
"According to Sturtivant & Page, the first batch of Scouts – 1259, 1261, 1262, 1263 & 1264 – were sent to Imbros in SS *Nankin* in August 1915, arriving with No. 3 Wing in September that year. They were transferred to No. 2 Wing in December that year. They were all the first batch of Type C Scouts manufactured under contract number CP 67209/14/X.

1259 suffered an engine failure on takeoff and was overturned by my Grandad in March 1916 and was written off.

1261 was written off around Dec 1916, probably still at Imbros.

1262 was written off after a landing accident with Flt SL Biscoe in March 1916.

1263 had an engine failure (Flt SL Busk) and landed in the sea in March 1916.

1264 was transferred to Thasos and was written off after being refurbished on HMS *Ark Royal,* put on a transport ship for delivery back to Thasos, but the transport ship was torpedoed.

The second batch of Bristol Scouts (also Type C, but with significant design changes), were delivered to Imbros in March 1916. They were serials 3017 – 3022. They all seem to have been returned to the UK in June 1916.

Two more Scout Cs, 3036 & 3037, were delivered to the Med in Dec 1915 and transferred to Thasos in May, when Thasos started operations.

We can't be too sure about armament. It's possible that all of the first batch had Lewis guns on the starboard side, but we don't have photographic confirmation. Some had bombs – 1259 and 1264 did, but I'm not sure about the others.

I have no information about the second batch.

3036 had a Lewis gun on the port side. It may have had one on the starboard side as well, but we've no information.

3037 had guns on the port side and over the top wing.

As for the performance data, I would be a little leery of that. I know our own weight and performance figures don't match those recorded at the time, and that applies to the Shuttleworth's Sopwith Pup as well. The increased weight of the EIII would have reduced the rate of climb but increased the maximum speed in a dive. It may also have affected the handling adversely. The rate of climb was only important in getting up to your adversary; once you were in combat it made less difference.

… The 80 le Rhone is said to deliver 92hp, but it does vary quite a bit from day to day. The 80 Gnome engine is said to deliver 65hp. I know grandad swapped 1264 from a Gnome to a le Rhone and got much improved figures. … There are many possible reasons for the difference in [weight] figures – most obviously the large amount of rigging needed to keep a monoplane wing rigid. But based on grandad's account (see below) I think that may be right; the Eindekker was faster in a dive, but the Bristol was faster on the level … Getting accurate time to climb data is notoriously difficult. Temperature, moisture, turbulence all have a huge effect on the numbers on the day. But the lighter weight of the Bristol, coupled with is low wing loading would have helped it a lot. The Sopwith Triplane was highly regarded for its rate of climb.

Probably the main reason the Bristol Scout was superior to the Eindekker was manoeuvrability. The Eindekkers – all of them – used wing warping whereas the Bristol had four ailerons. They are very effective for an aircraft of that date, as I can confirm from practical experience. I suspect the best evidence we have is my granddad's letter home after he engaged one of the Eindekkers on 16 March.

He was escorting a two seater Nieuport 12 home, along with Lt Savory in a Nieuport 11, when an Eindekker was spotted chasing them. He waited until the Eindekker got a bit closer, then turned back to face it so they were approaching head on. Grandad knew that the Eindekker would do a 'chandelle' (raise the nose to about 45deg, then apply stick and rudder to carry out a 180deg turn that rises and then falls) to the left. This was because the Eindekker's wing warping was ineffective and very dangerous – if you got the controls crossed the stick would lock over due to unbalanced aerodynamic loads and you couldn't get it back. A British builder/pilot, John Day, was killed this way a few years ago. Turning left is easier than turning right because of the precession effects of the engine.

Grandad waited until the German had started his turn and couldn't see him, then he did a vertically banked turn, also to the left, and completed a 270 degree turn in the time it took the Eindekker to do 90 degrees, ending up on his tail.

The Eindekker dived, and being a monoplane was faster in the dive, but when he levelled out grandad caught up with him and had another go at him. He saw bullets entering the Eindekker's fuselage, but nothing critical was hit.

You need to appreciate how very, very difficult it is to hit anything in air-to-air combat. Both you and the target are moving around randomly at great speed, and the only hits that count are to the pilot or the engine, with one or two other lucky strikes possible. So with a single gun firing 500 rounds a minute, the chances of hitting anything vital are very remote."

290. See Appendix I.
291. Kum Dere is actually the name of a small stream on the west coast of the peninsula, approximately midway between the town of Krithia and the headland at Gaba Tepe.

292. Bronnenkant, p. 16.
293. For example, see Franks, et al; p. 88 or the Aerodrome entry for Hans Buddecke.
294. Henshaw, pp. 84–85.
295. Bronnenkant, p. 17.
296. Professor Johannes Werner, *Knight of Germany: Oswald Boelcke – German Ace* (The Naval & Military Press, Ltd, Uckfield, England), p. 167.
297. Bronnenkant, pp. 17, 19. This is based upon photographic evidence.
298. He was stationed back in the Berlin area from late April 1915 to mid-May 1915 to prepare FFA 62 for deployment.
299. Werner, *op. cit.*, pp. 193-195.
300. Akhisar (modern spelling) is a small city about 45 mi (75 km) northeast of Smyrna (modern Izmir). The Magnesia to which he refers is the modern town of Manisa, roughly halfway between Akhisar and Izmir.
301. Leutnant Kurt Wintgens was the first German pilot to shoot down an enemy aircraft using a machine gun synchronized to fire through the propeller arc (a more advanced solution than Garros' metal deflectors). Walter Höhndorf (note the difference from Buddecke's spelling) was another early German fighter ace who scored most of his victories not while with a fighter squadron but while flying reconnaissance missions. He had been an aircraft designer and builder before the war. Oskar Gustav Rudolf Berthold downed an amazing 44 aircraft between 1916 and 1918. Even more amazing is that his final 16 victories were achieved after he was grievously wounded and had the use of only one arm. Fritz Otto Bernert was also a one-armed ace, having been invalided out of the infantry a crippling bayonet wound. He still managed to down 27 enemy aircraft. Of all these pilots, including Buddecke, only Berthold survived the war. He died in 1920 in street fighting during the postwar political chaos in Hamburg. Nothing is known of Stehle.
302. The Caudron was a type of French aircraft built by the firm Societé des Avions Caudron, founded by brothers Gaston and René Caudron in 1909. The aircraft mentioned here was probably a G.4 twin-engine bomber.

     On 6 September 1916, Buddecke was credited with a kill of an F.E.2b over Chaulnes at 1855. This is probably the same incident. Chaulnes is just north of Roye.
303. Note that the early Eindeckers – E.I, E.II, and E.III – only had one machine gun. Therefore the reference to "two machine guns" is puzzling.

304. Perhaps counter-intuitively, barrage or observation balloons could be quite difficult (and dangerous) to shoot down, and doing so usually required the use of special incendiary ammunition instead of the regular ball ammunition with which fighter planes were usually armed.
305. Berthold's seventh victory was recorded on 17 September. He had an unconfirmed victory on 22 September, another on 24 September, and his eighth confirmed victory on 26 September. Therefore this incident probably happened between 22-26 September 1916.
306. This is a reference to the Halberstadt D.II, a biplane fighter in use during 1916–17. It was the first biplane fighter employed by the Germans, gradually superseding the mono-wing Fokkers like the one Buddecke had been flying since his return from Turkey.
307. The town of Biaches, in the area called La Maisonnette, just across the Somme River SW of Péronne.
308. The Albatros was a series of German fighters, from the D.I (introduced in August 1916) through the D.V and D.Va (introduced May 1917). The model mentioned here is possibly the D.III, which was introduced in December 1916 and was flown by many German aces. More than 1,800 were built.
309. The date he left Turkey is derived from his and Boelcke's accounts. Buddecke was awarded the *Pour le Mérite* on 14 April and got word of its receipt while he was still in Turkey. His last kill there was on 4 April 1916. He was reported in Boelcke"s account to be in Smyrna on the 20th through the 25th of July 1916. His first kill on the Western Front was on 6 September 1916.

    Buddecke states in his account that "A week before me, Boelcke had returned from his visit to Smyrna to organize a fighter squadron on the Somme. I followed after him and thus returned to Roupy and Vaux."

    Boelcke left Smyrna on 26 July, left Constantinople on 1 August, and arrived at Dessau on 20 August. One could infer that Buddecke arrived on the Western Front in late August (27th?) and therefore had left Turkey a couple of weeks earlier than that.
310. France had a population of 41.4 million in 1911 according to their census. Germany had a population of 64.4 million in 1911, and 67.8 million at the start of the war. As such, the German population was almost 60 per cent larger.
311. Buddecke states in Chapter 17 that "After a four-month guest role in the West, it was back to the Dardanelles!"

312. Bronnenkant, p. 20, credits Immelmann with only 15. An official list of German Aces and their kill counts was published by the Germans shortly after the war. It was reproduced in *Cross & Cockade* 3:3, and on p. 216 gives Immelmann's count as 15.
313. Kilduff, p. 68, says Boelcke was ordered home on 11 August and Buddecke was ordered home a week later.
314. Kilduff, pp. 69–70. Wikipedia, referencing The Aerodrome website, claimed that Berthold was in command of the squadron from 25–28 August 1916, Buddecke was in command from 28 August to 14 December 1916, and then Althaus took command from 14 December 1916 to February 1917. The Aerodrome has Berthold commanding from 25 August–1 September 1916, Buddecke commanding from 1 September–14 December 1916 and Althaus is not listed.
315. Single-seat fighter plane.
316. His "confirmed" kill on 17 September appears to have been a plane that had engine trouble which he ended up claiming. See Kilduff, p. 70. His "confirmed" kill on 26 September was probably brought down by anti-aircraft fire, see Kilduff, pp. 72-73. Ironically, both of his unconfirmed kills appear to have been actual shoot downs. See Kilduff, pp. 70, 72.
317. Kilduff, p. 74.
318. Bronnenkant, p. 21.
319. Kilduff, p. 55.
320. Five of the previous awardees attended his award ceremony (Buddecke, Wintgens, Althaus, Frankl, and Höhndorf). Three others had already been killed in action.
321. Franks, et al, p. 88, has the date as 6 September (as does the Aerodrome website). Bronnenkant, pp. 20 and 37, states it was 16 September. He backs this up with a reference to the *Jasta 4* war diary which states that a "Vikkers" fell near Chaulnes on 16 September 1916. The British lost five F.E.2bs that day but none near Chaulnes. Also see Henshaw, pp. 107, 110.
322. For example see Henshaw, p. 112.
323. https://web.archive.org/web/20061018212527/http://www.crossandcockade.com/pdf/Buddecke.pdf. Also see Bronnenkant, p. 20, who seems to lean towards it being F.E.2b 6937 based upon photographic evidence. He includes a picture in his book on page 21 of Buddecke standing next to F.E.2b 6937 at Jasta 4's airfield at Roupy. These same pictures, along with a note on the back of the picture can be seen on Tobias Weber's website at http://www.buddecke.de/buddecke/albumbud/buddeckeplm.htm.

It is pretty probable from the photographic evidence and Buddecke's note that he forced down F.E.2b 6937. He identifies it in his memoir as his eleventh victory.

324. Smyrna (modern Izmir) was a major Ottoman port city on the Aegean coast. At this time, about half the residents of this city were of Greek descent. The nation of Greece officially joined the war by declaring war on the Central Powers on 30 June 1917.
325. As this is March 1917, his airplane is almost certainly not a Fokker Eindecker, which as previously mentioned only had one gun. It was perhaps an Albatros D.II or D.III which had two machine guns.
326. A hammam, or Turkish bath, is a public heated bath or steam bath usually connected with the Islamic world but modeled on the Roman *thermae*, the name of which was based (rather than from Latin) on the Greek *thermos*, or hot, as in Thermopylae, "the hot gates."
327. The Meander River (also spelled Maeander, or Büyük Menderes in modern Turkish) is a long, twisty river – hence the origin of the verb "to meander" in English – that is about 65 miles southeast of Smyrna at its closest point.
328. A cothurn is a stylized ancient Greek or Roman type of shoe, often used by stage actors, with laces that go partway up the lower leg.
329. Probably "Ali Anak" in Turkish.
330. The Seljuk (or Seljuq) Empire was a Sunni Muslim empire of the Middle Ages, lasting from 1037 to 1194. At its height (c. 1082) it included most of modern Turkey, Israel, Mesopotamia, Iran, Afghanistan, and on into the Hindu Kush and parts of the Arabian Peninsula.
331. Phidias was a renowned sculptor of ancient Greece, known for statues of Athena on the Acropolis and many other works in bronze and marble. The 41-foot-high statue of Zeus he created from ivory and gold for the temple at Olympia around 435 BC was one of the Seven Wonders of the ancient world.
332. Probably Akdağ (in Turkish, "white mountain").
333. See Bronnenkant, pages 21 and 25.
334. Bronnenkant, page 25.
335. As Dr. Cigdem Oguz noted in correspondence in February 2022: "At that time the most profitable job for the military-bureaucrats or the merchants was the so-called *vagon ticareti* ('railcar trade') because the usual transportation road was blocked at the sea. In the context of creating a Muslim bourgeoisie, the ruling party Committee of Union and Progress was providing the Muslim merchants with reserved railcars."

336. Bronnenkant, p. 25. According to correspondence with Bronnenkant, Serno's memoir was written in 1958. The late Dr. Dieter Gröschel obtained a copy and provided the translated passage about Buddecke in *Over the Front* 13:4, pp. 367–68.
337. Bronnenkant, p. 25.
338. The "Hans-Joachim Buddecke" page on The Aerodrome website is one of those that claims it was while he was with *Jasta 18*. However Kilduff, p. 108, states that: "Consequently, when Berthold requested that his friend join him at Jasta 18, Buddecke was able to leave his post at Jasta 30 and, on 8 March, the long-time comrades were reunited at Avelin."
339. Kilduff, p. 106.
340. Kilduff, page 108.
341. Quoted from Bronnenkant, p. 25; drawn from Wyngarden, Jasta 18, p. 63.
342. From website whealy.com: "Grandfather Arthur Treloar Whealy," maintained by grandson Chris Whealy.
343. Bronnenkant, pp. 25–26.
344. A review of his 27 claimed kills shows at least 19 were fighters. Five of his kills were shared.
345. See Bronnenkant, p. 28.
346. *Ibid.* He may have flown other planes at this time.
347. Bronnenkant, p. 29. He may have flown other planes at this time.
348. This is according to The Aerodrome website listing for *Jasta 4*, which states this plane was there in August 1916. Bronnenkant, p. 32, notes that the squadron was also armed with Halberstadt D.IIs.
349. Bronnenkant, p. 33.
350. The Iron Cross (or *Eiserneskreuz*, EK) came in two grades: 2nd Class (EKII) and 1st Class (EKI).
351. The Knight's Cross with Swords of the Hohenzollern House Order (KCHHO) was a very high decoration that was only awarded to officers who had already won the EKII and EKI, and was generally a precursor medal to the award of the *Pour le Mérite*.
352. The Military Order of St. Henry (*Militär-St. Heinrichs-Orden*) was not an Imperial German award but one given by the Kingdom of Saxony, which in 1915 was one of four constitutional monarchies that made up the 26 political entities that comprised the modern German Empire. It was named after St. Henry the Exuberant, last Saxon to be crowned Holy Roman Emperor (1014–1024).
353. As stated above, Buddecke was actually awarded the *Pour le Mérite* on 14 April 1916.

354. The Imtiyaz Medal (in Turkish, *Imtiyaz Madalyasi*) was an Ottoman military decoration that came in silver and gold classes. The gold class was the highest Ottoman medal for gallantry in combat.
355. There is possibly a picture of him in 1941 at https://www.asisbiz.com/il2/Dornier/NJG/pages/Dornier-Do-17Z6-4.NJG2-with-Hans-Georg-Schutz-at-the-controls-1941-ebay-01.html. His name is given as Hans Georg Schutz.
356. For example, see Franks et al., p. 88. This claim is also at The Aerodrome website listing for Buddecke, and it appears to have been drawn from Franks' book even though it is not sourced.

    We are indebted to The Aerodrome website for some of this information, much of which appears to come from the research and books by Franks and his associates. Still, their listing of kills for "Hans Buddecke" does not reference any sources, although their listings for Oswald Boelcke and Max Immelmann do. We assume their list was assembled from those same sources.

    This sources are listed as Norman Franks and Hal Giblin, *Under the Guns of the German Aces* (Grub Street, London, 1997), Norman Franks, Frank W. Bailey, and Russell Guest, A*bove the Lines: A Complete Record of the Fighter Aces of the German Air Services, Naval Air Service and Flanders Marine Corps, 1914–1918* (Grub Street, London, 1993), and Terry C. Treadwell and Alan C. Wood, G*erman Knights of the Air 1914–1918: The Holders of the Order Pour le Mérite* (Barnes and Noble Books, New York, 1998).

Bibliography

Books:

Barry, John M., *The Great Influenza: The Story of the Deadliest Pandemic in History* (Penguin Books, New York, 2004).

Bronnenkant, Lance J., PhD, *The Blue Max Airmen, German Airmen Awarded the Pour le Mérite, Volume 2, Buddecke, Wintgens, Mulzer* (Aeronaut Books, 2012).

Buddecke, Oberleutnant Hans Joachim (deceased), *El Schahin (Der Jagdfalke) Aus meinem Fleigerleben* or the *Hunting Falcon: from my life as a flyer.* With nine illustrations. Printed and published by August Scherl LLC, Berlin, probably in 1918.

Dierrikx, Marc., *Anthony Fokker: The Flying Dutchman Who Shaped American Aviation* (Smithsonian Books, Washington D.C., 2018).

Dobkin, Marjorie Houseplan, *Smyrna 1922: The Destruction of a City* (Newmark Press, 1998, originally published in 1972).

Dupuy, Trevor N., *A Genius for War: The German Army and General Staff 1807–1945* (Lume Books, 2018, first published in 1984).

Franks, Norman, Frank W. Bailey, Russell Guest, *Above the Lines: The Aces and Fighters Units of the German Air Service, Naval Air Service and Flanders Marine Corps, 1914–1918* (Grub Street, Oxford, 1993)

Fokker, Anthony H.G. and Bruce Gould, *Flying Dutchman: The Life of Anthony Fokker* (George Routledge & Sons, LTD., London, 1931).

Fromkin, David, *A Peace to End All Peace: The Fall of the Ottoman Empire and the Creation of the Modern Middle East* (Henry Hold and Company, New York, 1989),

Goerlitz, Walter, *History of the German General Staff 1657–1945* (Lucknow Books, 2015, first published in 1953).

Grosz, P.M., *Fokker E.II/II, Windsock Datafile 91*, (Albatros Productions Limited, Berkhamsted, UK, 2002).

Hawker, Tyrrell M., MC, *Hawker VC RFC Ace: The Life of Major Lanoe Hawker VC DSO 1890–1916.*

Henshaw, Trevor, *The Sky Their Battlefield: Air Fighting and the Complete List of Allied Air Casualties from Enemy Action in the First War: British,*

Commonwealth, and United States Air Services 1914–1918 (Grub Street Publishing, London, 1995).

Immelmann, Franz, *Immelmann: The Eagle of Lille* (Casemate, Philadelphia & Newbury, 2009). Translated by Claud W. Sykes, first published in Germany in 1934, first English edition published in 1935.

Kilduff, Peter, *Iron Man Rudolf Berthold: Germany's Indomitable Fighter Ace of World War I* (Grub Street, London, 2012).

Marvin, Thomas F., *Kurt Vonnegut: A Critical Companion* (Greenwood Press, Westport, Conn. & London, 2002).

Oliver, John, *The Air War in the Dardanelles* (self-published, 2017).

Pavelec, Sterling Michael, *Airpower over Gallipoli 1915–1916* (Naval Institute Press, Annapolis, Maryland, 2020).

Rance, Philip, *The Struggle for the Dardanelles: The Memoirs of a German Staff Officer in Ottoman Service* (Pen and Sword Military, Barnsley, UK, 2017). A translation of two reports by Major Erich R. Prigge first published in Germany in 1916.

Richthofen, Manfred von, *The Red Air Fighter* (Greenhill Books, London and Stackpole Books, Pennsylvania, 1999). First published in Germany in 1917, first English edition published in 1918.

Rickenbacker, Edward V., *Rickenbacker: An Autobiography* (Prentice-Hall, Inc., Englewood Cliffs, New Jersey, 1967), page 17.

von Sanders, Liman, *Five Years in Turkey* (Naval and Military Press, Uckfield, UK, 2015). First published in Germany in 1920.

Vonnegut, Kurt, *Palm Sunday* (Belacorte Press, New York, 1981).

Vonnegut, Kurt, *Fates Worse Than Death: An Autobiographical Collage* (Berkely Books, New York, 1991).

Werner, Professor Johannes, *Knight of Germany: Oswald Boelcke – German Ace* (The Naval & Military Press, Ltd, Uckfield, England). Translated by Claud W. Sykes, date of original book or the reprint not provided.

Wyngarden, Greg van, *Early German Aces of World War I* (Osprey Publishing, Oxford, 2006)

Articles and websites:

Air Attack 17th December 1915 – Gallipoli – The Great War (1914–1918) Forum (greatwarforum.org)

Air Attack 17th December 1915 – Page 2 – Gallipoli – The Great War (1914–1918) Forum (greatwarforum.org)

Aircraft at Gallipoli – Air personnel and the war in the air – The Great War (1914–1918) Forum (greatwarforum.org)

Air Force (Ottoman Empire) – zxc.wiki

"Air of mystery: Photos offer clues to trace life of 'Prof. Bumbaugh'" by Rick Steelhammer, *Charleston Gazette-Mail*, Jan. 28, 2017 at Air of mystery: Photos offer clues to trace life of 'Prof. Bumbaugh' | News | wvgazettemail.com;

Albert Wilhelm Friedrich Heinrich August Buddecke 1858–1931 – Ancestry®

The escadrille_524 (free.fr)

A rare dogfight over Anzac? – Gallipoli – The Great War (1914–1918) Forum (greatwarforum.org)

"Atlas Engine Works, Indianapolis, IN, U.S.A." in Vintage Machinery website at www.vintagemachinery.org

Average Height for Males and Females in 1912 and 2012 – A Hundred Years Ago

Average height of men by year of birth, 1996 (ourworldindata.org)

Bernard D., Aegean Air War: Brinsmead's unfortunate distinction. Bernard D. is Bernard de Broglio.

Bernard D., Aegean Air War: Gunners over Gallipoli. Bernard D. is Bernard de Broglio.

"Built Local: The Atlas Engine Works of Indianapolis" by Ed Fujawa dated 13 October 2019 on the Class 900: Indianapolis: A Blog About the History of the Circle City: Built Local: The Atlas Engine Works of Indianapolis (class900indy.com)

"Built Local: The Atlas Engine Works of Indianapolis" updated Aug 18, 2020 on Class 900: Indianapolis: A Blog about the History of the Circle City.

CANAKKALE AIR CAMPAIGN 6 (tayyareci.com)

CANAKKALE AIR CAMPAIGN 7 (tayyareci.com)

CANAKKALE AIR CAMPAIGN 8 (tayyareci.com)

CANAKKALE HAVA HAREKATI 1 (tayyareci.com)

CANAKKALE HAVA HAREKATI 6 (tayyareci.com)

Cecil Hoffnung Marks | British Jews in The First World War – We Were There Too (jewsfww.uk)

Cecil Marks | TheyServed Wiki | Fandom

Cicero Flying Field page: CICERO FLYING FIELD (lincolnbeachey.com).

Col Albert Buddecke (1858–1931) – Find A Grave Memorial

Colon, Raul: Air Effort over Gallipoli: A Brief Look at the Air Campaign over the Dardanelles – Aeroflight

Correspondence December 2021 – January 2022 with:

Sterling Michael Pavelec

Paschalis Palavouzis

David S. Bremner
Bernard de Broglio
croneiss.pdf (staatliche-bibliothek-regensburg.de)
"The Departure of the R.F.C. Expeditionary Force" on the Royal Flying Corps website: RFC home (airhistory.org.uk)
Eberhard Karls Universitat Tübingen, Universitatsbibliothek. See: El Schahin (der Jagdfalke) – OpenDigi (uni-tuebingen.de).
Enver Pasha, Ismail | International Encyclopedia of the First World War (WW1) (1914-1918-online.net)
The Ethnic Cleansing of Greeks from Gallipoli, April 1915 – Quadrant Online
Expeditionary Force page 3 (airhistory.org.uk)
Expeditionary Force page 4 (airhistory.org.uk
Expeditionary Force page 6 (airhistory.org.uk)
February | 2020 | Notes From The Indiana State Archives (wordpress.com).
Feldfliegerabteilung 23 (FFA 23) (frontflieger.de)
Feldfliegerabteilung 34 (FFA 34) (frontflieger.de)
Fliegerleutnant Ludwig Preußner | gallipoli1915
Fliegertruppe (Ottoman Empire)" HYPERLINK "https:/de.zxc.wiki/wiki/Fliegertruppe (Ottoman Empire) – Wikipedia, the free encyclopedia
The First Super Speedway website: 1909 Balloon Race | First Super Speedway and First Super Speedway
FOKKER E1 WW I Period TUAF AIRCRAFTS 1 nci dunya savasi dönemi Turk HvKK UCAKLARI (tayyareci.com)
Fokker E.II/E.III change-over. (theaerodrome.com)
Frontflieger.de – Die Soldaten der Deutschen Fliegertruppe 1914 1915 1916 1917 1918
Gallipoli casualties by country | NZHistory, New Zealand history online
General Hans Kettenbeil – Axis History Forum
Generalmajor Hans Schuez – Lexikon der Wehrmacht (lexikon-der-wehrmacht.de)
Gernot CRONEISS: généalogie par Gilles CRONEISS (croneiss) – Geneanet
Gilbert, Greg, "Air War over the Dardanelles," *Wartime Magazine*, Issue 61. Canberra: Australian War Memorial, 2013: pages 42–47.
Hans Acworth Busk | airwar19141918 (wordpress.com)
Hans Acworth Busk (rudgwickremembers.com)
Hans Acworth Busk (unknown-1916) – Find A Grave Memorial
"Harry P. Fletcher" from Indiana Memory website: Indiana Memory

Harold E. Morehouse, Flying Pioneers Biographies Collection at: Harold E. Morehouse Flying Pioneers Biographies Collection – Partridge and Keller: Elmer L. Partridge and Henry C. "Pop" Keller (si.edu).

Havaciligi, T.C. Bahriye, T.C. Sahil Guvenlik Komuntanligi, A History of Aircaft Operated by Turkish Sea Forces See: Microsoft Word – Turkish sea forces aircraft (ole-nikolajsen.com

HMS *Ribble* log book: http://www.naval-history.net/OWShips-WW1-10-HMS_Ribble.htm.

https://archiv-akh.de/filme/252#1

https://military.wikia.org/wiki/Ottoman_Air_Forcehttps://military.wikia.org/wiki/Ottoman_Air_Force#cite_note-Ordered_228-16

https://www.primidi.com/ottoman_air_force/world_war_i_operations

IMDB (Internet Movie Database) at www.imdb.com

"Indianapolis Collected: The Fall of the House of Fletcher" at the website HistoricalIndianapolis.com.

Indiana Memory website:https://digital.library.in.gov/Record/IHS_dc013-630

Indianapolis Brewing Company – Historic Indianapolis | All Things Indianapolis History

Iredale, Thomas P., Role of German Officers in the Gallipoli Campaign | International Encyclopedia of the First World War (WW1) (1914–1918-online.net)

ISL: Indianapolis Brewing Company

Indianapolis Brewing Company, Indianapolis, IN | Old Main Artifacts (wordpress.com)

Indy Speedway 1910 National Balloon Race at Indy Motor Speedway 1909-1910).

legacy.owensboro.kctcs.edu:

Albert Lieber (kctcs.edu).

Kurt Vonnegut (kctcs.edu).

Lt James Sydney Bolas (1892-1916) – Find A Grave Memorial

Major Erich Serno – Axis History Forum

Microsoft Word – Turkish sea forces aircraft (ole-nikolajsen.com).

ObLt Eric Muhra German Pilot – Air personnel and the war in the air – The Great War (1914-1918) Forum (greatwarforum.org)

Osborne, Dr John MG DDT PhD FSG, Fighter Aircraft in Support of the Gallipoli Campaign: armsregister.com/articles/articles_documents/nzar_a67_gallipoli_rnas_fighter_aircraft.pdf

Ottoman Air Force – Axis History Forum

Ottoman Air units – Axis History Forum

Ottoman Air units – Page 4 – Axis History Forum
Ottoman Air Force – Balkan Wars (liquisearch.com)
Ottoman Air Force – World War I Operations | World War Operations | Technology Trends (primidi.com)
So It Goes: Kurt Vonnegut's Beer Heritage – Brookston Beer Bulletin
Special cases – German nurses of the Great War (wordpress.com)
Spandauer Anwälte 4 (reinhardhillebrand.de)
Squadrons 1 & 6 | gallipoli1915
"Stoughton Fletcher(s)" on website: The First Super Speedway at Stoughton Fletcher(s) at Stoughton Fletcher(s) | First Super Speedway.
Sunrise and sunset times in Gallipoli Peninsula (timeanddate.com)
Sublunar Photography blog on Friday, June 19, 2015 in a blog post called "Indianapolis Coke" at Sublunar Photography: Indianapolis Coke.
Sunkel, Gwen, "In the Park: Riverside Amusement Park," Feb. 22, 2014 from Historic Indianapolis.com. In The Park: Riverside Amusement Park – Historic Indianapolis | All Things Indianapolis History
Tactical Decisions and Orders by Albert Buddecke, Kessinger Publishing, Hardcover – Anobii
TAYYARECİ-TÜRKİYENİN GERÇEK HAVACILIK SİTESİ www.tayyareci.com
T.C. Cumhurbaşkanlığı Devlet Arşivleri Başkanlığı (devletarsivleri.gov.tr)
Thams, Hames W., "Lawrence of Arabia's Family" at: Lawrence of Arabia's Family – St. David's Society of the State of New York (stdavidsny.org).
Theodor Croneiss – abcdef.wiki
Theodor Jakob Croneiss (theaerodrome.com)
The Aerodrome website: Welcome to The Aerodrome – Aces and Aircraft of World War I.
The Rise and Fall of the Billy Goat Beer – Historic Indianapolis | All Things Indianapolis History
THE SKY THEIR BATTLEFIELD II | THE EXPANDED EDITION OF TREVOR HENSHAW'S WW1 AVIATION CLASSIC (theskytheirbattlefield2.com)
U.S. Census Records: 1880, 1910, 1920 and 1930
U.S. Consumer Price Index from 1800 to present at: Consumer Price Index, 1800– | Federal Reserve Bank of Minneapolis (minneapolisfed.org).
Virtual Exhibition "100 Years First World War" – People – Albert Buddecke (1858–1931) (dnb.de)
Virtual Exhibition "100 Years First World War" – Persons (dnb.de)
Vonnegut genealogy website: Edith Sophia Vonnegut (Lieber) (1888 – 1944) – Genealogy (geni.com).

Wasserfliegerabteilung – Axis History Forum
Wayback Machine (archive.org)
Whealy.com: "Grandfather Arthur Treloar Whealy," maintained by grandson Chris Whealy.
Wikipedia (English language): multiple articles.
Wikipedia (German language): multipole articles.
Will Lawrence, Observer, RFC [Archive] – The Aerodrome Forum
Winchester College (winchestercollegeatwar.com)
Wings of Glory Aerodrome (wingsofwar.org)
WWI FACTS & FIGURES & MYTHS – Tommy 1418.com
#7 – Tactical decisions and orders : a study in troop-leading (based ... – Full View | HathiTrust Digital Library
10. Back to Imbros (wordpress.com)
23 October 1915 – "Sweeter than a small ladies' handkerchief" | airwar 1914–1918 (wordpress.com)
23 October 1915 | T.E. Lawrence Society (telsociety.org.uk)
6 January 1916 – Busk killed in Gallipoli | airwar19141918 (wordpress.com)
8 Jan 1916 (wordpress.com)

Newspaper Accounts

15 Oct 1913, Page 7 – *The Indianapolis Star* at Newspapers.com
06 Nov 1913, Page 7 – *The Indianapolis News* at Newspapers.com
16 Nov 1913, Page 43 – *The Indianapolis Star* at Newspapers.com
22 Nov 1913, Page 10 – *The Indianapolis Star* at Newspapers.com
22 Nov 1913, Page 16 – *The Indianapolis News* at Newspapers.com
25 Nov 1913, Page 9 – *The Indianapolis Star* at Newspapers.com
26 Nov 1913, Page 6 – *Asheville Gazette-News* at Newspapers.com
28 Nov 1913, Page 2 – *Asheville Citizen-Times* at Newspapers.com
22 Feb 1914, Page 12 – *The Indianapolis Star* at Newspapers.com
06 Mar 1914, Page 19 – *The Indianapolis News* at Newspapers.com
25 May 1914, Page 5 – *The Indianapolis News* at Newspapers.com
22 Jul 1914, Page 1 – *The Indianapolis Star* at Newspapers.com
31 Jul 1914, Page 14 – *The Indianapolis News* at Newspapers.com
04 Aug 1914, Page 6 – *The Indianapolis Star* at Newspapers.com
04 Aug 1914, Page 4 – *The Indianapolis News* at Newspapers.com
15 Nov 1914, Page 17 – *The Indianapolis Star* at Newspapers.com
11 Apr 1915, Page 15 – *The Indianapolis Star* at Newspapers.com
27 Aug 1915, Page 11 – *The Indianapolis News* at Newspapers.com
18 Jan 1916, Page 9 – *Palladium-Item* at Newspapers.com

13 Mar 1916, Page 3 – *The Star Press* at Newspapers.com

01 May 1916, Page 15 – *The Indianapolis News* at Newspapers.com

The Indianapolis Journal, Wednesday, November 12, 1884, page 7 has an article "The Estate of Stoughton A. Fletcher."

The Indianapolis Star on 22 July 1914

The Indianapolis Star, 25 November 1913.

The Indianapolis Star, 11 May 1916.

The Fort Wayne Daily News, 29 November 1906.

The Fort Wayne Daily News, 21 April 1914.

The Fort Wayne Daily News, 23 October 1915. "Among the Merchants."

The New York Times, 3 August 1914, front page.

The New York Times, 9 March 1918.

The New York Times, 28 December 1928.

The Washington Times, 26 August 1915.

"Harry Fletcher Talks Before the Quest Club," *The Fort Wayne Journal-Gazette*, 24 October 1914.

"Quest Club Holds Open House Thursday Evening, *The Fort Wayne News*, 30 January 1915.

Biographical Information

Jay Karamales is a software engineer by training, but has always had a keen interest in history and military affairs. He was hired by Trevor Dupuy in 1987 to design and build the database for the Ardennes Campaign Simulation Data Base project, of which Chris Lawrence was the manager. He was also called upon to use his knowledge of German to translate unit records for that effort, and thus began his thirty-five-year association with Chris and The Dupuy Institute, and his fascination with the Battle of the Bulge.

In 1989 Mr. Karamales was hired by the large consulting firm SAIC to conduct a quantitative analysis study of anti-tank warfare on the Western Front in World War II. From that research, he and his colleague Allyn Vannoy produced the book *Against the Panzers: United States Infantry versus German Tanks, 1944–45* (McFarland & Co., 1996). Realizing that any military history cannot properly be told without good maps, he taught himself the fundamentals of digital cartography and since has produced the maps for over one hundred books, including Mr. Lawrence's *Kursk: The Battle of Prokhorovka.*

Mr. Karamales and his wife live just outside Boise, Idaho, between the mountains and the desert, where he is Director and Chief Historian of the Dry Creek Historical Society and editor of the *DCHS Newsletter.* He also serves on the Ada County Historic Preservation Council.

Christopher A. Lawrence is a professional historian and military analyst. He is the Executive Director and President of The Dupuy Institute, an organization dedicated to scholarly research and objective analysis of historical data related to armed conflict and the resolution of armed conflict. TDI provides independent, historically-based analysis of lessons learned from modern military campaigns.

Mr. Lawrence was the program manager for the Ardennes Campaign Simulation Data Base, the Kursk Data Base, the Modern Insurgency Spread Sheets, and a number of other smaller combat data bases. He participated in studies on casualty estimates (including estimates for Bosnia and Iraq) and studies of air campaign modeling, enemy prisoner of war capture rates, medium weight armor, urban warfare, situational awareness, counterinsurgencies, and other subjects for the U.S. Army, Department of Defense, the Joint Staff, and the U.S. Air Force. He has also directed a number of studies related to the military impact of banning antipersonnel mines for the Joint Staff, the Los Alamos National Laboratories, and the Vietnam Veterans of America Foundation.

His published works include papers and monographs for the Congressional Office of Technology Assessment and Vietnam Veterans of America Foundation, in addition to over forty articles written for limited distribution newsletters and over sixty analytical reports prepared for the Department of Defense. He is the author of *America's Modern Wars: Understanding Iraq, Afghanistan and Vietnam* (Casemate Publishers, Philadelphia & Oxford, 2015); *Kursk: The Battle of Prokhorovka* (Aberdeen Books, Sheridan, CO, 2015); *War by Numbers: Understanding Conventional Combat* (Potomac Books, Lincoln, NE, 2017); *The Battle of Prokhorovka* (Stackpole Books, Mechanicsburg, PA, 2019); and *Aces at Kursk: The Battle for Aerial Supremacy on the Eastern Front, 1943* (Pen and Sword Books, Barnsley, UK, 2023).

Mr. Lawrence lives in northern Virginia near Washington, D.C., with his wife and son.

Index